Monetary Policy, Inflation, and the Business Cycle

Monetary Policy, Inflation, and the Business Cycle

An Introduction to the New Keynesian Framework

Jordi Galí

Princeton University Press

Princeton and Oxford

Published by Princeton University Press,
41 William Street, Princeton, New Jersey 08540

In the United Kingdom: Princeton University Press,
6 Oxford Street, Woodstock, Oxfordshire OX20 1TW

Library of Congress Cataloging-in-Publication Data

Galí, Jordi, 1961–
    Monetary policy, inflation, and the business cycle : an introduction
to the New Keynesian framework / Jordi Galí.
        p. cm.
    Includes bibliographical references and index.
    ISBN 978-0-691-13316-4 (hbk. : alk. paper)   1. Monetary policy.
2. Inflation (Finance).   3. Business cycles.   4. Keynesian economics.   I. Title.
HG230.3.G35 2008
339.5'3—dc22   2007044381

British Library Cataloging-in-Publication Data is available

This book has been composed in Times Roman by Westchester Book Group.

Printed on acid-free paper. ∞

press.princeton.edu

Printed in the United States of America

10   9   8   7   6   5   4   3

Als meus pares

Contents

Preface

This book brings together some of the lecture notes that I have developed over the past few years, and which have been the basis for graduate courses on monetary economics taught at different institutions, including Universitat Pompeu Fabra (UPF), Massachusetts Institute of Technology (MIT), and the Swiss Doctoral Program at Gerzensee. The book's main objective is to give an introduction to the New Keynesian framework and some of its applications. That framework has emerged as the workhorse for the analysis of monetary policy and its implications for inflation, economic fluctuations, and welfare. It constitutes the backbone of the new generation of medium-scale models under development at the International Monetary Fund, the Federal Reserve Board, the European Central Bank (ECB), and many other central banks. It has also provided the theoretical underpinnings to the inflation stability-oriented strategies adopted by the majority of central banks in the industrialized world.

A defining feature of this book is the use of a single reference model throughout the chapters. That benchmark framework, which I refer to as the "basic New Keynesian model," is developed in chapter 3. It features monopolistic competition and staggered price setting in goods markets, coexisting with perfectly competitive labor markets. The "classical model" introduced in chapter 2, characterized by perfect competition in goods markets and flexible prices, can be viewed as a limiting case of the benchmark model when both the degree of price stickiness and firms' market power vanish. The discussion of the empirical shortcomings of the classical monetary model provides the motivation for the development of the New Keynesian model, as discussed in the introductory chapter.

The implications for monetary policy of the basic New Keynesian model, including the desirability of inflation targeting, are analyzed in chapter 4. Each of the subsequent chapters then builds on the basic model and analyzes an extension of that model along some specific dimension. Once the reader has grasped the contents of chapters 1 through 4, each subsequent chapter can be read independently, and in any order. Thus, chapter 5 introduces a policy tradeoff in the form of an exogenous cost-push shock that serves as the basis for a discussion of the differences between the optimal policy with and without commitment. Chapter 6 extends the assumption of nominal rigidities to the labor market and examines the policy implications of the coexistence of sticky wages and sticky prices. Chapter 7 develops a small open economy version of the basic New Keynesian model, introducing explicitly in the analysis a number of variables inherent to open economies, including trade flows, nominal and real exchange rates, and the terms of trade. It should be emphasized that the extensions of the basic New Keynesian model covered in chapters 5 through 7 are only a sample of those found in the literature. In addition to some concluding comments, chapter 8 provides a brief description of several extensions not covered in this book, as well as a list of key references for each one.

Chapters 2 through 7 each contain a final section with a brief summary and discussion of the literature, including references to some of the key papers. Thus, references within the main text are kept to a minimum. The reader will also find at the end of each of these chapters a list of exercises related directly to the material covered.

The level of this book makes it suitable for use as a reference in a graduate course on monetary theory, possibly supplemented with readings covering some of the recent extensions not treated here. Chapters 1 through 5 could prove useful as the basis for the "monetary block" of a first-year graduate macro sequence or even in an advanced undergraduate course on monetary theory. Chapters 3 through 5 could be used as the basis for a short course that serves as an introduction to the New Keynesian framework.

Much of the material contained in this book overlaps with that found in two other (excellent) books on monetary theory published in recent years: Carl Walsh's *Monetary Theory and Policy* (MIT Press, second edition 2003) and Michael Woodford's *Interest and Prices* (Princeton University Press 2003). This book's focus on the New Keynesian model, with the use of a single, underlying framework throughout, represents the main difference from Walsh's, with the latter providing in many respects a more comprehensive, textbook-like coverage of the field of monetary theory, with a variety of models being used. On the other hand, the main difference with Woodford's comprehensive treatise lies in the more compact presentation of the basic New Keynesian model and the main associated results found here, which may facilitate its use as a textbook in an introductory graduate course. In addition, this book includes a chapter on open economy extensions of the basic New Keynesian model, a topic not covered in Woodford's book.

Many people have contributed to this book in important ways. First and foremost, I am in special debt to Rich Clarida, Mark Gertler, and Tommaso Monacelli with whom I coauthored the original articles underlying much of the material found here and, in particular, those of chapters 5, 7, and 8. I am also especially thankful to Olivier Blanchard who, as a teacher and thesis advisor at MIT, helped me discover the fascination of modern macroeconomics. Working with him as a coauthor in recent years has sharpened my understanding of many of the issues dealt with here. My interest in monetary theory was triggered by a course taught by Mike Woodford at MIT in the fall of 1988. His work in monetary economics (and in everything else) has always been a source of inspiration to me.

Many other colleagues have helped me to improve the original manuscript, either with specific comments on earlier versions of the chapters, or through discussions over the years on some of the covered topics. A nonexhaustive list includes Kosuke Aoki, Larry Christiano, José de Gregorio, Mike Kiley, Andy Levin, David López-Salido, Albert Marcet, Dirk Niepelt, Stephanie Schmitt-Grohé, Lars Svensson, and Lutz Weinke. I am also grateful to five anonymous reviewers for useful comments (and, of course, for a positive verdict on publication).

I owe special thanks to Davide Debortoli, for his excellent research assistance. Many other students uncovered algebra mistakes or made helpful suggestions on different chapters, including Suman Basu, Sevinc Cucurova, José Dorich, Elmar Mertens, Juan Carlos Odar, and Aron Tobias. Needless to say, I am solely responsible for any remaining errors.

I am also thankful to the Department of Economics at MIT, which I visited during the academic year 2005–2006, and where much of this book was written (and tested in the classroom). This book has also benefited from numerous conversations with many researchers at the European Central Bank, the Federal Reserve Board, and the Federal Reserve Banks of New York and Boston during my several visits to those institutions as an academic consultant.

I should also like to thank Richard Baggaley, from Princeton University Press, for his support of this project from day one.

Much of the research underlying this book has received the financial support of several sponsoring institutions, which I would like to acknowledge for their generosity. They include the European Commission, the National Science Foundation, the Ministerio de Ciencia y Tecnología (Government of Spain), the Fundación Ramón Areces, the Generalitat de Catalunya, and CREA-Barcelona Economics.

1

Introduction

The present monograph seeks to provide the reader with an overview of modern monetary theory. Over the past decade, monetary economics has been among the most fruitful research areas within macroeconomics. The effort of many researchers to understand the relationship between monetary policy, inflation, and the business cycle has led to the development of a framework—the so-called New Keynesian model—that is widely used for monetary policy analysis. The following chapters offer an introduction to that basic framework and a discussion of its policy implications.

The need for a framework that can help us understand the links between monetary policy and the aggregate performance of an economy seems self-evident. On the one hand, citizens of modern societies have good reason to care about developments in inflation, employment, and other economy-wide variables, for those developments affect to an important degree people's opportunities to maintain or improve their standard of living. On the other hand, monetary policy, as conducted by central banks, has an important role in shaping those macroeconomic developments, both at the national and supranational levels. Changes in interest rates have a direct effect on the valuation of financial assets and their expected returns, as well as on the consumption and investment decisions of households and firms. Those decisions can in turn have consequences for gross domestic product (GDP) growth, employment, and inflation. It is thus not surprising that the interest rate decisions made by the Federal Reserve system (Fed), the European Central Bank (ECB), or other prominent central banks around the world are given so much attention, not only by market analysts and the financial press, but also by the general public. It would thus seem important to understand how those interest rate decisions end up affecting the various measures of an economy's performance, both nominal and real. A key goal of monetary theory is to provide us with an account of the mechanisms through which those effects arise, i.e., the transmission mechanism of monetary policy.

Central banks do not change interest rates in an arbitrary or whimsical manner. Their decisions are meant to be purposeful, i.e., they seek to attain certain objectives, while taking as given the constraints posed by the workings of a market economy in which the vast majority of economic decisions are made in a decentralized manner by a large number of individuals and firms. Understanding what should be the objectives of monetary policy and how the latter should be conducted in order to attain those objectives constitutes another important aim of modern monetary theory in its normative dimension.

The following chapters present a framework that helps us understand both the transmission mechanism of monetary policy and the elements that come into play in the design of rules or guidelines for the conduct of monetary policy. The framework is, admittedly, highly stylized and should be viewed more as a pedagogical tool than a quantitative model that can be readily taken to the data. Nevertheless, and despite its simplicity, it contains the key elements (though not all the bells and whistles) found in the medium-scale monetary models that are currently being developed by the research teams of many central banks.[1]

The monetary framework that constitutes the focus of the present monograph has a core structure that corresponds to a Real Business Cycle (RBC) model, on which a number of elements characteristic of Keynesian models are superimposed. That confluence of elements has led some authors to label the new paradigm as the New Neoclassical Synthesis.[2] The following sections describe briefly each of those two influences in turn, in order to provide some historical background to the framework developed in subsequent chapters.

1.1   Background: Real Business Cycle (RBC) Theory and Classical Monetary Models

During the years following the seminal papers of Kydland and Prescott (1982) and Prescott (1986), RBC theory provided the main reference framework for the analysis of economic fluctuations and became to a large extent the core of macroeconomic theory. The impact of the RBC revolution had both a methodological and a conceptual dimension.

From a methodological point of view, RBC theory firmly established the use of dynamic stochastic general equilibrium (DSGE) models as a central tool for macroeconomic analysis. Behavioral equations describing aggregate variables were thus replaced by first-order conditions of intertemporal problems facing consumers and firms. Ad hoc assumptions on the formation of expectations gave way to rational expectations. In addition, RBC economists stressed the importance of the quantitative aspects of modelling, as reflected in the central role given to the calibration, simulation, and evaluation of their models.

---

[1] See, e.g., Bayoumi (2004) and Coenen, McAdam, and Straub (2006) for a description of the models under development at the International Monetary Fund and the European Central Bank, respectively. For descriptions of the Federal Reserve Board models, see Erceg, Guerrieri, and Gust (2006) and Edge, Kiley, and Laforte (2007).

[2] See Goodfriend and King (1997).

The most striking dimension of the RBC revolution was, however, conceptual. It rested on three basic claims:

- *The efficiency of business cycles.* The bulk of economic fluctuations observed in industrialized countries could be interpreted as an equilibrium outcome resulting from the economy's response to exogenous variations in real forces (most importantly, technology), in an environment characterized by perfect competition and frictionless markets. According to that view, cyclical fluctuations did not necessarily signal an inefficient allocation of resources (in fact, the fluctuations generated by the standard RBC model were fully optimal). That view had an important corollary: Stabilization policies may not be necessary or desirable, and they could even be counterproductive. This was in contrast with the conventional interpretation, tracing back to Keynes (1936), of recessions as periods with an inefficiently low utilization of resources that could be brought to an end by means of economic policies aimed at expanding aggregate demand.

- *The importance of technology shocks as a source of economic fluctuations.* That claim derived from the ability of the basic RBC model to generate "realistic" fluctuations in output and other macroeconomic variables, even when variations in total factor productivity—calibrated to match the properties of the Solow residual—are assumed to be the only exogenous driving force. Such an interpretation of economic fluctuations was in stark contrast with the traditional view of technological change as a source of long term growth, unrelated to business cycles.

- *The limited role of monetary factors.* Most important, given the subject of the present monograph, RBC theory sought to explain economic fluctuations with *no reference to monetary factors*, even abstracting from the existence of a monetary sector.

Its strong influence among academic researchers notwithstanding, the RBC approach had a very limited impact (if any) on central banks and other policy institutions. The latter continued to rely on large-scale macroeconometric models despite the challenges to their usefulness for policy evaluation (Lucas 1976) or the largely arbitrary identifying restrictions underlying the estimates of those models (Sims 1980).

The attempts by Cooley and Hansen (1989) and others to introduce a monetary sector in an otherwise conventional RBC model, while sticking to the assumptions of perfect competition and fully flexible prices and wages, were not perceived as yielding a framework that was relevant for policy analysis. As discussed in chapter 2, the resulting framework, which is referred to as the *classical monetary model*, generally predicts neutrality (or near neutrality) of monetary policy with respect to real variables. That finding is at odds with the widely held belief (certainly among central bankers) in the power of that policy to influence output and employment developments, at least in the short run. That belief is underpinned by a large body of empirical work, tracing back to the narrative evidence of Friedman and Schwartz (1963), up to the more recent work using time series techniques, as described in Christiano, Eichenbaum, and Evans (1999).[3]

In addition to the empirical challenges mentioned above, the normative implications of classical monetary models have also led many economists to call into question their relevance as a framework for policy evaluation. Thus, those models generally yield as a normative implication the optimality of the Friedman rule—a policy that requires central banks to keep the short term nominal rate constant at a zero level—even though that policy seems to bear no connection whatsoever with the monetary policies pursued (and viewed as desirable) by the vast majority of central banks. Instead, the latter are characterized by (often large) adjustments of interest rates in response to deviations of inflation and indicators of economic activity from their target levels.[4]

The conflict between theoretical predictions and evidence, and between normative implications and policy practice, can be viewed as a symptom that some elements that are important in actual economies may be missing in classical monetary models. As discussed in section 1.2, those shortcomings are the main motivation behind the introduction of some Keynesian assumptions, while maintaining the RBC apparatus as an underlying structure.

1.2 The New Keynesian Model: Main Elements and Features

Despite their different policy implications, there are important similarities between the RBC model and the New Keynesian monetary model.[5] The latter, whether in the canonical form presented below or in its more complex extensions, has at its core some version of the RBC model. This is reflected in the assumption of (i) an

---

[3] An additional challenge to RBC models has been posed by the recent empirical evidence on the effects of technology shocks. Some of that evidence suggests that technology shocks generate a negative short-run comovement between output and labor input measures, thus rejecting a prediction of the RBC model that is key to its ability to generate fluctuations that resemble actual business cycles (see, e.g., Galí 1999 and Basu, Fernald, and Kimball 2006). Other evidence suggests that the contribution of technology shocks to the business cycle has been quantitatively small (see, e.g., Christiano, Eichenbaum, and Vigfusson 2003), though investment-specific technology shocks may have played a more important role (Fisher 2006). See Galí and Rabanal (2004) for a survey of the empirical evidence on the effects of technology shocks.

[4] An exception to that pattern is given by the Bank of Japan, which kept its policy rate at a zero level over the period 1999–2006. Few, however, would interpret that policy as the result of a deliberate attempt to implement the Friedman rule. Rather, it is generally viewed as a consequence of the zero lower bound on interest rates becoming binding, with the resulting inability of the central banks to stimulate the economy out of a deflationary trap.

[5] See Galí and Gertler (2007) for an extended introduction to the New Keynesian model and a discussion of its main features.

infinitely-lived representative household that seeks to maximize the utility from consumption and leisure, subject to an intertemporal budget constraint, and (ii) a large number of firms with access to an identical technology, subject to exogenous random shifts. Though endogenous capital accumulation, a key element of RBC theory, is absent in canonical versions of the New Keynesian model, it is easy to incorporate and is a common feature of medium-scale versions.[6] Also, as in RBC theory, an equilibrium takes the form of a stochastic process for all the economy's endogenous variables consistent with optimal intertemporal decisions by households and firms, given their objectives and constraints and with the clearing of all markets.

The New Keynesian modelling approach, however, combines the DSGE structure characteristic of RBC models with assumptions that depart from those found in classical monetary models. Here is a list of some of the key elements and properties of the resulting models:

- *Monopolistic competition.* The prices of goods and inputs are set by private economic agents in order to maximize their objectives, as opposed to being determined by an anonymous Walrasian auctioneer seeking to clear all (competitive) markets at once.

- *Nominal rigidities.* Firms are subject to some constraints on the frequency with which they can adjust the prices of the goods and services they sell. Alternatively, firms may face some costs of adjusting those prices. The same kind of friction applies to workers in the presence of sticky wages.

- *Short run non-neutrality of monetary policy.* As a consequence of the presence of nominal rigidities, changes in short term nominal interest rates (whether chosen directly by the central bank or induced by changes in the money supply) are not matched by one-for-one changes in expected inflation, thus leading to variations in real interest rates. The latter bring about changes in consumption and investment and, as a result, on output and employment, because firms find it optimal to adjust the quantity of goods supplied to the new level of demand. In the long run, however, all prices and wages adjust, and the economy reverts back to its natural equilibrium.

It is important to note that the three aforementioned ingredients were already central to the New Keynesian literature that emerged in the late 1970s and 1980s, and which developed parallel to RBC theory. The models used in that literature, however, were often static or used reduced form equilibrium conditions that were not derived from explicit dynamic optimization problems facing firms and households. The emphasis of much of that work was instead on providing microfoundations, based on the presence of small menu costs, for the

---

[6] See, e.g., Smets and Wouters (2003)

stickiness of prices and the resulting monetary non-neutralities.[7] Other papers
emphasized the persistent effects of monetary policy on output, and the role that
staggered contracts played in generating that persistence.[8] The novelty of the new
generation of monetary models has been to embed those features in a fully specified DSGE framework, thus adopting the formal modelling approach that has been
the hallmark of RBC theory.

Not surprisingly, important differences with respect to RBC models emerge in
the new framework. First, the economy's response to shocks is generally inefficient. Second, the non-neutrality of monetary policy resulting from the presence of
nominal rigidities makes room for potentially welfare-enhancing interventions by
the monetary authority in order to minimize the existing distortions. Furthermore,
those models are arguably suited for the analysis and comparison of alternative
monetary regimes without being subject to the Lucas critique.[9]

1.2.1 Evidence of Nominal Rigidities and Monetary Policy Non-neutrality

The presence of nominal rigidities and the implied real effects of monetary policy
are two key ingredients of New Keynesian models. It would be hard to justify the
use of a model with those distinctive features in the absence of evidence in support
of their relevance. Next, some of that evidence is described briefly to provide the
reader with relevant references.

1.2.1.1 *Evidence of Nominal Rigidities*

Most attempts to uncover evidence on the existence and importance of price rigidities have generally relied on the analysis of micro data, i.e., data on the prices
of individual goods and services.[10] In an early survey of that research, Taylor
(1999) concludes that there is ample evidence of price rigidities, with the average frequency of price adjustment being about one year. In addition, he points to
the very limited evidence of synchronization of price adjustments, thus providing
some justification for the assumption of staggered price setting commonly found
in the New Keynesian model. The study of Bils and Klenow (2004), based on
the analysis of the average frequencies of price changes for 350 product cate-
gories underlying the U.S. consumer price index (CPI), called into question that
conventional wisdom by uncovering a median duration of prices between 4 and

---

[7] See, e.g., Akerlof and Yellen (1985), Mankiw (1985), Blanchard and Kiyotaki (1987), and Ball and
Romer (1990).

[8] See, e.g., Fischer (1977) and Taylor (1980).

[9] At least to the extent that the economy is sufficiently stable so that the log-linearized equilibrium
conditions remain a good approximation and that some of the parameters that are taken as "structural"
(including the degree of nominal rigidities) can be viewed as approximately constant.

[10] See, e.g., Cecchetti (1986) and Kashyap (1995) for early works examining the patterns of prices of
individual goods.

6 months. Nevertheless, more recent evidence by Nakamura and Steinsson (2006), using data on the individual prices underlying the U.S. CPI and excluding price changes associated with sales, has led to a reconsideration of the Bils–Klenow evidence, with an upward adjustment of the estimated median duration to a range between 8 and 11 months. Evidence for the euro area, discussed in Dhyne et al. (2006), points to a similar distribution of price durations to that uncovered by Nakamura and Steinsson for the United States.[11] It is worth mentioning that, in addition to evidence of substantial price rigidities, most studies find a large amount of heterogeneity in price durations across sectors/types of goods, with services being associated with the largest degree of price rigidities, and unprocessed food and energy with the smallest.

The literature also contains several studies based on micro data that provide analogous evidence of nominal rigidities for wages. Taylor (1999) surveys that literature and suggests an estimate of the average frequency of wage changes of about one year, the same frequency as for prices. A significant branch of the literature on wage rigidities has focused on the possible existence of asymmetries that make wage cuts very rare or unlikely. Bewley's (1999) detailed study of firms' wage policies based on interviews with managers finds ample evidence of downward nominal wage rigidities. More recently, the multicountry study of Dickens et al. (2007) uncovers evidence of significant downward nominal and real wage rigidities in most of the countries in their sample.

1.2.1.2 Evidence of Monetary Policy Non-neutralities

Monetary non-neutralities are, at least in theory, a natural consequence of the presence of nominal rigidities. As will be shown in chapter 3, if prices do not adjust in proportion to changes in the money supply (thus causing real balances to vary), or if expected inflation does not move one for one with the nominal interest rate when the latter is changed (thus leading to a change in the real interest rate), the central bank will generally be able to alter the level aggregate demand and, as a result, the equilibrium levels of output and employment. Is the evidence consistent with that prediction of models with nominal rigidities? And if so, are the effects of monetary policy interventions sufficiently important quantitatively to be relevant?

Unfortunately, identifying the effects of changes in monetary policy is not an easy task. The reason for this is well understood: An important part of the movements in whatever variable is taken as the instrument of monetary policy (e.g., the short term nominal rate) are likely to be endogenous, i.e., the result of a deliberate response of the monetary authority to developments in the economy.

---

[11] In addition to studies based on the analysis of micro data, some researchers have conducted surveys of firms' pricing policies. See, e.g., Blinder et al. (1998) for the United States and Fabiani et al. (2005) for several countries in the euro area. The conclusions from the survey-based evidence tend to confirm the evidence of substantial price rigidities coming out of the micro-data analysis.

Thus, simple correlations of interest rates (or the money supply) on output or other real variables cannot be used as evidence of non-neutralities. The direction of causality could well go, fully or in part, from movements in the real variable (resulting from nonmonetary forces) to the monetary variable. Over the years, a large literature has developed seeking to answer such questions while avoiding the pitfalls of a simple analysis of comovements. The main challenge facing that literature lies in identifying changes in policy that could be interpreted as autonomous, i.e., not the result of the central bank's response to movements in other variables. While alternative approaches have been pursued in order to meet that challenge, much of the recent literature has relied on time series econometrics techniques and, in particular, on structural (or identified) vector autoregressions.

The evidence displayed in figure 1.1, taken from Christiano, Eichenbaum, and Evans (1999), is representative of the findings in the recent literature seeking to estimate the effects of exogenous monetary policy shocks.[12] In the empirical model underlying figure 1.1, monetary policy shocks are identified as the residual from an estimated policy rule followed by the Federal Reserve. That policy rule determines the level of the federal funds rate (taken to be the instrument of monetary policy), as a linear function of its own lagged values, current and lagged values of GDP, the GDP deflator, and an index of commodity prices, as well as the lagged values of some monetary aggregates. Under the assumption that neither GDP nor the two price indexes can respond contemporaneously to a monetary policy shock, the coefficients of the previous policy rule can be estimated consistently with ordinary least squares (OLS), and the fitted residual can be taken as an estimate of the exogenous monetary policy shock. The response over time of any variable of interest to that shock is then given by the estimated coefficients of a regression of the current value of that variable on the current and lagged values of the fitted residual from the first-stage regression.

Figure 1.1 shows the dynamic responses of the federal funds rate, (log) GDP, (log) GDP deflator, and the money supply (measured by M2) to an exogenous tightening of monetary policy. The solid line represents the estimated response, with the dashed lines capturing the corresponding 95 percent confidence interval. The scale on the horizontal axis measures the number of quarters after the initial shock. Note that the path of the funds rate itself, depicted in the top left graph, shows an initial increase of about 75 basis points, followed by a gradual return to its original level. In response to that tightening of policy, GDP declines with a characteristic hump-shaped pattern. It reaches a trough after five quarters at a level about 50 basis points below its original level, and then it slowly reverts back to its original level. That estimated response of GDP can be viewed as

---

[12] Other references include Sims (1992), Galí (1992), Bernanke and Mihov (1998), and Uhlig (2005). Peersman and Smets (2003) provide similar evidence for the euro area. An alternative approach to identification, based on a narrative analysis of contractionary policy episodes can be found in Romer and Romer (1989).

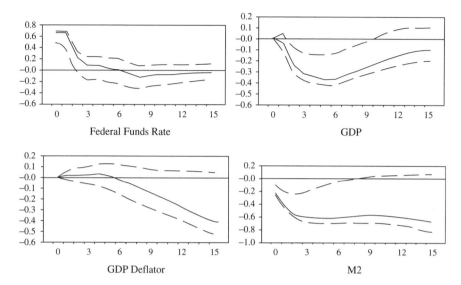

Figure 1.1 Estimated Dynamic Response to a Monetary Policy Shock

Source: Christiano, Eichenbaum, and Evans (1999).

evidence of sizable and persistent real effects of monetary policy shocks. On the other hand, the (log) GDP deflator displays a flat response for over a year, after which it declines. That estimated sluggish response of prices to the policy tightening is generally interpreted as evidence of substantial price rigidities.[13] Finally, note that (log) M2 displays a persistent decline in the face of the rise in the federal funds rate, suggesting that the Fed needs to reduce the amount of money in circulation in order to bring about the increase in the nominal rate. The observed negative comovement between money supply and nominal interest rates is known as *liquidity effect*. As will be discussed in chapter 2, that liquidity effect appears at odds with the predictions of a classical monetary model.

Having discussed the empirical evidence in support of the key assumptions underlying the New Keynesian framework, this introductory chapter ends with a brief description of the organization of the remaining chapters.

1.3 Organization of the Book

The book is organized into eight chapters, including this introduction. Chapters 2 through 7 progressively develop a unified framework, with new elements being incorporated in each chapter. Throughout the book, the references in the main text are kept to a minimum, and a section is added to the end of each chapter with

---

[13] Also, note that expected inflation hardly changes for several quarters and then declines. Combined with the path of the nominal rate, this implies a large and persistent increase in the real rate in response to the tightening of monetary policy, which provides another manifestation of the non-neutrality of monetary policy.

a discussion of the literature, including references to the key papers underlying the results presented in the chapter. In addition, each chapter contains a list of suggested exercises related to the material covered in the chapter.

Next, the content of each chapter is briefly described.

Chapter 2 introduces the assumptions on preferences and technology that will be used in most of the remaining chapters. The economy's equilibrium is determined and analyzed under the assumption of perfect competition in all markets and fully flexible prices and wages. Those assumptions define what is labeled as the *classical monetary economy*, which is characterized by neutrality of monetary policy and efficiency of the equilibrium allocation. In particular, the specification of monetary policy is shown to play a role only for the determination of nominal variables.

In the baseline model used in the first part of chapter 2, as in the rest of the book, money's role is limited to being the unit of account, i.e., the unit in terms of which prices of goods, labor services, and financial assets are quoted. Its potential role as a store of value (and hence as an asset in agents' portfolios), or as a medium of exchange, is ignored. As a result, there is generally no need to specify a money demand function, unless monetary policy itself is specified in terms of a monetary aggregate, in which case a simple log-linear money demand schedule is postulated. The second part of chapter 2, however, generates a motive to hold money by introducing real balances as an argument of the household's utility function, and examines its implications under the alternative assumptions of separability and nonseparability of real balances. In the latter case, in particular, the result of monetary policy neutrality is shown to break down, even in the absence of nominal rigidities. The resulting non-neutralities, however, are shown to be of limited interest empirically.

Chapter 3 introduces the basic New Keynesian model, by adding product differentiation, monopolistic competition, and staggered price setting to the framework developed in chapter 2. Labor markets are still assumed to be competitive. The solution is derived to the optimal price-setting problem of a firm in that environment with the resulting inflation dynamics. The log linearization of the optimality conditions of households and firms, combined with some market clearing conditions, leads to the canonical representation of the model's equilibrium, which includes the New Keynesian Phillips curve, a dynamic IS equation and a description of monetary policy. Two variables play a central role in the equilibrium dynamics: the output gap and the natural rate of interest. The presence of sticky prices is shown to make monetary policy non-neutral. This is illustrated by analyzing the economy's response to two types of shocks: an exogenous monetary policy shock and a technology shock.

In chapter 4, the role of monetary policy in the basic New Keynesian model is discussed from a normative perspective. In particular, it is shown that, under some assumptions, it is optimal to pursue a policy that fully stabilizes the price level (strict inflation targeting) and alternative ways in which that policy can be implemented are discussed (optimal interest rate rules). There follows a discussion of the likely practical difficulties in the implementation of the optimal policy, which motivates the introduction and analysis of simple monetary policy rules, i.e., rules that can be implemented with little or no knowledge of the economy's structure and/or realization of shocks. A welfare-based loss function that can be used for the evaluation and comparison of those rules is then derived and applied to two simple rules: a Taylor rule and a constant money growth rule.

A common criticism of the analysis of optimal monetary policy contained in chapter 4 is the absence of a conflict between inflation stabilization and output gap stabilization in the basic New Keynesian model. In chapter 5 that criticism is addressed by appending an exogenous additive shock to the New Keynesian Phillips curve, thus generating a meaningful policy tradeoff. In that context, and following the analysis in Clarida, Galí, and Gertler (1999), the optimal monetary policy under the alternative assumptions of discretion and commitment is discussed, emphasizing the key role played by the forward-looking nature of inflation as a source of the gains from commitment.

Chapter 6 extends the basic New Keynesian framework by introducing imperfect competition and staggered nominal wage setting in labor markets, in coexistence with staggered price setting and modelled in an analogous way, following the work of Erceg, Henderson, and Levin (2000). The presence of sticky nominal wages and the consequent variations in wage markups render a policy aimed at fully stabilizing price inflation as suboptimal. The reason is that fluctuations in wage inflation, in addition to variations in price inflation and the output gap, generate a resource misallocation and a consequent welfare loss. Thus, the optimal policy is one that seeks to strike the right balance between stabilization of those three variables. For a broad range of parameters, however, the optimal policy can be well approximated by a rule that stabilizes a weighted average of price and wage inflation, where the proper weights are a function of the relative stickiness of prices and wages.

Chapter 7 develops a small open economy version of the basic New Keynesian model. The analysis of the resulting model yields several results. First, the equilibrium conditions have a canonical representation analogous to that of the closed economy, including a New Keynesian Phillips curve, a dynamic IS equation, and an interest rate rule. In general, though, both the natural level of output and the natural real rate are a function of foreign, as well as domestic, shocks. Second, and under certain assumptions, the optimal policy consists in fully stabilizing domestic inflation while accommodating the changes in the exchange rate (and, as a result, in CPI inflation) necessary to bring about the desirable changes in the relative price of domestic goods. Thus, in general, policies that seek to stabilize the nominal exchange rate, including the limiting case of an exchange rate peg, are likely to be suboptimal.

Finally, chapter 8 reviews some of the general lessons that can be drawn from the previous chapters. In doing so, the focus is on two key insights generated by the new framework, namely, the key role of expectations in shaping the effects of monetary policy, and the importance of the natural levels of output and the interest rate for the design of monetary policy. Chapter 8 ends by describing briefly some of the extensions of the basic New Keynesian model that have not been covered in the book, and by discussing some of the recent developments in the literature.

References

Akerlof, George, and Janet Yellen (1985): "A Near-Rational Model of the Business Cycle with Wage and Price Inertia," *Quarterly Journal of Economics* 100, 823–838.

Ball, Laurence, and David H. Romer (1990): "Real Rigidities and the Nonneutrality of Money," *Review of Economic Studies* 57, 183–203.

Basu, Susanto, John Fernald, and Miles Kimball (2006): "Are Technology Improvements Contractionary?" *American Economic Review* 96, no. 5, 1418–1448.

Bayoumi, Tam (2004): "GEM: A New International Macroeconomic Model," *IMF Occasional Paper* no. 239.

Bernanke, Ben S., and Ilian Mihov (1998): "Measuring Monetary Policy," *Quarterly Journal of Economics* 113, no. 3, 869–902.

Bewley, Truman F. (1999): *Why Wages Don't Fall during a Recession?*, Harvard University Press, Cambridge, MA.

Bils, Mark, and Peter J. Klenow (2004): "Some Evidence on the Importance of Sticky Prices," *Journal of Political Economy* 112, no. 5, 947–985.

Blanchard, Olivier J., and Nobuhiro Kiyotaki (1987): "Monopolistic Competition and the Effects of Aggregate Demand," *American Economic Review* 77, no. 4, 647–666.

Blinder, Alan S., Elie R. D. Canetti, David E. Lebow, and Jeremy B. Rudd (1998): *Asking about Prices: A New Approach to Understanding Price Stickiness*, Russell Sage Foundation, New York.

Cecchetti, Stephen G. (1986): "The Frequency of Price Adjustment: A Study of Newsstand Prices of Magazines," *Journal of Econometrics* 31, no. 3, 255–274.

Christiano, Lawrence J., Martin Eichenbaum, and Charles L. Evans (1999): "Monetary Policy Shocks: What Have We Learned and to What End?" in J. B. Taylor and M. Woodford (eds.), *Handbook of Macroeconomics* 1A, Elsevier Science, Amsterdam, 65–148.

Christiano, Lawrence J., Martin Eichenbaum, and Robert Vigfusson (2003): "What Happens After a Technology Shock?" NBER WP#9819.

Clarida, Richard, Jordi Galí, and Mark Gertler (1999): " The Science of Monetary Policy: A New Keynesian Perspective," *Journal of Economic Literature* 37, 1661–1707.

Coenen, Günter, Peter McAdam, and Roland Straub (2006): " Tax Reform and Labour Market Performance in the Euro Area: A Simulation-Based Analysis Using the New Area-Wide Model," *Journal of Economic Dynamics and Control*, forthcoming.

Cooley, Thomas F., and Gary D. Hansen (1989): "Inflation Tax in a Real Business Cycle Model," *American Economic Review* 79, no. 4, 733–748.

Dhyne, Emmanuel, Luis J. Àlvarez, Daniel Dias, Johannes Hoffmann, Nicole Jonker, Hervé le Bihan, Patrick Lünnemann, Fabio Rumler, Giovanni Veronese, and Jouko Vilmunen

(2006): "Price Changes in the Euro Area and the United States: Some Facts from Individual Consumer Price Data," *Journal of Economic Perspectives* 20, no. 2, 171–192.

Dickens, William T., Lorenz Goette, Erica L. Groshen, Steinar Holden, Julian Messina, Mark E. Schweitzer, Jarkko Turunen, and Melanie E. Ward (2007): "How Wages Change: Micro Evidence from the International Wage Flexibility Project," *Journal of Economic Perspectives* 21, no. 2, 195–214.

Edge, Rochelle M., Michael T. Kiley, and Jean-Philippe Laforte (2007): "Documentation of the Research and Statistics Division's Estimated DSGE Model of the U.S. Economy: 2006 Version," Federal Reserve Board, Finance and Economics Discussion Series, no. 2007-52.

Erceg, Christopher J., Luca Guerrieri, and Christopher Gust (2006): "SIGMA: A New Open Economy Model for Policy Analysis," *International Journal of Central Banking* 2, no. 1, 1–50.

Erceg, Christopher J., Dale W. Henderson, and Andrew T. Levin (2000): "Optimal Monetary Policy with Staggered Wage and Price Contracts," *Journal of Monetary Economics* 46, no. 2, 281–314.

Fabiani, Silvia, Martine Druant, Ignacio Hernando, Claudia Kwapil, Bettina Landau, Claire Loupias, Fernando Martins, Thomas Y. Matha, Roberto Sabbatini, Harald Stahl, and Ad. C. J. Stokman (2005): "The Pricing Behavior of Firms in the Euro Area: New Survey Evidence," *ECB Working Paper* no. 535.

Fischer, Stanley (1977): "Long-Term Contracts, Rational Expectations, and the Optimal Money Supply," *Journal of Political Economy* 85, no. 1, 191–206.

Fisher, Jonas D. M. (2006): "The Dynamic Effects of Neutral and Investment-Specific Technology Shocks," *Journal of Political Economy* 114, no. 3, 413–451.

Friedman, Milton, and Anna J. Schwartz (1963): *A Monetary History of the United States, 1867–1960*, Princeton University Press, Princeton, NJ.

Galí, Jordi (1992): "How Well Does the IS-LM Model Fit Postwar U.S. Data?" *Quarterly Journal of Economics* 107, no. 2, 709–738.

Galí, Jordi (1999): "Technology, Employment, and the Business Cycle: Do Technology Shocks Explain Aggregate Fluctuations?" *American Economic Review* 89, no. 1, 249–271.

Galí, Jordi, and Mark Gertler (2007): "Macroeconomic Modeling for Monetary Policy Evaluation," *Journal of Economic Perspectives*, forthcoming.

Galí, Jordi, and Pau Rabanal (2004): "Technology Shocks and Aggregate Fluctuations: How Well Does the RBC Model Fit Postwar U.S. Data?," *NBER Macroeconomics Annual 2004*, MIT Press, Cambridge, MA.

Goodfriend, Marvin, and Robert G. King (1997): "The New Neoclassical Synthesis and the Role of Monetary Policy," *NBER Macroeconomics Annual 1997*, 231–282.

Kashyap, Anil K. (1995): "Sticky Prices: New Evidence from Retail Catalogues," *Quarterly Journal of Economics* 110, no. 1, 245–274.

Keynes, John Maynard (1936): *The General Theory of Employment, Interest and Money*, MacMillan and Co., London.

Kydland, Finn E., and Edward C. Prescott (1982): "Time to Build and Aggregate Fluctuations," *Econometrica* 50, no. 6, 1345–1370.

Lucas, Robert E. (1976): "Econometric Policy Evaluation: A Critique," *Carnegie–Rochester Conference Series on Public Policy* 1, 19–46.

Mankiw, Gregory (1985): "Small Menu Costs and Large Business Cycles: A Macroeconomic Model of Monopoly," *Quarterly Journal of Economy* 100, no. 2, 529–539.

Nakamura, Emi, and Jon Steinsson (2006): "Five Facts about Prices: A Reevaluation of Menu Costs Models," Harvard University Press, Cambridge, MA.

Peersman, Gert, and Frank Smets (2003): "The Monetary Transmission Mechanism in the Euro Area: More Evidence from VAR Analysis," in Angeloni et al. (eds.), *Monetary Policy Transmission in the Euro Area,* Cambridge University Press, New York.

Prescott, Edward C. (1986): "Theory Ahead of Business Cycle Measurement," *Quarterly Review* 10, 9–22, Federal Reserve Bank of Minneapolis, Minneapolis, MN.

Romer, Christina, and David Romer (1989): "Does Monetary Policy Matter? A New Test in the Spirit of Friedman and Schwartz," *NBER Macroeconomics Annual* 4, 121–170.

Sims, Christopher (1980): "Macroeconomics and Reality," *Econometrica* 48, no. 1, 1–48.

Sims, Christopher (1992): "Interpreting the Macroeconomic Time Series Facts: The Effects of Monetary Policy," *European Economic Review* 36, 975–1011.

Smets, Frank, and Raf Wouters (2003): "An Estimated Dynamic Stochastic General Equilibrium Model of the Euro Area," *Journal of the European Economic Association* 1, no. 5, 1123–1175.

Taylor, John B. (1980): "Aggregate Dynamics and Staggered Contracts," *Journal of Political Economy* 88, no. 1, 1–24.

Taylor, John B. (1999): "Staggered Price and Wage Setting in Macroeconomics," in J. B. Taylor and M. Woodford (eds.), *Handbook of Macroeconomics*, chap. 15, 1341–1397, Elsevier, New York.

Uhlig, Harald (2005): "What Are the Effects of Monetary Policy on Output? Results from an Anostic Identification Procedure," *Journal of Monetary Economics* 52, no. 2, 381–419.

Walsh, Carl E. (2003): *Monetary Theory and Policy*, Second Edition, MIT Press, Boston, MA.

Woodford, Michael (2003): *Interest and Prices: Foundations of a Theory of Monetary Policy*, Princeton University Press, Princeton, NJ.

2

A Classical Monetary Model

This chapter presents a simple model of a classical monetary economy, featuring perfect competition and fully flexible prices in all markets. As stressed below, many of the predictions of that classical economy are strongly at odds with the evidence reviewed in chapter 1. That notwithstanding, the analysis of the classical economy provides a benchmark that will be useful in subsequent chapters when some of its strong assumptions are relaxed. It also allows for the introduction of some notation, as well as assumptions on preferences and technology that are used in the remainder of the book.

Following much of the recent literature, the baseline classical model developed here attaches a very limited role to money. Thus, in the first four sections of this chapter, the only explicit role played by money is to serve as a unit of account. In that case, and as shown below, whenever monetary policy is specified in terms of an interest rate rule, no reference whatsoever is made to the quantity of money in circulation in order to determine the economy's equilibrium. When the specification of monetary policy involves the money supply, a "conventional" money demand equation is postulated in order to close the model without taking a stand on its microfoundations. In section 2.5, an explicit role for money is introduced, beyond that of serving as a unit of account. In particular, a model is analyzed in which real balances are assumed to generate utility to households, and the implications for monetary policy of alternative assumptions on the properties of that utility function are explored.

Independently of how money is introduced, the proposed framework assumes a representative household solving a dynamic optimization problem. That problem and the associated optimality conditions are described in section 2.1. Section 2.2 introduces the representative firm's technology and determines its optimal behavior under the assumption of price and wage-taking. Section 2.3 characterizes the equilibrium and shows how real variables are uniquely determined independent of monetary policy. Section 2.4 discusses the determination of the price level and other nominal variables under alternative monetary policy rules. Finally, section 2.5 analyzes a version of the model with money in the utility function, and discusses the extent to which the conclusions drawn from the earlier analysis need to be modified under that assumption.

2.1   Households

The representative household seeks to maximize the objective function

$$E_0 \sum_{t=0}^{\infty} \beta^t\, U(C_t, N_t) \tag{1}$$

where C_t is the quantity consumed of the single good, and N_t denotes hours of work or employment.[1] The period utility $U(C_t, N_t)$ is assumed to be continuous and twice differentiable, with $U_{c,t} \equiv \frac{\partial U(C_t, N_t)}{\partial C_t} > 0$, $U_{cc,t} \equiv \frac{\partial^2 U(C_t, N_t)}{\partial C_t^2} \leq 0$, $U_{n,t} \equiv \frac{\partial U(C_t, N_t)}{\partial N_t} \leq 0$, and $U_{nn,t} \equiv \frac{\partial^2 U(C_t, N_t)}{\partial N_t^2} \leq 0$. In words, the marginal utility of consumption $U_{c,t}$ is assumed to be positive and nonincreasing, while the marginal disutility of labor, $-U_{n,t}$, is positive and nondecreasing.

Maximization of (1) is subject to a sequence of flow budget constraints given by

$$P_t\, C_t + Q_t\, B_t \leq B_{t-1} + W_t\, N_t - T_t \tag{2}$$

for $t = 0, 1, 2, \ldots$ P_t is the price of the consumption good. W_t denotes the nominal wage, B_t represents the quantity of one-period, nominally riskless discount bonds purchased in period t and maturing in period $t+1$. Each bond pays one unit of money at maturity and its price is Q_t. T_t represents lump-sum additions or subtractions to period income (e.g., lump-sum taxes, dividends, etc.), expressed in nominal terms. When solving the problem above, the household is assumed to take as given the price of the good, the wage, and the price of bonds.

In addition to (2), it is assumed that the household is subject to a solvency constraint that prevents it from engaging in Ponzi-type schemes. The following constraint

$$\lim_{T \to \infty} E_t\{B_T\} \geq 0 \tag{3}$$

for all t is sufficient for our purposes.

2.1.1   Optimal Consumption and Labor Supply

The optimality conditions implied by the maximization of (1) subject to (2) are given by

$$-\frac{U_{n,t}}{U_{c,t}} = \frac{W_t}{P_t} \tag{4}$$

$$Q_t = \beta\, E_t\left\{ \frac{U_{c,t+1}}{U_{c,t}} \frac{P_t}{P_{t+1}} \right\} \tag{5}$$

for $t = 0, 1, 2, \ldots$.

---

[1] Note that N_t can be interpreted as the number of household members employed, assuming a large household and ignoring integer constraints.

The previous optimality conditions can be derived using a simple variational argument. Let us first consider the impact on utility of a small departure, in period t, from the household's optimal plan. That departure consists of an increase in consumption dC_t and an increase in hours dN_t, while keeping the remaining variables unchanged (including consumption and hours in other periods). If the household was following an optimal plan to begin with, it must be the case that

$$U_{c,t} \, dC_t + U_{n,t} \, dN_t = 0$$

for any pair (dC_t, dN_t) satisfying the budget constraint, i.e.,

$$P_t \, dC_t = W_t \, dN_t$$

for otherwise it would be possible to raise utility by increasing (or decreasing) consumption and hours, thus contradicting the assumption that the household is on an optimal plan. Note that by combining both equations the optimality condition (4) is obtained.

Similarly, consider the impact on expected utility as of time t of a reallocation of consumption between periods t and $t + 1$, while keeping consumption in any period other than t and $t + 1$, and hours worked (in all periods) unchanged. If the household is optimizing, it must be the case that

$$U_{c,t} \, dC_t + \beta \, E_t\{U_{c,t+1} \, dC_{t+1}\} = 0$$

for any pair (dC_t, dC_{t+1}) satisfying

$$P_{t+1}dC_{t+1} = -\frac{P_t}{Q_t} \, dC_t$$

where the latter equation determines the increase in consumption expenditures in period $t + 1$ made possible by the additional savings $-P_t dC_t$ allocated into one-period bonds. Combining the two previous equations yields the intertemporal optimality condition (5).

Much of what follows, assumes that the period utility takes the form

$$U(C_t, N_t) = \frac{C_t^{1-\sigma}}{1-\sigma} - \frac{N_t^{1+\varphi}}{1+\varphi}.$$

The consumer's optimality conditions (4) and (5) thus become

$$\frac{W_t}{P_t} = C_t^{\sigma} \, N_t^{\varphi} \tag{6}$$

$$Q_t = \beta \, E_t \left\{ \left(\frac{C_{t+1}}{C_t} \right)^{-\sigma} \frac{P_t}{P_{t+1}} \right\}. \tag{7}$$

Note, for future reference, that equation (6) can be rewritten in log-linear form as

$$w_t - p_t = \sigma\, c_t + \varphi\, n_t \tag{8}$$

where lowercase letters denote the natural logs of the corresponding variable (i.e., $x_t \equiv \log X_t$). The previous condition can be interpreted as a competitive labor supply schedule, determining the quantity of labor supplied as a function of the real wage, given the marginal utility of consumption (which under the assumptions is a function of consumption only).

As shown in appendix 2.1, a log-linear approximation of (7) around a steady state with constant rates of inflation and consumption growth is given by

$$c_t = E_t\{c_{t+1}\} - \frac{1}{\sigma}\,(i_t - E_t\{\pi_{t+1}\} - \rho) \tag{9}$$

where $i_t \equiv -\log Q_t$, $\rho \equiv -\log \beta$ and where $\pi_{t+1} \equiv p_{t+1} - p_t$ is the rate of inflation between t and $t+1$ (having defined $p_t \equiv \log P_t$). Notice that i_t corresponds to the log of the gross yield on the one-period bond; henceforth, it is referred to as the *nominal interest rate*.[2] Similarly, ρ can be interpreted as the household's discount rate.

While the previous framework does not explicitly introduce a motive for holding money balances, in some cases it will be convenient to postulate a demand for real balances with a log-linear form given by (up to an additive constant)

$$m_t - p_t = y_t - \eta\, i_t \tag{10}$$

where $\eta \geq 0$ denotes the interest semi-elasticity of money demand.

A money demand equation similar to (10) can be derived under a variety of assumptions. For instance, in section 2.5 it is derived as an optimality condition for the household when money balances yield utility.

2.2   Firms

A representative firm is assumed whose technology is described by a production function given by

$$Y_t = A_t\, N_t^{1-\alpha} \tag{11}$$

where A_t represents the level of technology, and $a_t \equiv \log A_t$ evolves exogenously according to some stochastic process.

Each period the firm maximizes profits

$$P_t\, Y_t - W_t\, N_t \tag{12}$$

subject to (11), taking the price and wage as given.

---

[2] The yield on the one period bond is defined by $Q_t \equiv (1 + yield)^{-1}$. Note that $i_t \equiv -\log Q_t = \log(1 + yield_t) \simeq yield_t$, where the latter approximation will be accurate as long as the nominal yield is "small."

Maximization of (12) subject to (11) yields the optimality condition

$$\frac{W_t}{P_t} = (1 - \alpha) \, A_t \, N_t^{-\alpha} \tag{13}$$

i.e., the firm hires labor up to the point where its marginal product equals the real wage. Equivalently, the marginal cost $\frac{W_t}{(1-\alpha)A_t \, N_t^{-\alpha}}$ must be equated to the price P_t.

In log-linear terms,

$$w_t - p_t = a_t - \alpha \, n_t + \log(1 - \alpha) \tag{14}$$

which can be interpreted as labor demand schedule, mapping the real wage into the quantity of labor demanded, given the level of technology.

2.3 Equilibrium

The baseline model abstracts from aggregate demand components like investment, government purchases, or net exports. Accordingly, the goods market clearing condition is given by

$$y_t = c_t \tag{15}$$

i.e., all output must be consumed.

By combining the optimality conditions of households and firms with (15) and the log-linear aggregate production relationship

$$y_t = a_t + (1 - \alpha) \, n_t \tag{16}$$

the equilibrium levels of employment and output are determined as a function of the level of technology

$$n_t = \psi_{na} \, a_t + \vartheta_n \tag{17}$$

$$y_t = \psi_{ya} \, a_t + \vartheta_y \tag{18}$$

where $\quad \psi_{na} \equiv \frac{1-\sigma}{\sigma(1-\alpha)+\varphi+\alpha}, \quad \vartheta_n \equiv \frac{\log(1-\alpha)}{\sigma(1-\alpha)+\varphi+\alpha}, \quad \psi_{ya} \equiv \frac{1+\varphi}{\sigma(1-\alpha)+\varphi+\alpha}, \quad$ and $\vartheta_y \equiv (1 - \alpha)\vartheta_n.$

Furthermore, given the equilibrium process for output, (9) can be used to determine the implied real interest rate, $r_t \equiv i_t - E_t\{\pi_{t+1}\}$, as

$$r_t = \rho + \sigma \, E_t\{\Delta y_{t+1}\}$$
$$= \rho + \sigma \psi_{ya} \, E_t\{\Delta a_{t+1}\}. \tag{19}$$

Finally, the equilibrium real wage $\omega_t \equiv w_t - p_t$ is given by

$$\omega_t = a_t - \alpha \, n_t + \log(1 - \alpha) \tag{20}$$
$$= \psi_{\omega a} \, a_t + \vartheta_\omega$$

where $\psi_{\omega a} \equiv \frac{\sigma+\varphi}{\sigma(1-\alpha)+\varphi+\alpha}$ and $\vartheta_\omega \equiv \frac{(\sigma(1-\alpha)+\varphi)\log(1-\alpha)}{\sigma(1-\alpha)+\varphi+\alpha}.$

Notice that the equilibrium dynamics of employment, output, and the real interest rate are determined *independently of monetary policy*. In other words, monetary policy is *neutral* with respect to those real variables. In the simple model, output and employment fluctuate in response to variations in technology, which is assumed to be the only real driving force.[3] In particular, output always rises in the face of a productivity increase, with the size of the increase being given by $\psi_{ya} > 0$. The same is true for the real wage. On the other hand, the sign of the employment is ambiguous, depending on whether σ (which measures the strength of the wealth effect of labor supply) is larger or smaller than one. When $\sigma < 1$, the substitution effect on labor supply resulting from a higher real wage dominates the negative effect caused by a smaller marginal utility of consumption, leading to an increase in employment. The converse is true whenever $\sigma > 1$. When the utility of consumption is logarithmic ($\sigma = 1$), employment remains unchanged in the face of technology variations, for substitution and wealth effects exactly cancel one another. Finally, the response of the real interest rate depends critically on the time series properties of technology. If the current improvement in technology is transitory so that $E_t\{a_{t+1}\} < a_t$, then the real rate will go down. Otherwise, if technology is expected to keep improving, then $E_t\{a_{t+1}\} > a_t$ and the real rate will increase with a rise in a_t.

What about nominal variables, like inflation or the nominal interest rate? Not surprisingly, and in contrast with real variables, their equilibrium behavior cannot be determined uniquely by real forces. Instead, it requires the specification of how monetary policy is conducted. Several monetary policy rules and their implied outcomes will be considered next.

2.4   Monetary Policy and Price Level Determination

Let us start by examining the implications of some interest rate rules. Rules that involve monetary aggregates will be introduced later. All cases will make use of the Fisherian equation

$$i_t = E_t\{\pi_{t+1}\} + r_t \tag{21}$$

that implies that the nominal rate adjusts one for one with expected inflation, given a real interest rate that is determined exclusively by real factors, as in (19).

2.4.1   An Exogenous Path for the Nominal Interest Rate

Let us first consider the case of the nominal interest rate following an *exogenous stationary process* $\{i_t\}$. Without loss of generality, assume that i_t has mean ρ,

---

[3] It would be straightforward to introduce other real driving forces like variations in government purchases or exogenous shifts in preferences. In general, real variables will be affected by all those real shocks in equilibrium.

which is consistent with a steady state with zero inflation and no secular growth. Notice that a particular case of this rule corresponds to a constant interest rate $i_t = i = \rho$ for all t.

Using (21), write

$$E_t\{\pi_{t+1}\} = i_t - r_t$$

where, as discussed above, r_t is determined independently of the monetary policy rule.

Note that expected inflation is pinned down by the previous equation but actual inflation is not. Because there is no other condition that can be used to determine inflation, it follows that any path for the price level that satisfies

$$p_{t+1} = p_t + i_t - r_t + \xi_{t+1}$$

is consistent with equilibrium, where ξ_{t+1} is a shock, possibly unrelated to economic fundamentals, satisfying $E_t\{\xi_{t+1}\} = 0$ for all t. Such shocks are often referred to in the literature as *sunspot shocks*. An equilibrium in which such nonfundamental factors may cause fluctuations in one or more variables is referred to as an *indeterminate equilibrium*. The example above shows how an exogenous nominal interest rate leads to *price level indeterminacy*.

Notice that when (10) is operative the equilibrium path for the money supply (which is endogenous under the present policy regime) is given by

$$m_t = p_t + y_t - \eta\, i_t.$$

Hence, the money supply will inherit the indeterminacy of p_t. The same will be true of the nominal wage (which, in logs, equals the real wage, which is determined by (20) plus the price level, which is indeterminate).

2.4.2 A Simple Inflation-Based Interest Rate Rule

Suppose that the central bank adjusts the nominal interest rate according to the rule

$$i_t = \rho + \phi_\pi\, \pi_t$$

where $\phi_\pi \geq 0$.

Combining the previous rule with the Fisherian equation (21) yields

$$\phi_\pi\, \pi_t = E_t\{\pi_{t+1}\} + \widehat{r}_t \tag{22}$$

where $\widehat{r}_t \equiv r_t - \rho$. A distinction is made between two cases, depending on whether the coefficient on inflation in the above rule, ϕ_π, is larger or smaller than one.

If $\phi_\pi > 1$, the previous difference equation has only one stationary solution, i.e., a solution that remains in a neighborhood of the steady state. That solution can be obtained by solving (22) forward, which yields

$$\pi_t = \sum_{k=0}^{\infty} \phi_\pi^{-(k+1)} E_t\{\widehat{r}_{t+k}\}. \tag{23}$$

The previous equation fully determines inflation (and, hence, the price level) as a function of the path of the real interest rate, which in turn is a function of fundamentals, as shown in (19). Consider, for the sake of illustration, the case in which technology follows the stationary AR(1) process

$$a_t = \rho_a\, a_{t-1} + \varepsilon_t^a$$

where $\rho_a \in [0, 1)$. Then, (19) implies $\widehat{r}_t = -\, \sigma \psi_{ya}(1 - \rho_a)\, a_t$, which combined with (23) yields the following expression for equilibrium inflation

$$\pi_t = -\frac{\sigma \psi_{ya}(1 - \rho_a)}{\phi_\pi - \rho_a}\, a_t.$$

Note that a central bank following a rule of the form considered here can influence the degree of inflation volatility by choosing the size of ϕ_π. The larger is the latter parameter the smaller will be the impact of the real shock on inflation.

On the other hand, if $\phi_\pi < 1$, the stationary solutions to (22) take the form

$$\pi_{t+1} = \phi_\pi\, \pi_t - \widehat{r}_t + \xi_{t+1} \tag{24}$$

where $\{\xi_t\}$ is, again, an arbitrary sequence of shocks, possibly unrelated to fundamentals, satisfying $E_t\{\xi_{t+1}\} = 0$ for all t.

Accordingly, any process $\{\pi_t\}$ satisfying (24) is consistent with equilibrium, while remaining in a neighborhood of the steady state. So, as in the case of an exogenous nominal rate, the price level (and, hence, inflation and the nominal rate) are not determined uniquely when the interest rate rule implies a weak response of the nominal rate to changes in inflation. More specifically, the condition for a determinate price level, $\phi_\pi > 1$, requires that the central bank adjust nominal interest rates more than one for one in response to any change in inflation, a property known as the *Taylor principle*. The previous result can be viewed as a particular instance of the need to satisfy the Taylor principle in order for an interest rate rule to bring about a determinate equilibrium.

2.4.3 An Exogenous Path for the Money Supply

Suppose that the central bank sets an exogenous path for the money supply $\{m_t\}$. Using (10) to eliminate the nominal interest rate in (21), the following difference equation for the price level can be derived as

$$p_t = \left(\frac{\eta}{1+\eta}\right) E_t\{p_{t+1}\} + \left(\frac{1}{1+\eta}\right) m_t + u_t$$

where $u_t \equiv (1+\eta)^{-1}(\eta\, r_t - y_t)$ evolves independently of $\{m_t\}$.

Assuming $\eta > 0$ and solving forward obtains

$$p_t = \frac{1}{1+\eta} \sum_{k=0}^{\infty} \left(\frac{\eta}{1+\eta}\right)^k E_t\{m_{t+k}\} + u_t'$$

where $u_t' \equiv \sum_{k=0}^{\infty} (\frac{\eta}{1+\eta})^k E_t\{u_{t+k}\}$ is, again, independent of monetary policy.

Equivalently, the previous expression can be rewritten in terms of expected future growth rate of money as

$$p_t = m_t + \sum_{k=1}^{\infty} \left(\frac{\eta}{1+\eta}\right)^k E_t\{\Delta m_{t+k}\} + u_t'. \tag{25}$$

Hence, an arbitrary exogenous path for the money supply always determines the price level uniquely. Given the price level, as determined above, (10) can be used to solve for the nominal interest rate

$$i_t = \eta^{-1}\left[y_t - (m_t - p_t)\right]$$
$$= \eta^{-1} \sum_{k=1}^{\infty} \left(\frac{\eta}{1+\eta}\right)^k E_t\{\Delta m_{t+k}\} + u_t''$$

where $u_t'' \equiv \eta^{-1}(u_t' + y_t)$ is independent of monetary policy.

For example, consider the case in which money growth follows the AR(1) process

$$\Delta m_t = \rho_m\, \Delta m_{t-1} + \varepsilon_t^m.$$

For simplicity, assume the absence of real shocks, thus implying a constant output and a constant real rate. Without loss of generality, set $r_t = y_t = 0$ for all t. Then, it follows from (25) that

$$p_t = m_t + \frac{\eta\rho_m}{1+\eta(1-\rho_m)}\, \Delta m_t.$$

Hence, in response to an exogenous monetary policy shock, and as long as $\rho_m > 0$ (the empirically relevant case, given the observed positive autocorrelation of money growth), the price level should respond more than one for one with the increase in the money supply, a prediction that contrasts starkly with the sluggish response of the price level observed in empirical estimates of the effects of monetary policy shocks as discussed in chapter 1.

The nominal interest rate is in turn given by

$$i_t = \frac{\rho_m}{1 + \eta(1 - \rho_m)} \Delta m_t$$

i.e., in response to an expansion of the money supply, and as long as $\rho_m > 0$, the nominal interest rate is predicted to go up. In other words, the model implies the absence of a liquidity effect, in contrast with the evidence discussed in chapter 1.

2.4.4 Optimal Monetary Policy

The analysis of the baseline classical economy above has shown that while real variables are independent of monetary policy, the latter can have important implications for the behavior of nominal variables and, in particular, of prices. Yet, and given that the household's utility is a function of consumption and hours only—two real variables that are invariant to the way monetary policy is conducted—it follows that there is no policy rule that is better than any other. Thus, in the classical model above, a policy that generates large fluctuations in inflation and other nominal variables (perhaps as a consequence of following a policy rule that does not guarantee a unique equilibrium for those variables) is no less desirable than one that succeeds in stabilizing prices in the face of the same shocks.

The previous result, which is clearly extreme and empirically unappealing, can be overcome once versions of the classical monetary model are considered in which a motive to keep part of a household's wealth in the form of monetary assets is introduced explicitly. Section 2.5 discusses one such model in which real balances are assumed to yield utility.

The overall assessment of the classical monetary model as a framework to understand the joint behavior of nominal and real variables and their connection to monetary policy cannot be positive. The model cannot explain the observed real effects of monetary policy on real variables. Its predictions regarding the response of the price level, the nominal rate, and the money supply to exogenous monetary policy shocks are also in conflict with the empirical evidence. Those empirical failures are the main motivation behind the introduction of nominal frictions in otherwise similar models, a task that will be undertaken in chapter 3.

2.5 Money in the Utility Function

In the model developed in the previous sections, and in much of the recent monetary literature, the only role played by money is to serve as a numéraire, i.e., a unit of account in which prices, wages, and securities' payoffs are stated.[4] Economies

---

[4] Readers not interested in this extension may skip this section and proceed to section 2.6 without any loss of continuity.

with that characteristic are often referred to as *cashless economies*. Whenever a simple log-linear money demand function was postulated, it was done in an ad-hoc manner without an explicit justification for why agents would want to hold an asset that is dominated in return by bonds while having identical risk properties. Even though in the analysis of subsequent chapters the assumption of a cashless economy is held, it is useful to understand how the basic framework can incorporate a role for money other than that of a unit of account and, in particular, how it can generate a demand for money. The discussion in this section focuses on models that achieve the previous objective by assuming that real balances are an argument of the utility function.

The introduction of money in the utility function requires modifying the household's problem in two ways. First, preferences are now given by

$$E_0 \sum_{t=0}^{\infty} \beta^t \, U\left(C_t, \frac{M_t}{P_t}, N_t\right) \tag{26}$$

where M_t denotes holdings of money in period t. Assume that period utility is increasing and concave in real balances M_t/P_t. Second, the flow budget constraint incorporates monetary holdings explicitly, taking the form

$$P_t \, C_t + Q_t \, B_t + M_t \le B_{t-1} + M_{t-1} + W_t \, N_t - T_t.$$

By letting $A_t \equiv B_{t-1} + M_{t-1}$ denote total financial wealth at the beginning of the period t (i.e., before consumption and portfolio decisions are made), the previous flow budget constraint can be rewritten as

$$P_t \, C_t + Q_t A_{t+1} + (1 - Q_t) M_t \le A_t + W_t \, N_t - T_t \tag{27}$$

with the solvency constraint now taking the form

$$\lim_{T \to \infty} E_t\{A_T\} \ge 0, \quad \text{for all } t.$$

The previous representation of the budget constraint can be thought of as equivalent to that of an economy in which all financial assets (represented by A_t) yield a gross nominal return Q_t^{-1} ($= \exp\{i_t\}$), and where agents can purchase the utility-yielding "services" of money balances at a unit price $(1 - Q_t) = 1 - \exp\{-i_t\} \simeq i_t$. Thus, the implicit price for money services roughly corresponds to the nominal interest rate, which in turn is the opportunity cost of holding one's financial wealth in terms of monetary assets, instead of interest-bearing bonds.

Consider next the household's problem, which consists of maximizing (26) subject to (27). Two of the implied optimality conditions are the same as those obtained for the cashless model, i.e., (4) and (5), with the marginal utility terms being now defined over (and evaluated at) the triplet $(C_t, \frac{M_t}{P_t}, N_t)$. In addition to (4) and (5), there is an additional optimality condition given by

$$\frac{U_{m,t}}{U_{c,t}} = 1 - \exp\{-i_t\} \tag{28}$$

where $U_{m,t} \equiv \frac{\partial U(C_t, M_t/P_t, N_t)}{\partial (M_t/P_t)} > 0$.

Again, in order to derive that optimality condition a simple variational argument can be used. Suppose that the household is considering deviating from the optimal plan by adjusting consumption and money holdings in period t by amounts dC_t and dM_t, respectively, while keeping all other variables unchanged at their optimal values. Optimality of the initial plan requires that utility cannot be raised as a result of the deviation, i.e.,

$$U_{c,t}\, dC_t + U_{m,t}\, \frac{1}{P_t}\, dM_t = 0$$

for any pair (dC_t, dM_t) satisfying

$$P_t\, dC_t + (1 - Q_t)\, dM_t = 0$$

which guarantees that the budget constraint is met without the need to adjust any other variable. Combining the previous two equations and using the definition of the nominal rate $i_t \equiv -\log Q_t$ yields the optimality condition (28).

In order to be able to make any statements about the consequences of having money in the utility function, more precision is needed about the way money balances interact with other variables in yielding utility. In particular, whether the utility function is separable or not in real balances determines the extent to which the neutrality properties derived above for the cashless economy carry over to the economy with money in the utility function. That point is illustrated by considering, in turn, two example economies with separable and nonseparable utility.

2.5.1 An Example with Separable Utility

Specifically, the household's utility function is assumed to have the functional form

$$U\left(C_t, \frac{M_t}{P_t}, N_t\right) = \frac{C_t^{1-\sigma}}{1-\sigma} + \frac{(M_t/P_t)^{1-\nu}}{1-\nu} - \frac{N_t^{1+\varphi}}{1+\varphi}.$$

Note that, given the assumed separability, neither $U_{c,t}$ nor $U_{n,t}$ depend on the level of real balances. As a result, (6) and (7), as well as their log-linear counterparts, (8) and (9), continue to hold unchanged. It follows that the equilibrium values for output, employment, the real rate, and the real wage can be determined by following the same steps as above and without any reference to monetary policy.

The introduction of money in the utility function allows a money demand equation to be derived from the household's optimal behavior. Using the above specification of utility, the optimality condition (28) can be rewritten as

$$\frac{M_t}{P_t} = C_t^{\sigma/\nu} \, (1 - \exp\{-i_t\})^{-1/\nu} \tag{29}$$

which can be naturally interpreted as a demand for real balances. The latter is increasing in consumption and inversely related to the nominal interest rate, as in conventional specifications.

Using the first-order Taylor approximation $\log(1 - \exp\{-i_t\}) \simeq const. + \frac{1}{\exp\{i\}-1} i_t$, (29) can be rewritten in approximate log-linear form (and up to an uninteresting constant) as

$$m_t - p_t = \frac{\sigma}{\nu} \, c_t - \eta \, i_t \tag{30}$$

where $\eta \equiv \frac{1}{\nu(\exp\{i\}-1)} \simeq \frac{1}{\nu i}$ is the implied interest semi-elasticity of money demand.

The particular case of $\nu = \sigma$ is an appealing one, because it implies a unit elasticity with respect to consumption. Under that assumption, a conventional linear demand for real balances is obtained as

$$m_t - p_t = c_t - \eta \, i_t$$
$$= y_t - \eta \, i_t \tag{31}$$

where the second equality holds in the baseline model economy, in which all output is consumed. The previous specification is often assumed in subsequent chapters, without the need to invoke its source explicitly.

As in the analysis of the cashless economy, the usefulness of (30), or (31), is confined to the determination of the equilibrium values for inflation and other nominal variables whenever the description of monetary policy involves the quantity of money in circulation. Otherwise, the only use of the money demand equation is to determine the quantity of money that the central bank will need to supply in order to support, in equilibrium, the nominal interest rate implied by the policy rule.

2.5.2 An Example with Nonseparable Utility

Let us consider an economy in which period utility is given by

$$U \left(C_t, \frac{M_t}{P_t}, N_t \right) = \frac{X_t^{1-\sigma}}{1 - \sigma} - \frac{N_t^{1+\varphi}}{1 + \varphi}$$

where X_t is a composite index of consumption and real balances defined as

$$X_t \equiv \left[(1 - \vartheta) \, C_t^{1-v} + \vartheta \left(\frac{M_t}{P_t} \right)^{1-v} \right]^{\frac{1}{1-v}} \quad \text{for } v \neq 1$$

$$\equiv C_t^{1-\vartheta} \left(\frac{M_t}{P_t} \right)^{\vartheta} \quad \text{for } v = 1$$

with v representing the (inverse) elasticity of substitution between consumption and real balances, and ϑ the relative weight of real balances in utility.

Notice that the marginal utilities of consumption and real balances are now given, respectively, by

$$U_{c,t} = (1 - \vartheta) \, X_t^{v-\sigma} \, C_t^{-v}$$

$$U_{m,t} = \vartheta \, X_t^{v-\sigma} \left(\frac{M_t}{P_t} \right)^{-v}$$

whereas the marginal (dis)utility of labor is, as before, given by $U_{n,t} = -N_t^{\varphi}$. The optimality conditions of the household's problem, (4), (5), and (28), can now be written as

$$\frac{W_t}{P_t} = N_t^{\varphi} \, X_t^{\sigma-v} \, C_t^{v} \, (1 - \vartheta)^{-1} \tag{32}$$

$$Q_t = \beta \, E_t \left\{ \left(\frac{C_{t+1}}{C_t} \right)^{-v} \left(\frac{X_{t+1}}{X_t} \right)^{v-\sigma} \frac{P_t}{P_{t+1}} \right\} \tag{33}$$

$$\frac{M_t}{P_t} = C_t \, (1 - \exp\{-i_t\})^{-\frac{1}{v}} \left(\frac{\vartheta}{1 - \vartheta} \right)^{\frac{1}{v}} \tag{34}$$

Notice that in the particular case in which the intertemporal and intratemporal elasticities of substitution coincide (i.e., $v = \sigma$), optimality conditions (32) and (33) match exactly those obtained in the case of separable utility, and thus lead to the same equilibrium implications derived for that case and discussed in section 2.5.1

In the general case, however, both the labor supply equation (32) and the Euler equation (33) are influenced by the level of real balances through the dependence of the index X_t on the latter. The level of real balances depends, in turn, on the nominal interest rate, as implied by (34). Those features imply that monetary policy is no longer neutral in the case of nonseparable utility considered here. In particular, to the extent that different monetary policy rules have different implications for the path of the nominal rate (as will generally be the case), they will also have different effects on real balances and—through the latter's influence on the marginal utility of consumption—on the position of the labor supply schedule and, hence, on employment and output. This mechanism is analyzed formally below.

Notice that the implied money demand equation (34) can be rewritten in log-linear form (and up to an additive constant) as in (31), i.e.,

$$m_t - p_t = c_t - \eta \, i_t \tag{35}$$

where, again, $\eta = \frac{1}{v(\exp\{i\}-1)}$. Thus, the implied interest semi-elasticity of demand η is now proportional to the elasticity of substitution between real balances and consumption v^{-1}.

On the other hand, log-linearization of (32) around the zero inflation steady state yields

$$w_t - p_t = \sigma c_t + \varphi n_t + (v - \sigma)(c_t - x_t).$$

Log-linearizing the expression defining X_t around a zero inflation steady state and combining the resulting expression with (34), yields

$$w_t - p_t = \sigma c_t + \varphi n_t + \chi (v - \sigma) \left[c_t - (m_t - p_t) \right]$$
$$= \sigma c_t + \varphi n_t + \chi \eta (v - \sigma) \, i_t$$

where $\chi \equiv \frac{\vartheta^{\frac{1}{v}}(1-\beta)^{1-\frac{1}{v}}}{(1-\vartheta)^{\frac{1}{v}} + \vartheta^{\frac{1}{v}}(1-\beta)^{1-\frac{1}{v}}} \in [0, 1)$, and where the second equality makes use of (35).

For future reference, it is convenient to rewrite the previous optimality conditions in terms of the steady state ratio $k_m \equiv \frac{M/P}{C}$, i.e., the inverse consumption velocity. Using the money demand equation, $k_m = \left(\frac{\vartheta}{(1-\beta)(1-\vartheta)} \right)^{\frac{1}{v}}$. Noting that $\chi = \frac{k_m(1-\beta)}{1+k_m(1-\beta)}$, and using the definition of η evaluated at the zero inflation steady state, the optimality condition above can be rewritten as

$$w_t - p_t = \sigma c_t + \varphi n_t + \omega \, i_t \tag{36}$$

where $\omega \equiv \frac{k_m \beta(1-\frac{\sigma}{v})}{1+k_m(1-\beta)}$. Thus, the sign of the effect of the nominal interest rate on labor supply is determined by the sign of $v - \sigma$. When $v > \sigma$ (implying $\omega > 0$), the reduction in real balances induced by an increase in the nominal rate brings down the marginal utility of consumption (for any given c_t), lowering the quantity of labor supplied at any given real wage. The opposite effect is obtained when $v < \sigma$. Note, however, that $v \simeq \frac{1}{i\eta}$ is likely to be larger than σ for any plausible values of η and σ. Thus, the case of $U_{cm} > 0$ (and, hence, $\omega > 0$) appears as the most plausible one, conditional on the specification of preferences analyzed here.

The corresponding log-linear approximation to (33) is given by

$$c_t = E_t\{c_{t+1}\} - \frac{1}{\sigma} (i_t - E_t\{\pi_{t+1}\} - (v-\sigma) \, E_t\{(c_{t+1} - x_{t+1}) - (c_t - x_t)\} - \rho)$$

$$= E_t\{c_{t+1}\} - \frac{1}{\sigma} (i_t - E_t\{\pi_{t+1}\} - \chi(v-\sigma) \, E_t\{\Delta c_{t+1} - \Delta(m_{t+1} - p_{t+1})\} - \rho)$$

$$= E_t\{c_{t+1}\} - \frac{1}{\sigma} (i_t - E_t\{\pi_{t+1}\} - \omega \, E_t\{\Delta i_{t+1}\} - \rho) \tag{37}$$

where, again, the last equality makes use of (35). Thus, when $v > \sigma$ (and, hence, $\omega > 0$), the anticipation of a nominal rate increase (and, hence, of a decline in real balances) lowers the expected one period ahead level of the marginal utility of consumption (for any expected c_{t+1}), which induces an increase in current consumption (in order to smooth marginal utility over time).

In order to reflect the changes implied by nonseparable utility, the economy's log-linearized equilibrium conditions need to be modified. Thus, combining (36) with the labor demand schedule (14) yields the labor market clearing condition

$$\sigma c_t + \varphi n_t + \omega \, i_t = y_t - n_t + \log(1 - \alpha) \tag{38}$$

which can be rewritten, using the goods market clearing condition (15) and the log-linear production relationship (16) as (ignoring an uninteresting additive constant)

$$y_t = \psi_{ya} \, a_t - \psi_{yi} \, i_t \tag{39}$$

where $\psi_{yi} \equiv \frac{\omega(1-\alpha)}{\sigma+\varphi+\alpha(1-\sigma)}$.

Condition (39) points to a key implication of the property of nonseparability ($\omega \neq 0$): Equilibrium output is no longer invariant to monetary policy, at least to the extent that the latter implies variations in the nominal interest rate. In other words, monetary policy is not neutral. As a result, equilibrium condition (39) does not suffice to determine the equilibrium level of output, in contrast to the economy with separable utility analyzed above. In order to pin down the equilibrium path of output and other endogenous variables (39) is combined with the remaining equilibrium conditions, including a description of monetary policy.

One such additional condition can be obtained by imposing the goods market clearing condition $y_t = c_t$ on Euler equation (37), which yields an equation relating the nominal interest rate to the expected path of output and expected inflation

$$y_t = E_t\{y_{t+1}\} - \frac{1}{\sigma} (i_t - E_t\{\pi_{t+1}\} - \omega \, E_t\{\Delta i_{t+1}\} - \rho) \,. \tag{40}$$

Finally, an equation that describes how monetary policy is conducted is needed. For the purposes of illustration, assume that the central bank follows the simple inflation-based interest rate rule

$$i_t = \rho + \phi_\pi \, \pi_t + v_t \tag{41}$$

where v_t now represents an exogenous policy disturbance, assumed to follow the stationary AR(1) process

$$v_t = \rho_v \, v_{t-1} + \varepsilon_t^v.$$

Similarly, and for concreteness, assume that the technology parameter follows the AR(1) process

$$a_t = \rho_a \, a_{t-1} + \varepsilon_t^a.$$

Using (41) to eliminate the nominal rate in (39) and (40) and combining the resulting two equations yields (after some algebraic manipulation) the following closed-form expressions for the equilibrium level of inflation, the nominal rate, and output

$$\pi_t = -\frac{\sigma(1-\rho_a)\psi_{ya}}{\phi_\pi(1+\omega\psi)(1-\Theta\rho_a)}a_t - \frac{1+(1-\rho_v)\omega\psi}{\phi_\pi(1+\omega\psi)(1-\Theta\rho_v)}v_t$$

$$i_t = -\frac{\sigma(1-\rho_a)\psi_{ya}}{(1+\omega\psi)(1-\Theta\rho_a)}a_t - \frac{\rho_v}{\phi_\pi(1+\omega\psi)(1-\Theta\rho_v)}v_t$$

$$y_t = \psi_{ya}\left(1+\frac{\sigma(1-\rho_a)\psi_{yi}}{(1+\omega\psi)(1-\Theta\rho_a)}\right)a_t + \frac{\rho_v\psi_{yi}}{\phi_\pi(1+\omega\psi)(1-\Theta\rho_v)}v_t$$

where $\Theta \equiv \frac{1+\omega\psi\phi_\pi}{(1+\omega\psi)\phi_\pi}$ and $\psi \equiv \frac{\alpha+\varphi}{\sigma(1-\alpha)+\alpha+\varphi}$.

A few remarks regarding the impact of monetary policy on the economy's equilibrium are in order. First, note that the interest rate multiplier of output, conditional on an exogenous monetary policy shock, is given by $\frac{dy_t}{di_t} = \frac{dy_t/dv_t}{di_t/dv_t} = -\psi_{yi}$. In order to get a sense for the magnitude of that multiplier, recall that $\psi_{yi} \equiv \frac{\omega(1-\alpha)}{\sigma+\varphi+\alpha(1-\sigma)}$. Let us assume parameter values $\sigma = \varphi = 1$ and $\alpha = 1/3$, as in the baseline calibration that will be introduced in chapter 3. Using the definition of ω, and the fact that $\nu = \frac{1}{\eta\rho}$ is "large" for any reasonable values of η, $\psi_{yi} \simeq \frac{k_m}{3}$, and so the size of the inverse velocity k_m is a key determinant of the quantitative importance of monetary non-neutralities in the model. Unfortunately, the magnitude of k_m depends crucially on the definition of money used. Thus, and focusing on postwar U.S. data, $k_m \simeq 0.3$ if the monetary base is taken as the relevant measure of money.[5] In that case $\psi_{yi} \simeq 0.1$, which implies a relatively small multiplier: A monetary policy shock that raised the nominal rate by one percentage point (expressed at an annual rate) would generate a decrease in output of about 0.025 percent. By way of contrast, by using M2 as the definition of money, $k_m \simeq 3$, and so the impact on output of an analogous monetary policy shock is a 0.25 percent decline. The latter value, while small, appears to be closer to the estimated output effects of a monetary policy shock found in the literature. Yet, even in the latter case, there are other aspects of the transmission of monetary policy shocks implied by the model that are clearly at odds with the evidence, e.g., the response of inflation and the real interest rate. Thus, note that

$$\frac{d\pi_t}{di_t} = \frac{d\pi_t/dv_t}{di_t/dv_t} = (1+(1-\rho_v)\omega\psi)\rho_v^{-1} > 0$$

$$\frac{dr_t}{di_t} = 1 - \frac{dE_t\{\pi_{t+1}\}/dv_t}{di_t/dv_t} = -(1-\rho_v)\omega\psi < 0$$

i.e., in response to a monetary policy shock that raises the nominal interest rate and lowers output, inflation tends to increase, and the real rate tends to go down (as a result of the dominant effect of higher expected inflation). This contrasts with

---

[5] This is the approach followed in Woodford (2003, chapter 2).

the downward adjustment of inflation and the rise in the real rate observed as part of the economy's response following a contractionary monetary policy shock.

Finally, there is an additional argument that can be brought up and which calls into question the relevance of the transmission mechanism underlying the classical model with nonseparable preferences and that has to do with its implications regarding the long-run effects of monetary policy. To see this, consider an exogenous monetary policy intervention that raises the nominal rate permanently. The implied permanent change in output is determined by (39) and given by $-\psi_{yi}$. Thus, the long-run tradeoff between output and the nominal rate is identical to the short-run tradeoff. How about the inflation–output tradeoff? Equation (40), evaluated at the steady state, requires a long-run increase in inflation of the same size as the increase in the nominal rate. Hence, the long-run tradeoff between inflation and output is also given by $-\psi_{yi}$. But note that the same coefficient describes the short-run inflation–output tradeoff because, in the relevant case of a permanent policy change ($\rho_v = 1$), $\frac{dy_t/dv_t}{d\pi_t/dv_t} = -\psi_{yi}$.

As argued above, for a most plausible range of parameter values $\psi_{yi} > 0$. Thus, in the present model a permanent increase in inflation will be associated with a permanent decline in output. Given the determinants of ψ_{yi}, whether that long-run tradeoff is large or small will depend largely on the size of inverse velocity k_m and, hence, on the relevant measure of money. Thus, the lack of a significant empirical relationship between long-run inflation and economic activity (at least at low levels of inflation), suggests a low value for k_m and ψ_{yi}, as implied by a narrow definition of money. Unfortunately, in the present model, and as argued above, any calibration with the desirable feature of a negligible long-run tradeoff will also be associated with negligible (and, hence, counterfactual) short run effects of monetary policy.

2.5.3 Optimal Monetary Policy in a Classical Economy with Money in the Utility Function

This section derives the form of the optimal monetary policy in the presence of money in the utility function. The problem facing a hypothetical social planner seeking to maximize the utility of the representative household is presented and solved.

Note that, under the assumptions, there are no aggregate intertemporal links in the simple model: Even though each individual household can reallocate its own consumption over time through financial markets, there are no mechanisms that make this possible for the economy as a whole. Thus, the social planner would solve a sequence of static problems of the form

$$\max U\left(C_t, \frac{M_t}{P_t}, N_t\right)$$

subject to the resource constraint

$$C_t = A_t N_t^{1-\alpha}.$$

The optimality conditions for that problem are given by

$$-\frac{U_{n,t}}{U_{c,t}} = (1-\alpha) A_t N_t^{-\alpha} \tag{42}$$

$$U_{m,t} = 0. \tag{43}$$

Condition (42) requires that the marginal rate of substitution between hours of work and consumption be equated to the marginal product of labor. Condition (43) equates the marginal utility of real balances to the "social" marginal cost of producing real balances, which is implicitly assumed to be zero in the setting.

Under what conditions does the equilibrium of the decentralized economy satisfy efficiency conditions (42) and (43)? First note that condition (42) is implied by the combined effect of profit maximization by firms (see equation (13), which equates the real wage to the marginal product of labor) and the optimal labor supply choice by the household (see equation (4), which equates the real wage to the marginal rate of substitution between hours of work and consumption). Hence, (42) will be satisfied independently of monetary policy. On the other hand, and as shown above, the household's optimal choice of money balances requires

$$\frac{U_{m,t}}{U_{c,t}} = 1 - \exp\{-i_t\}.$$

Accordingly, efficiency condition (43) will be satisfied, if and only if, $i_t = 0$ for all t, a policy known as the *Friedman rule*. The rationale for that policy is quite intuitive: While the social cost of producing real balances is zero, the private (opportunity) cost is given by the nominal interest rate. As a result, only when the nominal interest rate is zero are the private and social costs of holding money equated. Note that such a policy implies an average (steady state) rate of inflation

$$\pi = -\rho < 0$$

i.e., prices will decline on average at the rate of time preference. In other words: Under the Friedman rule the economy experiences a (moderate) deflation in the long run.

Implementation of the Friedman rule requires some discussion. As shown earlier, a policy rule of the form $i_t = 0$ for all t leaves the price level indeterminate in the model. Even though that indeterminacy should not have any welfare consequences (because (42) and (43) uniquely pin down consumption, employment, and real balances), a central bank could avoid that indeterminacy by following a rule of the form

$$i_t = \phi(r_{t-1} + \pi_t)$$

for some $\phi > 1$. Combined with (21), that rule implies the difference equation

$$E_t\{i_{t+1}\} = \phi i_t$$

whose only stationary solution is $i_t = 0$ for all t. Under that rule, equilibrium inflation is fully predictable and given by

$$\pi_t = -r_{t-1}.$$

More generally, any rule that makes the central bank adjust its policy settings (e.g., the money supply) to guarantee that current inflation moves inversely, and one for one with the lagged real interest rate, will imply a zero nominal interest rate and, thus, an efficient amount of real balances.

2.6 Notes on the Literature

The modelling approach favored in much of the recent monetary literature, and the one adopted in this book (with the exception of section 2.5 of this chapter), does not incorporate money explicitly in the analysis. Under that approach the main role played by money is that of a unit of account. Such model economies can be viewed as a limiting case (the cashless limit) of an economy in which money is valued and held by households. Woodford (2003) provides a detailed discussion and a forceful defense of that approach.

Models that introduce monetary assets explicitly rely on one of two alternative formalisms in order to generate a demand for an asset that—as is the case with money—is dominated in its rate of return by alternative assets that have identical risk characteristics: they either assume (i) that real balances generate utility to households or, alternatively, (ii) that the presence of some transaction costs in the purchases of goods can be reduced by a household's holding of monetary assets.

The first of those approaches—money in the utility function—traces back to Sidrauski (1967), who introduced that assumption in an otherwise standard neoclassical growth model (with inelastic labor supply). Woodford (2003) offers a detailed analysis of the implications of alternative assumptions on the specification of utility and, in particular, of the likely degree of monetary non-neutralities arising from the nonseparability of real balances. Walsh (2003, chapter 2) develops an RBC model with money in the utility function, and analyzes the equilibrium properties of a calibrated version of that model. Both analyses conclude, in a way consistent with the discussion above, that even under a utility that is nonseparable in real balances, the real effects of monetary policy are quantitatively very small for plausible calibrations of the models.

A common approach to the modelling of a transaction's motive for holding money builds on the assumption, originally due to Clower (1967), that cash must be held in advance in order to purchase certain goods. Early examples of classical monetary models in which a demand for money is generated by postulating a cash-in-advance constraint can be found in the work of Lucas (1982) and Svensson (1985). Cooley and Hansen (1989) analyze an otherwise standard RBC model augmented with a cash-in-advance constraint for consumption goods, showing that monetary policy is nearly neutral for plausible calibrations of that model. Walsh (2003, chapter 3) provides a detailed description of classical monetary models with cash-in-advance constraints and their implications for the role of monetary policy.

The practice, followed in this monograph, of appending a money demand equation to a set of equilibrium conditions that have been derived in the context of a cashless economy is often found in the literature. King and Watson (1995) constitutes an example of that practice.

The analysis of the form of the optimal monetary policy in a classical economy goes back to Friedman (1969), where a case is made for a policy that keeps the nominal interest rate constant at a zero level. More recent treatments of the conditions under which that rule is optimal include Woodford (1990) and Correia and Teles (1999).

Finally, the reader can find two useful discussions of the notion of monetary neutrality and its evolution in macroeconomic thinking in Patinkin (1987) and Lucas (1996).

Appendix

2.1 A Useful Log-Linear Approximation

The consumer's Euler equation can be rewritten as

$$1 = E_t\{\exp(i_t - \sigma \Delta c_{t+1} - \pi_{t+1} - \rho)\}. \tag{44}$$

In a perfect foresight steady state with constant inflation π and constant growth γ

$$i = \rho + \pi + \sigma\gamma$$

with the steady state real rate being given by

$$r \equiv i - \pi$$
$$= \rho + \sigma\gamma.$$

A first-order Taylor expansion of $\exp(i_t - \sigma \Delta c_{t+1} - \pi_{t+1} - \rho)$ around that steady state yields

$$\exp(i_t - \sigma \Delta c_{t+1} - \pi_{t+1} - \rho) \simeq 1 + (i_t - i) - \sigma(\Delta c_{t+1} - \gamma) - (\pi_{t+1} - \pi)$$
$$= 1 + i_t - \sigma \Delta c_{t+1} - \pi_{t+1} - \rho$$

which can be used in (44) to obtain, after some rearrangement of terms, the log-linearized Euler equation

$$c_t = E_t\{c_{t+1}\} - \frac{1}{\sigma}\,(i_t - E_t\{\pi_{t+1}\} - \rho).$$

References

Clower, Robert (1967): "A Reconsideration of the Microeconomic Foundations of Monetary Theory," *Western Economic Journal* 6, 1–8.

Cooley, Thomas F., and Gary D. Hansen (1989): "Inflation Tax in a Real Business Cycle Model," *American Economic Review* 79, no. 4, 733–748.

Correia, Isabel, and Pedro Teles (1999): "The Optimal Inflation Tax," *Review of Economic Dynamics* 2, no. 2, 325–346.

Friedman, Milton (1969): *The Optimum Quantity of Money and Other Essays*, Aldine Press, Chicago, IL.

King, Robert G., and Mark Watson (1995): "Money, Prices, Interest Rates, and the Business Cycle," *Review of Economics and Statistics* 58, no. 1, 35–53.

Lucas, Robert E. (1982): "Interest Rates and Currency Prices in a Two-Country World," *Journal of Monetary Economics* 10, no. 3, 335–359.

Lucas, Robert E. (1996): "Nobel Lecture: Monetary Neutrality," *Journal of Political Economy* 104, no. 4, 661–682.

Patinkin, Don (1987): "Neutrality of Money," in J. Eatwell, M. Milgate, and P. Newman (eds.), *The New Palgrave: A Dictionary of Economics*, W. W. Norton, New York.

Sidrauski, Miguel (1967): "Inflation and Economic Growth," *Journal of Political Economy* 75, no. 6, 796–816.

Svensson, Lars E. O. (1985): "Money and Asset Prices in a Cash in Advance Economy," *Journal of Political Economy* 93, no. 5, 919–944.

Walsh, Carl E. (2003): *Monetary Theory and Policy*, Second Edition, The MIT Press, Cambridge, MA.

Woodford, Michael (1990): "The Optimum Quantity of Money," in B. M. Friedman and F. H. Hahn (eds.), *Handbook of Monetary Economics* 2, Elsevier-Science, New York.

Woodford, Michael (2003): *Interest and Prices: Foundations of a Theory of Monetary Policy*, Princeton University Press, Princeton, NJ.

Exercises

2.1   Optimality Conditions under Nonseparable Leisure

Derive the log-linearized optimality conditions of the household problem under the following specification of the period utility function with nonseparable leisure.

$$U\,(C_t, N_t) = \frac{1}{1 - \sigma}\left[C_t\,(1 - N_t)^\nu\right]^{1-\sigma}$$

2.2 Alternative Interest Rules for the Classical Economy

Consider the simple classical economy described in the text, in which the following approximate equilibrium relationships must be satisfied

$$y_t = E_t\{y_{t+1}\} - \frac{1}{\sigma}(i_t - E_t\{\pi_{t+1}\} - \rho)$$

and

$$r_t \equiv i_t - E_t\{\pi_{t+1}\}$$
$$= \rho + \sigma E_t\{\Delta y_{t+1}\}$$

and where y_t and, hence, r_t, are determined independently of monetary policy. Next analyze, in turn, two alternative monetary policy rules and their implications. When relevant, assume that the money market clearing condition takes the form

$$m_t - p_t = y_t - \eta i_t + \varepsilon_t^m$$

where ε_t^m is a stochastic money demand disturbance.

a) *Strict Inflation Targeting*

(i) Derive an interest rate rule that guarantees full stabilization of inflation, i.e., $\pi_t = \pi^*$ for all t where π^* is an inflation target assumed to be "close to" zero (so that the log-linearized equilibrium conditions remain valid).

(ii) Determine the behavior of money growth that is consistent with the strict inflation targeting policy analyzed in (i).

(iii) Explain why a policy characterized by a constant rate of money growth $\Delta m_t = \pi$ will generally not succeed in stabilizing inflation in that economy.

b) *Price Level Targeting*

(i) Consider the interest rate rule

$$i_t = \rho + \phi_p (p_t - p^*)$$

where $\phi_p > 0$ and p^* is a (constant) target for the (log) price level. Determine the equilibrium behavior of the price level under this rule. (Hint: you may find it useful to introduce a new variable $\widehat{p}_t \equiv p_t - p^*$ —the deviation of the price level from target—to ease some of the algebraic manipulations.)

(ii) Consider instead the money targeting rule

$$m_t = p^*.$$

Determine the equilibrium behavior of the price level under this rule.

(iii) Show that the money targeting rule considered in (ii) can be combined with the money market clearing condition and rewritten as a price level targeting rule of the form

$$i_t = \rho + \psi (p_t - p^*) + u_t$$

where ψ is a coefficient and u_t is a stochastic process to be determined.

(iv) Suppose that the central bank wants to minimize the volatility of the price level. Discuss the advantages and disadvantages of the interest rate rule in (i) versus the money targeting rule in (ii) in light of your findings above.

2.3 Nonseparable Preferences and Money Superneutrality

Assume that the representative consumer's period utility is given by

$$U\left(C_t, \frac{M_t}{P_t}, N_t\right) = \frac{1}{1-\sigma}\left[(1-\vartheta)\, C_t^{1-\nu} + \vartheta \left(\frac{M_t}{P_t}\right)^{1-\nu}\right]^{\frac{1-\sigma}{1-\nu}} - \frac{N_t^{1+\varphi}}{1+\varphi}.$$

a) Derive the optimality conditions of the associated consumer's problem.

b) Assume that the representative firm has access to a simple technology $Y_t = N_t$ and that the monetary authority keeps a constant money growth γ_m. Derive the economy's steady state equilibrium under the assumption of perfect competition.

c) Discuss the effects on inflation and output of a permanent change in the rate of money growth γ_m, and relate it to the existing evidence.

2.4 Optimal Monetary Policy in a Classical Economy with an Exact Equilibrium Representation

Consider a version of the classical economy with money in the utility function, where the representative consumer maximizes $E_0 \sum_{t=0}^{\infty} \beta^t\, U(C_t, \frac{M_t}{P_t}, N_t)$ subject to the sequence of dynamic budget constraints

$$P_t C_t + M_t + Q_t B_t \leq M_{t-1} + B_{t-1} + W_t\, N_t - T_t.$$

Assume a period utility given by

$$U\left(C_t, \frac{M_t}{P_t}, N_t\right) = \log C_t + \log \frac{M_t}{P_t} - \frac{N_t^{1+\varphi}}{1+\varphi}. \tag{45}$$

Suppose there is a representative perfectly competitive firm, producing the single consumption good. The firm has access to the linear production function $Y_t(i) = A_t\, N_t(i)$, where productivity evolves according to

$$\frac{A_t}{A_{t-1}} = (1+\gamma_a)\, \exp\{\varepsilon_t^a\}$$

with $\{\varepsilon_t^a\}$ as an i.i.d., random process, normally distributed, with mean 0 and variance σ_a^2.

The money supply varies exogenously according to the process

$$\frac{M_t}{M_{t-1}} = (1 + \gamma_m) \, \exp\{\varepsilon_t^m\} \tag{46}$$

where $\{\varepsilon_t^m\}$ is an i.i.d., normally distributed process with mean 0 and variance σ_m^2. Assume that $\{\varepsilon_t^m\}$ evolves exogenously, outside the control of the monetary authority (e.g., could reflect shocks in the monetary multiplier that prevent the monetary authority from fully controlling the money supply). Finally, assume that all output is consumed, so that equilibrium $Y_t = C_t$ for all t.

a) Derive the optimality conditions for the problem of households and firms.

b) Determine the equilibrium levels of aggregate employment, output, and inflation (Hint: show that a constant velocity $\frac{P_t Y_t}{M_t} = V$ for all t is a solution).

c) Discuss how utility depends on the two parameters describing monetary policy, γ_m and σ_m^2 (recall that the nominal interest rate is constrained to be non-negative, i.e., $Q_t \leq 1$ for all t). Show that the optimal policy must satisfy the Friedman rule ($i_t = 0$ for all t) and discuss alternative ways of supporting that rule in equilibrium.

2.5 A Shopping Time Model (based on Walsh 2003)

Assume that the transaction technology is such that consuming C_t requires a quantity of shopping time $N_t^s = s(C_t, \frac{M_t}{P_t})$, where $s_c > 0$ and $s_m \leq 0$. Hence, the amount of time diverted from leisure is given by $N_t + N_t^s$, where N_t denotes hours of work. Let the original period utility be given by $V(C_t, L_t)$ where $L_t = 1 - N_t - N_t^s$ denotes leisure.

a) Derive the condition determining the optimal allocation of time.

b) Derive the implied utility function in terms of consumption, hours, and real balances and discuss its properties.

2.6 A Model with Cash and Credit Goods

Assume that the utility of the representative household is given by

$$V(C_{1t}, C_{2t}, N_t) \tag{47}$$

where C_{1t} denotes consumption of a "cash-good" (i.e., a good that requires cash in order to be purchased), C_{2t} is consumption of a "credit-good" (which does not require cash), and N_t is labor supply. For simplicity, assume that the price of the two goods is identical and equal to P_t (this will be the case if the production function of the representative firm is given by $Y_{1t} + Y_{2t} = N_t$ and there is perfect competition). Purchases of cash-goods have to be settled in cash, whereas credit-goods can be financed by issuing one-period riskless nominal bonds.

The budget constraint is given by

$$P_t(C_{1t} + C_{2t}) + Q_t B_t + M_t = B_{t-1} + M_{t-1} + W_t N_t + T_t.$$

Finally, the cash-in-advance (CIA) constraint is given by

$$P_t C_{1t} \leq M_{t-1} + T_t$$

where, in equilibrium, $T_t = \Delta M_t$, i.e., transfers to households correspond to money tranfers made by the central bank, which consumers take as given. For simplicity, assume no uncertainty.

a) Derive the first-order conditions associated with the household's problem.

b) Note that whenever the CIA constraint is binding reduced form period utility can be defined as

$$U\left(C_t, \frac{M_t}{P_t}, N_t\right) \equiv V\left(\frac{M_t}{P_t}, C_t - \frac{M_t}{P_t}, N_t\right)$$

where $C_t = C_{1t} + C_{2t}$. Show that $U_m \geq 0$, given the optimality conditions derived in (a).

3

The Basic New Keynesian Model

The present chapter describes the key elements of the baseline model that will be used as a reference framework in the remainder of the book. In doing so there is a departure from the assumptions of the classical monetary economy discussed in chapter 2. First, imperfect competition in the goods market is introduced by assuming that each firm produces a differentiated good for which it sets the price (instead of taking the price as given). Second, some constraints are imposed on the price adjustment mechanism by assuming that only a fraction of firms can reset their prices in any given period. In particular, and following much of the literature, a model of staggered price setting due to Calvo (1983) and characterized by random price durations is adopted.[1] The resulting framework is referred to as the *basic New Keynesian model*. As discussed in chapter 1, that model has become in recent years the workhorse for the analysis of monetary policy, fluctuations, and welfare.

The introduction of differentiated goods requires that the household problem be modified slightly relative to the one considered in the previous chapter. That modification is discussed before turning to the firms' optimal price-setting problem and the implied inflation dynamics.

3.1 Households

Once again, assume a representative infinitely-lived household, seeking to maximize

$$E_0 \sum_{t=0}^{\infty} \beta^t U(C_t, N_t)$$

where C_t is now a consumption index given by

$$C_t \equiv \left(\int_0^1 C_t(i)^{1-\frac{1}{\varepsilon}} \, di \right)^{\frac{\varepsilon}{\varepsilon-1}}$$

with $C_t(i)$ representing the quantity of good i consumed by the household in period t. Assume the existence of a continuum of goods represented by the interval $[0, 1]$.

---

[1] The resulting inflation dynamics can also be derived under the assumption of quadratic costs of price adjustment. See, e.g., Rotemberg (1982).

The period budget constraint now takes the form

$$\int_0^1 P_t(i)\, C_t(i)\, di + Q_t\, B_t \le B_{t-1} + W_t\, N_t + T_t$$

for $t = 0, 1, 2 \ldots$, where $P_t(i)$ is the price of good i, and where the remaining variables are defined as in chapter 2: N_t denotes hours of work (or the measure of household members employed), W_t is the nominal wage, B_t represents purchases of one-period bonds (at a price Q_t), and T_t is a lump-sum component of income (which may include, among other items, dividends from ownership of firms). The above sequence of period budget constraints is supplemented with a solvency condition of the form $\lim_{T \to \infty} E_t\{B_T\} \ge 0$ for all t.

In addition to the consumption/savings and labor supply decision analyzed in chapter 2, the household now must decide how to allocate its consumption expenditures among the different goods. This requires that the consumption index C_t be maximized for any given level of expenditures $\int_0^1 P_t(i)\, C_t(i)\, di$. As shown in appendix 3.1, the solution to that problem yields the set of demand equations

$$C_t(i) = \left(\frac{P_t(i)}{P_t} \right)^{-\varepsilon} C_t \tag{1}$$

for all $i \in [0, 1]$, where $P_t \equiv \left[\int_0^1 P_t(i)^{1-\varepsilon}\, di \right]^{\frac{1}{1-\varepsilon}}$ is an aggregate price index. Furthermore, and conditional on such optimal behavior,

$$\int_0^1 P_t(i)\, C_t(i)\, di = P_t\, C_t$$

i.e., total consumption expenditures can be written as the product of the price index times the quantity index. Plugging the previous expression into the budget constraint yields

$$P_t\, C_t + Q_t\, B_t \le B_{t-1} + W_t\, N_t + T_t$$

which is formally identical to the constraint facing households in the single good economy analyzed in chapter 2. Hence, the optimal consumption/savings and labor supply decisions are identical to the ones derived therein, and described by the conditions

$$-\frac{U_{n,t}}{U_{c,t}} = \frac{W_t}{P_t}$$

$$Q_t = \beta\, E_t \left\{ \frac{U_{c,t+1}}{U_{c,t}} \frac{P_t}{P_{t+1}} \right\}.$$

Under the assumption of a period utility given by

$$U(C_t, N_t) = \frac{C_t^{1-\sigma}}{1-\sigma} - \frac{N_t^{1+\varphi}}{1+\varphi}$$

and as shown in chapter 2, the resulting log-linear versions of the above optimality conditions take the form

$$w_t - p_t = \sigma\, c_t + \varphi\, n_t \tag{2}$$

$$c_t = E_t\{c_{t+1}\} - \frac{1}{\sigma}\,(i_t - E_t\{\pi_{t+1}\} - \rho) \tag{3}$$

where $i_t \equiv -\log Q_t$ is the short term nominal rate and $\rho \equiv -\log \beta$ is the discount rate, and where lowercase letters are used to denote the logs of the original variables. As before, the previous conditions will be supplemented, when necessary, with an ad-hoc log-linear money demand equation of the form

$$m_t - p_t = y_t - \eta\, i_t. \tag{4}$$

3.2 Firms

Assume a continuum of firms indexed by $i \in [0, 1]$. Each firm produces a differentiated good, but they all use an identical technology, represented by the production function

$$Y_t(i) = A_t\, N_t(i)^{1-\alpha} \tag{5}$$

where A_t represents the level of technology, assumed to be common to all firms and to evolve exogenously over time.

All firms face an identical isoelastic demand schedule given by (1), and take the aggregate price level P_t and aggregate consumption index C_t as given.

Following the formalism proposed in Calvo (1983), each firm may reset its price only with probability $1 - \theta$ in any given period, independent of the time elapsed since the last adjustment. Thus, each period a measure $1 - \theta$ of producers reset their prices, while a fraction θ keep their prices unchanged. As a result, the average duration of a price is given by $(1 - \theta)^{-1}$. In this context, θ becomes a natural index of price stickiness.

3.2.1 Aggregate Price Dynamics

As shown in appendix 3.2, the above environment implies that the aggregate price dynamics are described by the equation

$$\Pi_t^{1-\varepsilon} = \theta + (1 - \theta)\left(\frac{P_t^*}{P_{t-1}}\right)^{1-\varepsilon} \tag{6}$$

where $\Pi_t \equiv \frac{P_t}{P_{t-1}}$ is the gross inflation rate between $t - 1$ and t, and P_t^* is the price set in period t by firms reoptimizing their price in that period. Notice that, as shown below, all firms will choose the same price because they face an identical problem. It follows from (6) that in a steady state with zero inflation ($\Pi = 1$),

$P_t^* = P_{t-1} = P_t$ for all t. Furthermore, a log-linear approximation to the aggregate price index around that steady state yields

$$\pi_t = (1 - \theta) \, (p_t^* - p_{t-1}). \tag{7}$$

The previous equation makes clear that, in the present setup, inflation results from the fact that firms reoptimizing in any given period choose a price that differs from the economy's average price in the previous period. Hence, and in order to understand the evolution of inflation over time, one needs to analyze the factors underlying firms' price-setting decisions, a question which is discussed next.

3.2.2   Optimal Price Setting

A firm reoptimizing in period t will choose the price P_t^* that maximizes the current market value of the profits generated while that price remains effective. Formally, it solves the problem

$$\max_{P_t^*} \sum_{k=0}^{\infty} \theta^k \, E_t \left\{ Q_{t,t+k} \left(P_t^* \, Y_{t+k|t} - \Psi_{t+k}(Y_{t+k|t}) \right) \right\}$$

subject to the sequence of demand constraints

$$Y_{t+k|t} = \left(\frac{P_t^*}{P_{t+k}} \right)^{-\varepsilon} C_{t+k} \tag{8}$$

for $k = 0, 1, 2, \ldots$ where $Q_{t,t+k} \equiv \beta^k \, (C_{t+k}/C_t)^{-\sigma} \, (P_t/P_{t+k})$ is the stochastic discount factor for nominal payoffs, $\Psi_t(\cdot)$ is the cost function, and $Y_{t+k|t}$ denotes output in period $t + k$ for a firm that last reset its price in period t.

The first-order condition associated with the problem above takes the form

$$\sum_{k=0}^{\infty} \theta^k \, E_t \left\{ Q_{t,t+k} \, Y_{t+k|t} \left(P_t^* - \mathcal{M} \, \psi_{t+k|t} \right) \right\} = 0 \tag{9}$$

where $\psi_{t+k|t} \equiv \Psi'_{t+k}(Y_{t+k|t})$ denotes the (nominal) marginal cost in period $t + k$ for a firm which last reset its price in period t and $\mathcal{M} \equiv \frac{\varepsilon}{\varepsilon-1}$.

Note that in the limiting case of no price rigidities ($\theta = 0$), the previous condition collapses to the familiar optimal price-setting condition under flexible prices

$$P_t^* = \mathcal{M} \, \psi_{t|t}$$

which allows us to interpret $\mathcal{M}$ as the desired markup in the absence of constraints on the frequency of price adjustment. Henceforth, $\mathcal{M}$ is referred to as the desired or frictionless markup.

Next, the optimal price-setting condition (9) is linearized around the zero inflation steady state. Before doing so, however, it is useful to rewrite it in terms of variables that have a well-defined value in that steady state. In particular, dividing by P_{t-1} and letting $\Pi_{t,t+k} \equiv P_{t+k}/P_t$, equation (9) can be written as

$$\sum_{k=0}^{\infty} \theta^k \, E_t \left\{ Q_{t,t+k} Y_{t+k|t} \left(\frac{P_t^*}{P_{t-1}} - \mathcal{M} \, MC_{t+k|t} \, \Pi_{t-1,t+k} \right) \right\} = 0 \qquad (10)$$

where $MC_{t+k|t} \equiv \psi_{t+k|t}/P_{t+k}$ is the real marginal cost in period $t+k$ for a firm whose price was last set in period t.

In the zero inflation steady state, $P_t^*/P_{t-1} = 1$ and $\Pi_{t-1,t+k} = 1$. Furthermore, constancy of the price level implies that $P_t^* = P_{t+k}$ in that steady state, from which it follows that $Y_{t+k|t} = Y$ and $MC_{t+k|t} = MC$, because all firms will be producing the same quantity of output. In addition, $Q_{t,t+k} = \beta^k$ must hold in that steady state. Accordingly, $MC = 1/\mathcal{M}$. A first-order Taylor expansion of (10) around the zero inflation steady state yields

$$p_t^* - p_{t-1} = (1 - \beta\theta) \sum_{k=0}^{\infty} (\beta\theta)^k \, E_t \{ \widehat{mc}_{t+k|t} + (p_{t+k} - p_{t-1}) \} \qquad (11)$$

where $\widehat{mc}_{t+k|t} \equiv mc_{t+k|t} - mc$ denotes the log deviation of marginal cost from its steady state value $mc = -\mu$, and where $\mu \equiv \log \mathcal{M}$ is the log of the desired gross markup (which, for $\mathcal{M}$ close to one, is approximately equal to the net markup $\mathcal{M} - 1$).

In order to gain some intuition about the factors determining a firm's price-setting decision it is useful to rewrite (11) as

$$p_t^* = \mu + (1 - \beta\theta) \sum_{k=0}^{\infty} (\beta\theta)^k \, E_t \{ mc_{t+k|t} + p_{t+k} \}.$$

Hence, firms resetting their prices will choose a price that corresponds to the desired markup over a weighted average of their current and expected (nominal) marginal costs, with the weights being proportional to the probability of the price remaining effective at each horizon θ^k.

3.3 Equilibrium

Market clearing in the goods market requires

$$Y_t(i) = C_t(i)$$

for all $i \in [0, 1]$ and all t. Letting aggregate output be defined as $Y_t \equiv \left(\int_0^1 Y_t(i)^{1-\frac{1}{\varepsilon}} \, di \right)^{\frac{\varepsilon}{\varepsilon-1}}$ it follows that

$$Y_t = C_t$$

must hold for all t. One can combine the above goods market clearing condition with the consumer's Euler equation to yield the equilibrium condition

$$y_t = E_t\{y_{t+1}\} - \frac{1}{\sigma}(i_t - E_t\{\pi_{t+1}\} - \rho). \tag{12}$$

Market clearing in the labor market requires

$$N_t = \int_0^1 N_t(i)\, di.$$

Using (5),

$$N_t = \int_0^1 \left(\frac{Y_t(i)}{A_t}\right)^{\frac{1}{1-\alpha}} di$$

$$= \left(\frac{Y_t}{A_t}\right)^{\frac{1}{1-\alpha}} \int_0^1 \left(\frac{P_t(i)}{P_t}\right)^{-\frac{\varepsilon}{1-\alpha}} di$$

where the second equality follows from (1) and the goods market clearing condition. Taking logs,

$$(1-\alpha)\, n_t = y_t - a_t + d_t$$

where $d_t \equiv (1-\alpha)\log \int_0^1 (P_t(i)/P_t)^{-\frac{\varepsilon}{1-\alpha}}$ and di is a measure of price (and, hence, output) dispersion across firms. In appendix 3.3 it is shown that, in a neighborhood of the zero inflation steady state, d_t is equal to zero up to a first-order approximation. Hence, one can write the following approximate relation between aggregate output, employment, and technology as

$$y_t = a_t + (1-\alpha)\, n_t. \tag{13}$$

Next an expression is derived for an individual firm's marginal cost in terms of the economy's average real marginal cost. The latter is defined by

$$mc_t = (w_t - p_t) - mpn_t$$
$$= (w_t - p_t) - (a_t - \alpha n_t) - \log(1-\alpha)$$
$$= (w_t - p_t) - \frac{1}{1-\alpha}(a_t - \alpha y_t) - \log(1-\alpha)$$

for all t, where the second equality defines the economy's average marginal product of labor, mpn_t, in a way consistent with (13). Using the fact that

$$mc_{t+k|t} = (w_{t+k} - p_{t+k}) - mpn_{t+k|t}$$
$$= (w_{t+k} - p_{t+k}) - \frac{1}{1-\alpha}(a_{t+k} - \alpha y_{t+k|t}) - \log(1-\alpha)$$

then

$$mc_{t+k|t} = mc_{t+k} + \frac{\alpha}{1-\alpha} (y_{t+k|t} - y_{t+k})$$

$$= mc_{t+k} - \frac{\alpha\varepsilon}{1-\alpha} (p_t^* - p_{t+k}) \quad (14)$$

where the second equality follows from the demand schedule (1) combined with the market clearing condition $c_t = y_t$. Notice that under the assumption of constant returns to scale ($\alpha = 0$), $mc_{t+k|t} = mc_{t+k}$, i.e., marginal cost is independent of the level of production and, hence, it is common across firms.

Substituting (14) into (11) and rearranging terms yields

$$p_t^* - p_{t-1} = (1 - \beta\theta) \sum_{k=0}^{\infty} (\beta\theta)^k E_t \{\Theta \widehat{mc}_{t+k} + (p_{t+k} - p_{t-1})\}$$

$$= (1 - \beta\theta)\Theta \sum_{k=0}^{\infty} (\beta\theta)^k E_t\{\widehat{mc}_{t+k}\} + \sum_{k=0}^{\infty} (\beta\theta)^k E_t\{\pi_{t+k}\}$$

where $\Theta \equiv \frac{1-\alpha}{1-\alpha+\alpha\varepsilon} \leq 1$. Notice that the above discounted sum can be rewritten more compactly as the difference equation

$$p_t^* - p_{t-1} = \beta\theta E_t\{p_{t+1}^* - p_t\} + (1 - \beta\theta)\Theta \widehat{mc}_t + \pi_t. \quad (15)$$

Finally, combining (7) and (15) yields the inflation equation

$$\pi_t = \beta E_t\{\pi_{t+1}\} + \lambda \widehat{mc}_t \quad (16)$$

where

$$\lambda \equiv \frac{(1-\theta)(1-\beta\theta)}{\theta} \Theta$$

is strictly decreasing in the index of price stickiness θ, in the measure of decreasing returns α, and in the demand elasticity ε.

Solving (16) forward, inflation is expressed as the discounted sum of current and expected future deviations of real marginal costs from steady state

$$\pi_t = \lambda \sum_{k=0}^{\infty} \beta^k E_t\{\widehat{mc}_{t+k}\}.$$

Equivalently, and defining the average markup in the economy as $\mu_t = -mc_t$, it is seen that inflation will be high when firms expect average markups to be below their steady state (i.e., desired) level μ, for in that case firms that have the opportunity to reset prices will choose a price above the economy's average price level in order to realign their markup closer to its desired level.

It is worth emphasizing here that the mechanism underlying fluctuations in the aggregate price level and inflation as laid out above has little in common with the mechanism at work in the classical monetary economy. Thus, in the present model, inflation results from the aggregate consequences of purposeful price-setting decisions by firms, which adjust their prices in light of current and anticipated cost conditions. By contrast, in the classical monetary economy analyzed in chapter 2, inflation is a consequence of the changes in the aggregate price level that, given the monetary policy rule in place, are required in order to support an equilibrium allocation that is independent of the evolution of nominal variables, with no account given of the mechanism (other than an invisible hand) that will bring about those price level changes.

Next, a relation is derived between the economy's real marginal cost and a measure of aggregate economic activity. Notice that independent of the nature of price setting, average real marginal cost can be expressed as

$$
\begin{aligned}
mc_t &= (w_t - p_t) - mpn_t \\
&= (\sigma \, y_t + \varphi \, n_t) - (y_t - n_t) - \log(1 - \alpha) \\
&= \left(\sigma + \frac{\varphi + \alpha}{1 - \alpha}\right) y_t - \frac{1 + \varphi}{1 - \alpha} a_t - \log(1 - \alpha) \quad (17)
\end{aligned}
$$

where derivation of the second and third equalities make use of the household's optimality condition (2) and the (approximate) aggregate production relation (13).

Furthermore, and as shown at the end of section 3.2.2, under *flexible prices* the real marginal cost is constant and given by $mc = -\mu$. Defining the *natural level of output*, denoted by y_t^n, as the equilibrium level of output under flexible prices

$$
mc = \left(\sigma + \frac{\varphi + \alpha}{1 - \alpha}\right) y_t^n - \frac{1 + \varphi}{1 - \alpha} a_t - \log(1 - \alpha) \quad (18)
$$

thus implying

$$
y_t^n = \psi_{ya}^n \, a_t + \vartheta_y^n \quad (19)
$$

where $\vartheta_y^n \equiv -\frac{(1-\alpha)\,(\mu - \log(1-\alpha))}{\sigma(1-\alpha)+\varphi+\alpha} > 0$ and $\psi_{ya}^n \equiv \frac{1+\varphi}{\sigma(1-\alpha)+\varphi+\alpha}$. Notice that when $\mu = 0$ (perfect competition), the natural level of output corresponds to the equilibrium level of output in the classical economy, as derived in chapter 2. The presence of market power by firms has the effect of lowering that output level uniformly over time, without affecting its sensitivity to changes in technology.

Subtracting (18) from (17) obtains

$$
\widehat{mc}_t = \left(\sigma + \frac{\varphi + \alpha}{1 - \alpha}\right) (y_t - y_t^n) \quad (20)
$$

i.e., the log deviation of real marginal cost from steady state is proportional to the log deviation of output from its flexible price counterpart. Following convention, henceforth that deviation is referred to as the *output gap*, and is denoted by $\widetilde{y}_t \equiv y_t - y_t^n$.

By combining (20) with (16) one can obtain an equation relating inflation to its one period ahead forecast and the output gap

$$\pi_t = \beta \, E_t\{\pi_{t+1}\} + \kappa \, \widetilde{y}_t \tag{21}$$

where $\kappa \equiv \lambda \left(\sigma + \frac{\varphi + \alpha}{1 - \alpha}\right)$. Equation (21) is often referred to as the *New Keynesian Phillips curve* (or NKPC, for short), and constitutes one of the key building blocks of the basic New Keynesian model.

The second key equation describing the equilibrium of the New Keynesian model can be obtained by rewriting (12) in terms of the output gap as

$$\widetilde{y}_t = -\frac{1}{\sigma} \, (i_t - E_t\{\pi_{t+1}\} - r_t^n) + E_t\{\widetilde{y}_{t+1}\} \tag{22}$$

where r_t^n is the *natural rate of interest*, given by

$$r_t^n \equiv \rho + \sigma \, E_t\{\Delta y_{t+1}^n\}$$
$$= \rho + \sigma \psi_{ya}^n \, E_t\{\Delta a_{t+1}\}. \tag{23}$$

Henceforth (22) is referred to as the *dynamic IS equation* (or DIS, for short). Under the assumption that the effects of nominal rigidities vanish asymptotically, $\lim_{T \to \infty} E_t\{\widetilde{y}_{t+T}\} = 0$. In that case one can solve equation (22) forward to yield the expression

$$\widetilde{y}_t = -\frac{1}{\sigma} \sum_{k=0}^{\infty} (r_{t+k} - r_{t+k}^n) \tag{24}$$

where $r_t \equiv i_t - E_t\{\pi_{t+1}\}$ is the expected real return on a one period bond (i.e., the real interest rate). The previous expression emphasizes the fact that the output gap is proportional to the sum of current and anticipated deviations between the real interest rate and its natural counterpart.

Equations (21) and (22), together with an equilibrium process for the natural rate r_t^n (which in general will depend on all the real exogenous forces in the model), constitute the non-policy block of the basic New Keynesian model. That block has a simple recursive structure: The NKPC determines inflation given a path for the output gap, whereas the DIS equation determines the output gap given a path for the (exogenous) natural rate *and* the actual real rate. In order to close the model, supplement those two equations with one or more equations determining how the nominal interest rate i_t evolves over time, i.e., with a description of how monetary policy is conducted. Thus, and in contrast with the classical model analyzed in chapter 2, when prices are sticky the equilibrium path of real variables cannot be determined independently of monetary policy. In other words: Monetary policy is non-neutral.

In order to illustrate the workings of the basic model just developed, two alternative specifications of monetary policy are considered and some of their equilibrium implications are analyzed.

3.4 Equilibrium Dynamics under Alternative Monetary Policy Rules

3.4.1 Equilibrium under an Interest Rate Rule

The equilibrium is first analyzed under a simple interest rate rule of the form

$$i_t = \rho + \phi_\pi \pi_t + \phi_y \tilde{y}_t + v_t \tag{25}$$

where v_t is an exogenous (possibly stochastic) component with zero mean. Assume ϕ_π and ϕ_y are non-negative coefficients, chosen by the monetary authority. Note that the choice of the intercept ρ makes the rule consistent with a zero inflation steady state.

Combining (21), (22), and (25) represents the equilibrium conditions by means of the following system of difference equations.

$$\begin{bmatrix} \tilde{y}_t \\ \pi_t \end{bmatrix} = \mathbf{A}_T \begin{bmatrix} E_t\{\tilde{y}_{t+1}\} \\ E_t\{\pi_{t+1}\} \end{bmatrix} + \mathbf{B}_T \, (\hat{r}_t^n - v_t) \tag{26}$$

where $\hat{r}_t^n \equiv r_t^n - \rho$, and

$$\mathbf{A}_T \equiv \Omega \begin{bmatrix} \sigma & 1 - \beta\phi_\pi \\ \sigma\kappa & \kappa + \beta(\sigma + \phi_y) \end{bmatrix} ; \quad \mathbf{B}_T \equiv \Omega \begin{bmatrix} 1 \\ \kappa \end{bmatrix}$$

with $\Omega \equiv \frac{1}{\sigma + \phi_y + \kappa\phi_\pi}$.

Given that both the output gap and inflation are nonpredetermined variables, the solution to (26) is locally unique, if and only if, $\mathbf{A}_T$ has both eigenvalues within the unit circle.[2] Under the assumption of non-negative coefficients (ϕ_π, ϕ_y) it can be shown that a necessary and sufficient condition for uniqueness is given by[3]

$$\kappa \, (\phi_\pi - 1) + (1 - \beta) \, \phi_y > 0 \tag{27}$$

which is assumed to hold, unless stated otherwise. An economic interpretation to the previous condition will be offered in chapter 4.

Next the economy's equilibrium response to two exogenous shocks—a monetary policy shock and a technology shock—is examined when the central bank follows the interest rate rule (25).

3.4.1.1 *The Effects of a Monetary Policy Shock*

Let us assume that the exogenous component of the interest rate, v_t, follows an AR(1) process

$$v_t = \rho_v \, v_{t-1} + \varepsilon_t^v$$

---

[2] See, e.g., Blanchard and Kahn (1980).
[3] See Bullard and Mitra (2002) for a proof.

where $\rho_v \in [0, 1)$. Note that a positive (negative) realization of ε_t^v should be interpreted as a contractionary (expansionary) monetary policy shock, leading to a rise (decline) in the nominal interest rate, *given* inflation, and the output gap.

Because the natural rate of interest is not affected by monetary shocks $\widehat{r}_t^n = 0$ is set for all t for the purposes of the present exercise. Next, guess that the solution takes the form $\widetilde{y}_t = \psi_{yv} \, v_t$ and $\pi_t = \psi_{\pi v} \, v_t$, where ψ_{yv} and $\psi_{\pi v}$ are coefficients to be determined. Imposing the guessed solution on (22) and (21) and using the method of undetermined coefficients,

$$\widetilde{y}_t = -(1 - \beta \rho_v) \Lambda_v \, v_t$$

and

$$\pi_t = -\kappa \Lambda_v \, v_t$$

where $\Lambda_v \equiv \frac{1}{(1 - \beta \rho_v)[\sigma(1 - \rho_v) + \phi_y] + \kappa(\phi_\pi - \rho_v)}$. It can be easily shown that as long as (27) is satisfied, $\Lambda_v > 0$. Hence, an exogenous increase in the interest rate leads to a persistent decline in the output gap and inflation. Because the natural level of output is unaffected by the monetary policy shock, the response of output matches that of the output gap.

One can use (22) to obtain an expression for the real interest rate, expressed as deviations from its steady state value.

$$\widehat{r}_t = \sigma(1 - \rho_v)(1 - \beta \rho_v) \Lambda_v \, v_t$$

which is thus shown to increase unambiguously in response to an exogenous increase in the nominal rate.

The response of the nominal interest rate combines both the direct effect of v_t and the variation induced by lower output gap and inflation. It is given by

$$\widehat{i}_t = \widehat{r}_t + E_t\{\pi_{t+1}\} = [\sigma(1 - \rho_v)(1 - \beta \rho_v) - \rho_v \kappa] \, \Lambda_v \, v_t.$$

Note that if the persistence of the monetary policy shock ρ_v is sufficiently high, the nominal rate will decline in response to a rise in v_t. This is a result of the downward adjustment in the nominal rate induced by the decline in inflation and the output gap more than offsetting the direct effect of a higher v_t. In that case, and despite the lower nominal rate, the policy shock still has a contractionary effect on output, because the latter is inversely related to the real rate, which goes up unambiguously.

Finally, one can use (4) to determine the change in the money supply required to bring about the desired change in the interest rate. In particular, the response of m_t on impact is given by

$$\frac{dm_t}{d\varepsilon_t^v} = \frac{dp_t}{d\varepsilon_t^v} + \frac{dy_t}{d\varepsilon_t^v} - \eta \frac{di_t}{d\varepsilon_t^v}$$

$$= -\Lambda_v \left[(1 - \beta\rho_v)(1 + \eta\sigma(1 - \rho_v)) + \kappa(1 - \eta\rho_v) \right].$$

Hence, the sign of the change in the money supply that supports the exogenous policy intervention is, in principle, ambiguous. Even though the money supply needs to be tightened to raise the nominal rate *given output and prices*, the decline in the latter induced by the policy shocks combined with the possibility of an induced nominal rate decline make it impossible to rule out a countercyclical movement in money in response to an interest rate shock. Note, however, that $di_t/d\varepsilon_t^v > 0$ is a sufficient condition for a contraction in the money supply, as well as for the presence of a liquidity effect (i.e., a negative short-run comovement of the nominal rate and the money supply in response to an exogenous monetary policy shock).

The previous analysis can be used to quantify the effects of a monetary policy shock, given numerical values for the model's parameters. Next a baseline calibration of the model is briefly presented that takes the relevant period to correspond to a quarter.

In the baseline calibration of the model's preference parameters it is assumed $\beta = 0.99$, which implies a steady state real return on financial assets of about 4 percent. It is also assumed $\sigma = 1$ (log utility) and $\varphi = 1$ (a unitary Frisch elasticity of labor supply), $\alpha = 1/3$, and $\varepsilon = 6$, values commonly found in the business cycle literature. The interest semi-elasticity of money demand, η, is set to equal 4.[4] In addition it is assumed $\theta = 2/3$, which implies an average price duration of three quarters, a value consistent with the empirical evidence.[5] As to the interest rate rule coefficients, it is assumed $\phi_\pi = 1.5$ and $\phi_y = 0.5/4$, which are roughly consistent with observed variations in the Federal Funds rate over the Greenspan era.[6] Finally, $\rho_v = 0.5$, a set value associated with a moderately persistent shock.

Figure 3.1 illustrates the dynamic effects of an expansionary monetary policy shock. The shock corresponds to an increase of 25 basis points in ε_t^v, which, in the absence of a further change induced by the response of inflation or the output gap, would imply an increase of 100 basis points in the annualized nominal rate on impact. The responses of inflation and the two interest rates shown in figure

---

[4] The calibration of η is based on the estimates of an OLS regression of (log) M2 inverse velocity on the 3 month Treasury Bill rate (quarterly rate, per unit), using quarterly data over the period 1960: 1–1988:1. The focus is on that period because it is characterized by a highly stable relationship between velocity and the nominal rate, which is consistent with the model.

[5] See, in particular, the estimates in Galí, Gertler, and López-Salido (2001) and Sbordone (2002), based on aggregate data and the discussion of the micro evidence in chapter 1.

[6] See, e.g., Taylor (1999). Note that empirical interest rate rules are generally estimated using inflation and interest rate data expressed in annual rates. Conversion to quarterly rates requires that the output gap coefficient be divided by 4.

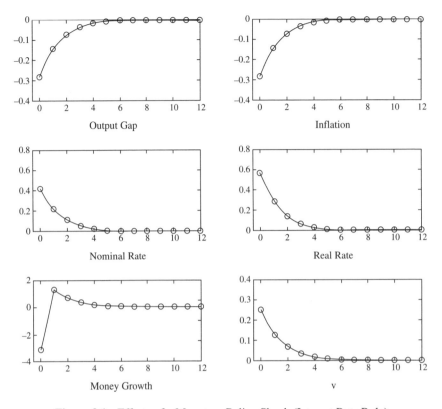

Figure 3.1 Effects of a Monetary Policy Shock (Interest Rate Rule)

3.1 are expressed in annual terms (i.e., they are obtained by multiplying by 4 the responses of π_t, i_t, and r_t in the model).

In a way consistent with the analytical results above it is seen that the policy shock generates an increase in the real rate, and a decrease in inflation and output (whose response corresponds to that of the output gap, because the natural level of output is not affected by the monetary policy shock). Note that under the baseline calibration the nominal rate goes up, though by less than its exogenous component—as a result of the downward adjustment induced by the decline in inflation and the output gap. In order to bring about the observed interest rate response, the central bank must engineer a reduction in the money supply. The calibrated model thus displays a liquidity effect. Note also that the response of the real rate is larger than that of the nominal rate as a result of the decrease in expected inflation.

Overall, the dynamic responses to a monetary policy shock shown in figure 3.1 are similar, at least in a qualitative sense, to those estimated using structural vector autoregressive (VAR) methods, as described in chapter 1. Nevertheless, and as emphasized in Christiano, Eichenbaum, and Evans (2005), among others, matching some of the quantitative features of the empirical impulse responses requires that the basic New Keynesian model be enriched in a variety of dimensions.

3.4.1.2   The Effects of a Technology Shock

In order to determine the economy's response to a technology shock first a process must be specified for the technology parameter $\{a_t\}$ and then an implied process can be derived for the natural rate. Assume the following AR(1) process for $\{a_t\}$

$$a_t = \rho_a \, a_{t-1} + \varepsilon_t^a \tag{28}$$

where $\rho_a \in [0, 1]$ and $\{\varepsilon_t^a\}$ is a zero mean white noise process. Given (23), the implied natural rate expressed in terms of deviations from steady state, is given by

$$\widehat{r}_t^n = -\sigma \psi_{ya}^n \, (1 - \rho_a) a_t.$$

Setting $v_t = 0$, for all t (i.e., turning off monetary shocks), and guessing that output gap and inflation are proportional to $\widehat{r}_t^n$, the method of undetermined coefficients can be applied in a way analogous to the previous subsection, or the fact that $\widehat{r}_t^n$ enters the equilibrium conditions in a way symmetric to v_t, but with the opposite sign, can be exploited to obtain

$$\begin{aligned} \widetilde{y}_t &= (1 - \beta\rho_a)\Lambda_a \, \widehat{r}_t^n \\ &= -\sigma \psi_{ya}^n (1 - \rho_a)(1 - \beta\rho_a)\Lambda_a \, a_t \end{aligned}$$

and

$$\begin{aligned} \pi_t &= \kappa \Lambda_a \, \widehat{r}_t^n \\ &= -\sigma \psi_{ya}^n (1 - \rho_a)\kappa \Lambda_a \, a_t \end{aligned}$$

where $\Lambda_a \equiv \frac{1}{(1 - \beta\rho_a)[\sigma(1 - \rho_a) + \phi_y] + \kappa(\phi_\pi - \rho_a)} > 0$.

Hence, and as long as $\rho_a < 1$, a positive technology shock leads to a persistent decline in both inflation and the output gap. The implied equilibrium responses of output and employment are given by

$$\begin{aligned} y_t &= y_t^n + \widetilde{y}_t \\ &= \psi_{ya}^n \, (1 - \sigma(1 - \rho_a)(1 - \beta\rho_a)\Lambda_a) \, a_t \end{aligned}$$

and

$$\begin{aligned} (1 - \alpha) \, n_t &= y_t - a_t \\ &= [(\psi_{ya}^n - 1) - \sigma \psi_{ya}^n (1 - \rho_a)(1 - \beta\rho_a)\Lambda_a] a_t. \end{aligned}$$

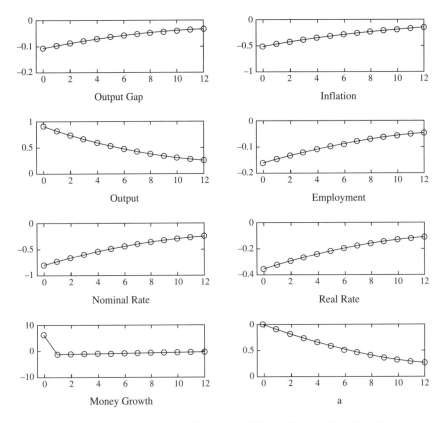

Figure 3.2 Effects of a Technology Shock (Interest Rate Rule)

Hence, the sign of the response of output and employment to a positive technology shock is in general ambiguous, depending on the configuration of parameter values, including the interest rate rule coefficients. In the baseline calibration, $\sigma = 1$, which in turn implies $\psi_{ya}^n = 1$. In that case, a technological improvement leads to a persistent employment decline. Such a response of employment is consistent with much of the recent empirical evidence on the effects of technology shocks.[7]

Figure 3.2 shows the responses of a number of variables to a favorable technology shock, as implied by the baseline calibration and under the assumption of $\rho_a = 0.9$. Notice that the improvement in technology is partly accommodated by the central bank, which lowers nominal and real rates, while increasing the quantity of money in circulation. That policy, however, is not sufficient to close a negative output gap, which is responsible for the decline in inflation. Under the

---

[7] See Galí and Rabanal (2004) for a survey of that empirical evidence.

baseline calibration, output increases (though less than its natural counterpart) and employment declines in a way consistent with the evidence mentioned above.

3.4.2 Equilibrium under an Exogenous Money Supply

Next the equilibrium dynamics of the basic New Keynesian model is analyzed under an exogenous path for the growth rate of the money supply, Δm_t. As a preliminary step, it is useful to rewrite the money market equilibrium condition in terms of the output gap

$$\widetilde{y}_t - \eta\, i_t = l_t - y_t^n \tag{29}$$

where $l_t \equiv m_t - p_t$. Substituting the latter equation into (22) yields

$$(1 + \sigma\eta)\ \widetilde{y}_t = \sigma\eta\ E_t\{\widetilde{y}_{t+1}\} + l_t + \eta\ E_t\{\pi_{t+1}\} + \eta\ \widehat{r}_t^n - y_t^n. \tag{30}$$

Note also that real balances are related to inflation and money growth through the identity

$$l_{t-1} = l_t + \pi_t - \Delta m_t. \tag{31}$$

Hence, the equilibrium dynamics for real balances, output gap, and inflation are described by equations (30) and (31) together with the NKPC equation (21). They can be summarized compactly by the system

$$\mathbf{A_{M,0}} \begin{bmatrix} \widetilde{y}_t \\ \pi_t \\ l_{t-1} \end{bmatrix} = \mathbf{A_{M,1}} \begin{bmatrix} E_t\{\widetilde{y}_{t+1}\} \\ E_t\{\pi_{t+1}\} \\ l_t \end{bmatrix} + \mathbf{B_M} \begin{bmatrix} \widehat{r}_t^n \\ y_t^n \\ \Delta m_t \end{bmatrix} \tag{32}$$

where

$$\mathbf{A_{M,0}} \equiv \begin{bmatrix} 1+\sigma\eta & 0 & 0 \\ -\kappa & 1 & 0 \\ 0 & -1 & 1 \end{bmatrix} ;\ \mathbf{A_{M,1}} \equiv \begin{bmatrix} \sigma\eta & \eta & 1 \\ 0 & \beta & 0 \\ 0 & 0 & 1 \end{bmatrix} ;\ \mathbf{B_M} \equiv \begin{bmatrix} \eta & -1 & 0 \\ 0 & 0 & 0 \\ 0 & 0 & -1 \end{bmatrix}.$$

The system above has one predetermined variable (l_{t-1}) and two non-predetermined variables ($\widetilde{y}_t$ and π_t). Accordingly, a stationary solution will exist and be unique, if and only if, $\mathbf{A_M} \equiv \mathbf{A_{M,0}^{-1}}\mathbf{A_{M,1}}$ has two eigenvalues inside and one outside (or on) the unit circle. The latter condition can be shown to be always satisfied so, in contrast with the interest rate rule discussed above, the equilibrium is always determined under an exogenous path for the money supply.[8]

Next the equilibrium responses of the economy to a monetary policy shock and a technology shock are examined.

---

[8] That result is based on numerical analysis of the eigenvalues for a broad range of calibrations of the model's parameter values.

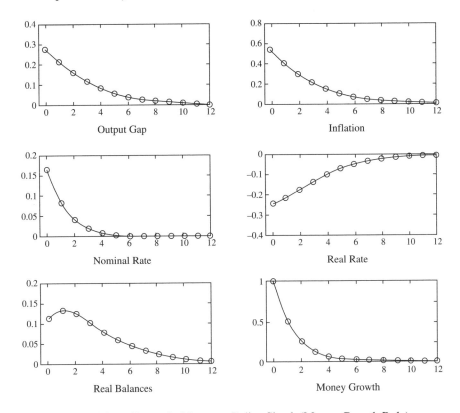

Figure 3.3 Effects of a Monetary Policy Shock (Money Growth Rule)

3.4.2.1 The Effects of a Monetary Policy Shock

In order to illustrate how the economy responds to an exogenous shock to the money supply, assume that Δm_t follows the AR(1) process

$$\Delta m_t = \rho_m \, \Delta m_{t-1} + \varepsilon_t^m \tag{33}$$

where $\rho_m \in [0, 1)$ and $\{\varepsilon_t^m\}$ is white noise.

The economy's response to a monetary policy shock can be obtained by determining the stationary solution to the dynamical system consisting of (32) and (33) and tracing the effects of a shock to ε_t^m (while setting $\widehat{r}_t^n = y_t^n = 0$, for all t).[9] In doing so, assume $\rho_m = 0.5$, a value roughly consistent with the first-order autocorrelation of money growth in postwar U.S. data.

Figure 3.3 displays the dynamic responses of several variables of interest to an expansionary monetary policy shock that takes the form of positive realization of ε_t^m of size 0.25. That impulse corresponds to a one percent increase, on impact,

---

[9] See, e.g., Blanchard and Kahn (1980) for a description of a solution method.

in the annualized rate of money growth, as shown in figure 3.3. The sluggishness in the adjustment of prices implies that real balances rise in response to the increase in the money supply. As a result, clearing of the money market requires either a rise in output and/or a decline in the nominal rate. Under the calibration considered here, output increases by about a third of a percentage point on impact, after which it slowly reverts back to its initial level. The nominal rate, however, shows a slight increase. Hence, and in contrast with the case of an interest rate rule considered above, a liquidity effect does not emerge here. Note, however, that the rise in the nominal rate does not prevent the real rate from declining persistently (due to higher expected inflation), leading in turn to an expansion in aggregate demand and output, as implied by (24), and, as a result, a persistent rise in inflation, which follows from (21).

It is worth noting that the absence of a liquidity effect is not a necessary feature of the exogenous money supply regime considered here, but instead a consequence of the calibration used. To see this, note that one can combine equations (4) and (22) to obtain the difference equation

$$i_t = \frac{\eta}{1+\eta} E_t\{i_{t+1}\} + \frac{\rho_m}{1+\eta} \Delta m_t + \frac{\sigma - 1}{1+\eta} E_t\{\Delta y_{t+1}\}$$

whose forward solution yields

$$i_t = \frac{\rho_m}{1+\eta(1-\rho_m)} \Delta m_t + \frac{\sigma - 1}{1+\eta} \sum_{k=0}^{\infty} \left(\frac{\eta}{1+\eta}\right)^k E_t\{\Delta y_{t+1+k}\}.$$

Note that when $\sigma = 1$, as in the baseline calibration underlying figure 3.3, the nominal rate always comoves positively with money growth. Nevertheless, and given that quite generally the summation term will be negative (because for most calibrations output tends to adjust monotonically to its original level after the initial increase), a liquidity effect emerges given values of σ sufficiently above one combined with sufficiently low (absolute) values of ρ_m.[10]

3.4.2.2   The Effects of a Technology Shock

Finally, turn to the analysis of the effects of a technology shock under a monetary policy regime characterized by an exogenous money supply. Once again, assume the technology parameter a_t follows the stationary process given by (28). That assumption, combined with (19) and (23), is used to determine the implied path of $\widehat{r}_t^n$ and y_t^n as a function of a_t, as needed to solve (32). In a way consistent with the assumption of exogenous money, let us set $\Delta m_t = 0$ for all t for the purpose of the present exercise.

Figure 3.4 displays the dynamic responses to a one percent increase in the technology. A comparison with the responses shown in figure 3.2 (corresponding

---

[10] See Galí (2003) for a detailed analysis.

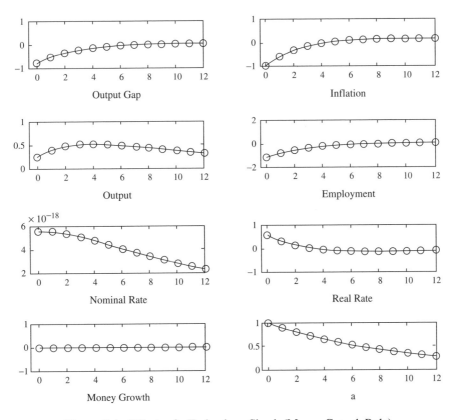

Figure 3.4 Effects of a Technology Shock (Money Growth Rule)

to the analogous exercise under an interest rate rule) reveals many similarities: In both cases the output gap (and, hence, inflation) display a negative response to the technology improvement as a result of output failing to increase as much as its natural level. Note, however, that in the case of exogenous money the gap between output and its natural level is much larger, which also explains the larger decline in employment. This is due to the upward response of the real rate implied by the unchanged money supply, which contrasts with its decline (in response to the negative response of inflation and the output gap) under the interest rate rule. Because the natural real rate also declines in response to the positive technology shock (in order to support the transitory increase in output and consumption), the response of interest rates generated under the exogenous money regime becomes highly contractionary, as illustrated in figure 3.4.

The previous simulations have served several goals. First, they have helped illustrate the workings of the New Keynesian model, i.e., how the model can be used to answer some specific questions about the behavior of the economy under different assumptions. Second, under a plausible calibration, it was seen how the simulated responses to monetary and technology shocks display notable similarities (at least qualitative) with the empirical evidence on the effects of those shocks. Third, the previous analysis has made clear that monetary policy in the New Keynesian model can have large and persistent effects on both real and nominal variables. The latter feature leads one to raise a natural question, which is the focus of the next chapter: How should monetary policy be conducted?

3.5   Notes on the Literature

Early examples of microfounded monetary models with monopolistic competition and sticky prices can be found in Akerlof and Yellen (1985), Mankiw (1985), Blanchard and Kiyotaki (1987), and Ball and Romer (1990).

An early version and analysis of the baseline New Keynesian model can be found in Yun (1996), which used a discrete-time version of the staggered price-setting model originally developed in Calvo (1983). King and Wolman (1996) provide a detailed analysis of the steady state and dynamic properties of that model. King and Watson (1996) compare its predictions regarding the cyclical properties of money, interest rates, and prices with those of flexible price models. Woodford (1996) incorporates a fiscal sector in the model and analyzes its properties under a non-Ricardian fiscal policy regime.

An inflation equation identical to the New Keynesian Phillips curve can be derived under the assumption of quadratic costs of price adjustment, as shown in Rotemberg (1982). Hairault and Portier (1993) developed and analyzed an early version of a monetary model with quadratic costs of price adjustment and compared its second-moment predictions with those of the French and U.S. economies.

Two main alternatives to the Calvo random price duration model can be found in the literature. The first one is given by staggered price-setting models with a deterministic price duration, originally proposed by Taylor (1980) in the context of a non-microfounded model. A microfounded version of the Taylor model can be found in Chari, Kehoe, and McGrattan (2000) who analyzed the output effects of exogenous monetary policy shocks. An alternative price-setting structure is given by state dependent models in which the timing of price adjustments is influenced by the state of the economy. A quantitative analysis of a state dependent pricing model can be found in Dotsey, King, and Wolman (1999) and, more recently, in Golosov and Lucas (2007) and Gertler and Leahy (2006).

The empirical performance of the New Keynesian Phillips curve has been the object of numerous criticisms. An early critical assessment can be found in Fuhrer and Moore (1986). Mankiw and Reis (2002) give a quantitative review of the perceived shortcomings of the NKPC and propose an alternative price-setting structure based on the assumption of sticky information. Galí and Gertler (1999), Sbordone (2002), and Galí, Gertler, and López-Salido (2001) provide favorable evidence of the empirical fit of the equation relating inflation to marginal costs, and discuss the difficulties in estimating or testing the NKPC given the unobservability of the output gap.

Rotemberg and Woodford (1999) and Christiano, Eichenbaum, and Evans (2005) provide empirical evidence on the effects of monetary policy shocks, and discuss a number of modifications of the baseline New Keynesian model aimed at improving the model's ability to match the estimated impulse responses.

Evidence on the effects of technology shocks and its implications for the relevance of alternative models can be found in Galí (1999) and Basu, Fernald, and Kimball (2004), among others. Recent evidence, as well as alternative interpretations, are surveyed in Galí and Rabanal (2004).

Appendix

3.1 Optimal Allocation of Consumption Expenditures

The problem of maximization of C_t for any *given* expenditure level

$$\int_0^1 P_t(i)\, C_t(i)\, di \equiv Z_t$$

can be formalized by means of the Lagrangean

$$\mathcal{L} = \left[\int_0^1 C_t(i)^{1-\frac{1}{\varepsilon}}\, di \right]^{\frac{\varepsilon}{\varepsilon-1}} - \lambda \left(\int_0^1 P_t(i)\, C_t(i)\, di - Z_t \right)$$

The associated first-order conditions are

$$C_t(i)^{-\frac{1}{\varepsilon}}\, C_t^{\frac{1}{\varepsilon}} = \lambda\, P_t(i)$$

for all $i \in [0, 1]$. Thus, for any two goods (i, j),

$$C_t(i) = C_t(j) \left(\frac{P_t(i)}{P_t(j)} \right)^{-\varepsilon}$$

which can be substituted into the expression for consumption expenditures to yield

$$C_t(i) = \left(\frac{P_t(i)}{P_t} \right)^{-\varepsilon} \frac{Z_t}{P_t}$$

for all $i \in [0, 1]$. The latter condition can then be substituted into the definition of C_t to obtain

$$\int_0^1 P_t(i)\, C_t(i)\, di = P_t\, C_t.$$

Combining the two previous equations yields the demand schedule

$$C_t(i) = \left(\frac{P_t(i)}{P_t} \right)^{-\varepsilon} C_t.$$

3.2 Aggregate Price Level Dynamics

Let $S(t) \subset [0, 1]$ represent the set of firms not reoptimizing their posted price in period t. Using the definition of the aggregate price level and the fact that all firms resetting prices will choose an identical price P_t^*,

$$P_t = \left[\int_{S(t)} P_{t-1}(i)^{1-\varepsilon} \, di + (1 - \theta) \, (P_t^*)^{1-\varepsilon} \right]^{\frac{1}{1-\varepsilon}}$$
$$= \left[\theta \, (P_{t-1})^{1-\varepsilon} + (1 - \theta) \, (P_t^*)^{1-\varepsilon} \right]^{\frac{1}{1-\varepsilon}}$$

where the second equality follows from the fact that the distribution of prices among firms not adjusting in period t corresponds to the distribution of effective prices in period $t - 1$, though with total mass reduced to θ.

Dividing both sides by P_{t-1},

$$\Pi_t^{1-\varepsilon} = \theta + (1 - \theta) \left(\frac{P_t^*}{P_{t-1}} \right)^{1-\varepsilon} \tag{34}$$

where $\Pi_t \equiv \frac{P_t}{P_{t-1}}$. Notice that in a steady state with zero inflation $P_t^* = P_{t-1} = P_t$ for all t.

Log-linearization of (34) around $\Pi_t = 1$ and $\frac{P_t^*}{P_{t-1}} = 1$ yields

$$\pi_t = (1 - \theta) \, (p_t^* - p_{t-1}). \tag{35}$$

3.3 Price Dispersion

From the definition of the price index

$$1 = \int_0^1 \left(\frac{P_t(i)}{P_t} \right)^{1-\varepsilon} di$$
$$= \int_0^1 \exp\{(1 - \varepsilon)(p_t(i) - p_t)\} \, di$$
$$\simeq 1 + (1 - \varepsilon) \int_0^1 (p_t(i) - p_t) \, di + \frac{(1 - \varepsilon)^2}{2} \int_0^1 (p_t(i) - p_t)^2 \, di$$

where the approximation results from a second-order Taylor expansion around the zero inflation steady state. Thus, and up to second order,

$$p_t \simeq E_i\{p_t(i)\} + \frac{(1 - \varepsilon)}{2} \int_0^1 (p_t(i) - p_t)^2 \, di$$

where $E_i\{p_t(i)\} \equiv \int_0^1 p_t(i)\,di$ is the cross-sectional mean of (log) prices.
In addition,

$$\int_0^1 \left(\frac{P_t(i)}{P_t}\right)^{-\frac{\varepsilon}{1-\alpha}} di$$

$$= \int_0^1 \exp\left\{-\frac{\varepsilon}{1-\alpha}\,(p_t(i)-p_t)\right\} di$$

$$\simeq 1 - \frac{\varepsilon}{1-\alpha} \int_0^1 (p_t(i)-p_t)\,di + \frac{1}{2}\left(\frac{\varepsilon}{1-\alpha}\right)^2 \int_0^1 (p_t(i)-p_t)^2\,di$$

$$\simeq 1 + \frac{1}{2}\frac{\varepsilon(1-\varepsilon)}{1-\alpha} \int_0^1 (p_t(i)-p_t)^2\,di + \frac{1}{2}\left(\frac{\varepsilon}{1-\alpha}\right)^2 \int_0^1 (p_t(i)-p_t)^2\,di$$

$$= 1 + \frac{1}{2}\left(\frac{\varepsilon}{1-\alpha}\right) \frac{1}{\Theta} \int_0^1 (p_t(i)-p_t)^2\,di$$

$$\simeq 1 + \frac{1}{2}\left(\frac{\varepsilon}{1-\alpha}\right) \frac{1}{\Theta}\, var_i\{p_t(i)\} > 1$$

where $\Theta \equiv \frac{1-\alpha}{1-\alpha+\alpha\varepsilon}$, and where the last equality follows from the observation that, up to second order,

$$\int_0^1 (p_t(i)-p_t)^2\,di \simeq \int_0^1 (p_t(i)-E_i\{p_t(i)\})^2\,di$$
$$\equiv var_i\{p_t(i)\}$$

Finally, using the definition of d_t,

$$d_t \equiv (1-\alpha)\log \int_0^1 \left(\frac{P_t(i)}{P_t}\right)^{-\frac{\varepsilon}{1-\alpha}} di \simeq \frac{1}{2}\frac{\varepsilon}{\Theta}\, var_i\{p_t(i)\}.$$

References

Akerlof, George, and Janet Yellen (1985): "A Near-Rational Model of the Business Cycle with Wage and Price Inertia," *Quarterly Journal of Economics* 100, supplement, 823–838.

Ball, Laurence, and David Romer (1990): "Real Rigidities and the Non-Neutrality of Money," *Review of Economic Studies* 57, 183–203.

Basu, Susanto, John Fernald, and Miles Kimball (2004): "Are Technology Improvements Contractionary?" *American Economic Review*, 96, no. 5, 1418–1448.

Blanchard, Olivier J., and Charles Kahn (1980): "The Solution of Linear Difference Equations under Rational Expectations," *Econometrica* 48, no. 5, 1305–1311.

Blanchard, Olivier J., and Nobuhiro Kiyotaki (1987): "Monopolistic Competition and the Effects of Aggregate Demand," *American Economic Review* 77, no. 4, 647–666.

Bullard, James, and Kaushik Mitra (2002): "Learning about Monetary Policy Rules," *Journal of Monetary Economics* 49, no. 6, 1005–1129.

Calvo, Guillermo (1983): "Staggered Prices in a Utility Maximizing Framework," *Journal of Monetary Economics* 12, no. 3, 383–398.

Chari, V. V., Patrick J. Kehoe, and Ellen R. McGrattan (2000): "Sticky Price Models of the Business Cycle: Can the Contract Multiplier Solve the Persistence Problem?" *Econometrica* 68, no. 5, 1151–1180.

Christiano, Lawrence J., Martin Eichenbaum, and Charles L. Evans (2005): "Nominal Rigidities and the Dynamic Effects of a Shock to Monetary Policy," *Journal of Political Economy* 113, no. 1, 1–45.

Dotsey, Michael, Robert G. King, and Alexander L. Wolman (1999): "State Dependent Pricing and the General Equilibrium Dynamics of Money and Output," *Quarterly Journal of Economics* 114, no. 2, 655–690.

Fuhrer, Jeffrey C., and George R. Moore (1995): "Inflation Persistence," *Quarterly Journal of Economics* 440, no. 2, 127–159.

Galí, Jordi (1999): "Technology, Employment, and the Business Cycle: Do Technology Shocks Explain Aggregate Fluctuations?" *American Economic Review* 89, no. 1, 249–271.

Galí, Jordi (2003): "New Perspectives on Monetary Policy, Inflation, and the Business Cycle," in M. Dewatripont, L. Hansen, and S. Turnovsky (eds.), *Advances in Economics and Econometrics* 3, 151–197, Cambridge University Press, Cambridge, MA.

Galí, Jordi, and Mark Gertler (1999): "Inflation Dynamics: A Structural Econometric Analysis," *Journal of Monetary Economics* 44, no. 2, 195–222.

Galí, Jordi, Mark Gertler, and David López-Salido (2001): "European Inflation Dynamics," *European Economic Review* 45, no. 7, 1237–1270.

Galí, Jordi, and Pau Rabanal (2004): "Technology Shocks and Aggregate Fluctuations: How Well Does the RBC Model Fit Postwar U.S. Data?" *NBER Macroeconomics Annual 2004*, 225–288.

Gertler, Mark, and John Leahy (2006): "A Phillips Curve with an Ss Foundation," NBER Working Paper No. 11971.

Golosov, Mikhail, and Robert E. Lucas (2007): "Menu Costs and Phillips Curves," *Journal of Political Economy* 115, no. 2, 171–199.

Hairault, Jean-Olivier, and Franck Portier (1993): "Money, New Keynesian Macroeconomics, and the Business Cycle," *European Economic Review* 37, no. 8, 33–68.

King, Robert G., and Mark Watson (1996): "Money, Prices, Interest Rates, and the Business Cycle," *Review of Economics and Statistics* 58, no. 1, 35–53.

King, Robert G., and Alexander L. Wolman (1996): "Inflation Targeting in a St. Louis Model of the 21st Century," *Federal Reserve Bank of St. Louis Review* 78, no. 3, 83–107.

Mankiw, Gregory (1985): "Small Menu Costs and Large Business Cycles: A Macroeconomic Model of Monopoly," *Quarterly Journal of Economy* 100, no. 2, 529–539.

Mankiw, N. Gregory, and Ricardo Reis (2002): "Sticky Information vs. Sticky Prices: A Proposal to Replace the New Keynesian Phillips Curve," *Quarterly Journal of Economics* 117, issue 4, 1295–1328.

Rotemberg, Julio (1982): "Monopolistic Price Adjustment and Aggregate Output," *Review of Economic Studies* 49, 517–531.

Rotemberg, Julio, and Michael Woodford (1999): "Interest Rate Rules in an Estimated Sticky Price Model," in J. B. Taylor (ed.), *Monetary Policy Rules*, University of Chicago Press, Chicago, IL.

Sbordone, Argia (2002): "Prices and Unit Labor Costs: Testing Models of Pricing Behavior," *Journal of Monetary Economics* 45, no. 2, 265–292.

Taylor, John (1980): "Aggregate Dynamics and Staggered Contracts," *Journal of Political Economy* 88, no. 1, 1–24.

Taylor, John B. (1999): "A Historical Analysis of Monetary Policy Rules," in J. B. Taylor (ed.), *Monetary Policy Rules*, University of Chicago Press, Chicago, IL.

Woodford, Michael (1996): "Control of the Public Debt: A Requirement for Price Stability," NBER WP 5684.

Yun, Tack (1996): "Nominal Price Rigidity, Money Supply Endogeneity, and Business Cycles," *Journal of Monetary Economics* 37, no. 2, 345–370.

Exercises

3.1 Interpreting Discrete-Time Records of Data on Price Adjustment Frequency

Suppose firms operate in continuous time, with the *pdf* for the duration of the price of an individual good being $f(t) = \phi \exp(-\phi t)$, where $t \in \mathbb{R}^+$ is expressed in month units.

a) Show that the implied instantaneous probability of a price change is constant over time and given by ϕ.

b) What is the *mean* duration of a price? What is the *median* duration? What is the relationship between the two?

c) Suppose that the prices of individual goods are recorded once a month (say, on the first day, for simplicity). Let λ_t denote the fraction of items in a given goods category whose price in month t is different from that recorded in month $t-1$ (Note: of course, the price may have changed more than once since the previous record). How would you go about estimating parameter ϕ?

d) Given information on monthly frequencies of price adjustment, how would you go about calibrating parameter θ in a quarterly Calvo model?

3.2 Introducing Government Purchases in the Basic New Keynesian Model

Assume that the government purchases quantity $G_t(i)$ of good i, for all $i \in [0, 1]$. Let $G_t \equiv \left[\int_0^1 G_t(i)^{1-\frac{1}{\varepsilon}} di \right]^{\frac{\varepsilon}{\varepsilon-1}}$ denote an index of public consumption, which the government seeks to maximize for any level of expenditures $\int_0^1 P_t(i) G_t(i) di$. Assume government expenditures are financed by means of lump-sum taxes.

a) Derive an expression for total demand facing firm i.

b) Derive a log-linear aggregate goods market clearing condition that is valid around a steady state with a constant public consumption share $S_G \equiv \frac{G}{Y}$.

c) Derive the corresponding expression for average real marginal cost as a function of aggregate output, government purchases, and technology and provide some intuition for the effect of government purchases.

d) How is the equilibrium relationship linking interest rates to current and expected output affected by the presence of government purchases?

3.3   Government Purchases and Sticky Prices

Consider a model economy with the following equilibrium conditions. The household's log-linearized Euler equation takes the form

$$c_t = -\frac{1}{\sigma}(i_t - E_t\{\pi_{t+1}\} - \rho) + E_t\{c_{t+1}\}$$

where c_t is consumption, i_t is the nominal rate, and $\pi_{t+1} \equiv p_{t+1} - p_t$ is the rate of inflation between t and $t+1$ (Note: as in the text, lowercase letters denote the logs of the original variable). The household's log-linearized labor supply is given by

$$w_t - p_t = \sigma\, c_t + \varphi\, n_t$$

where w_t denotes the nominal wage, p_t is the price level, and n_t is employment.
  Firms' technology is given by

$$y_t = n_t.$$

The time between price adjustments is random, which gives rise to an inflation equation

$$\pi_t = \beta\, E_t\{\pi_{t+1}\} + \kappa\, \widetilde{y}_t$$

where $\widetilde{y}_t \equiv y_t - y_t^n$ is the output gap (with y_t^n representing the natural level of output). Assume that in the absence of constraints on price adjustment firms would set a price equal to a constant markup over marginal cost given by μ (in logs).

  Suppose that the government purchases a fraction τ_t of the output of each good, with τ_t varying exogenously. Government purchases are financed through lump-sum taxes (Remark: the possibility of capital accumulation or the existence of an external sector is ignored).

  a) Derive a log-linear version of the goods market clearing condition of the form $y_t - c_t + g_t$, where $g_t \equiv -\log(1 - \tau_t)$.

  b) Derive an expression for (log) real marginal cost mc_t as a function of y_t and g_t.

  c) Determine the behavior of the natural level of output y_t^n as a function of g_t and discuss the mechanism through which a fiscal expansion leads to an increase in output when prices are flexible.

  d) Assume that $\{g_t\}$ follows a simple AR(1) process with autoregressive coefficient $\rho_g \in [0, 1]$. Derive the DIS equation

$$\widetilde{y}_t = E_t\{\widetilde{y}_{t+1}\} - \frac{1}{\sigma}(i_t - E_t\{\pi_{t+1}\} - r_t^n)$$

together for an expression for the natural rate r_t^n as a function of g_t.

3.4 Indexation and the New Keynesian Phillips Curve

Consider the Calvo model of staggered price setting with the following modification: In the periods between price reoptimizations firms mechanically adjust their prices according to some indexation rule. Formally, a firm that reoptimizes its price in period t (an event that occurs with probability $1 - \theta$) sets a price P_t^* in that period. In subsequent periods (i.e., until it reoptimizes prices again), its price is adjusted according to one of the following two alternative rules:

Rule 1: full indexation to steady state inflation Π,

$$P_{t+k|t} = P_{t+k-1|t}\Pi.$$

Rule 2: partial indexation to past inflation (assuming zero inflation in the steady state),

$$P_{t+k|t} = P_{t+k-1|t}(\Pi_{t+k-1})^{\omega}$$

for $k = 1, 2, 3, \ldots$ and

$$P_{t,t} = P_t^*$$

where $P_{t+k|t}$ denotes the price effective in period $t + k$ for a firm that last reoptimized its price in period t, $\Pi_t \equiv \frac{P_t}{P_{t-1}}$ is the aggregate gross inflation rate, and $\omega \in [0, 1]$ is an exogenous parameter that measures the degree of indexation. (Notice that when $\omega = 0$, the standard Calvo model is recovered with the price remaining constant between reoptimization periods.)

Suppose that all firms have access to the same constant returns to scale technology and face a demand schedule with a constant price elasticity ε.

The objective function for a firm reoptimizing its price in period t (i.e., choosing P_t^*) is given by

$$\max_{P_t^*} \sum_{k=0}^{\infty} \theta^k\, E_t\left\{Q_{t,t+k}\,[P_{t+k|t}\, Y_{t+k|t} - \Psi_{t+k}(Y_{t+k|t})]\right\}$$

subject to a sequence of demand constraints, and the rules of indexation described above. $Y_{t+k|t}$ denotes the output in period $t + k$ of a firm that last reoptimized its price in period t, $Q_{t,t+k} \equiv \beta^k \left(\frac{C_{t+k}}{C_t}\right)^{-\sigma}\frac{P_t}{P_{t+k}}$ is the usual stochastic discount factor for nominal payoffs, Ψ is the cost function, and θ is the probability of not being able to reoptimize the price in any given period. For each indexation rule:

a) Using the definition of the price level index $P_t \equiv \left[\int_0^1 P_t(i)^{1-\varepsilon}\, di\right]^{\frac{1}{1-\varepsilon}}$, derive a log-linear expression for the evolution of inflation π_t as a function of the average price adjustment term $p_t^* - p_{t-1}$.

b) Derive the first-order condition for the firm's problem that determines the optimal price P_t^*.

c) Log-linearize the first-order condition around the corresponding steady state and derive an expression for p_t^* (i.e., the approximate log-linear price-setting rule).

d) Combine the results of (a) and (c) to derive an inflation equation of the form

$$\widehat{\pi}_t = \beta \; E_t\{\widehat{\pi}_{t+1}\} + \lambda \; \widehat{mc}_t$$

where $\widehat{\pi}_t \equiv \pi_t - \pi$ in the case of rule 1, and

$$\pi_t = \gamma_b \; \pi_{t-1} + \gamma_f \; E_t\{\pi_{t+1}\} + \lambda \; \widehat{mc}_t$$

in the case of rule 2.

3.5   Optimal Price Setting and Equilibrium Dynamics in the Taylor Model

Assume a continuum of firms indexed by $i \in [0, 1]$. Each firm produces a differentiated good, with a technology

$$Y_t(i) = A_t \; N_t(i)$$

where A_t represents the level of technology, and $a_t \equiv \log A_t$ evolves exogenously according to some stationary stochastic process.

During each period a fraction $\frac{1}{N}$ of firms reset their prices, which then remain effective for N periods. Hence, a firm i setting a new price P_t^* in period t will seek to maximize

$$\sum_{k=0}^{N-1} E_t \left\{ Q_{t,t+k} \left(P_t^* \; Y_{t+k|t} - \Psi_{t+k}(Y_{t+k|t}) \right) \right\}$$

subject to

$$Y_{t+k|t} = (P_t^* / P_{t+k})^{-\varepsilon} \; C_{t+k}$$

where $Q_{t,t+k} \equiv \beta^k \left(\frac{C_{t+k}}{C_t} \right)^{-\sigma} \left(\frac{P_t}{P_{t+k}} \right)$ is the usual stochastic discount factor for nominal payoffs.

a) Show that P_t^* must satisfy the first-order condition

$$\sum_{k=0}^{N-1} E_t \left\{ Q_{t,t+k} \; Y_{t+k|t}^d \left[P_t^* - \mathcal{M} \; \psi_{t+k} \right] \right\} = 0$$

where $\psi_t \equiv \Psi_t'$ is the nominal marginal cost and $\mathcal{M} \equiv \frac{\varepsilon}{\varepsilon - 1}$.

b) Derive the following log-linearized optimal price-setting rule (around a zero inflation steady state)

$$p_t^* = \mu + \sum_{k=0}^{N-1} \omega_k \; E_t \{\psi_{t+k}\}$$

where $\omega_k \equiv \frac{\beta^k (1-\beta)}{1-\beta^N}$ and $\mu \equiv \log \mathcal{M}$. Show that in the limiting case of $\beta = 1$ (no discounting) the above equation can be rewritten as

$$p_t^* = \mu + \frac{1}{N} \sum_{k=0}^{N-1} E_t \{\psi_{t+k}\}.$$

How does the previous price-setting rule differ from the one generated by the Calvo model?

c) Recalling the expression for the aggregate price index $P_t \equiv [\int_0^1 P_t(i)^{1-\varepsilon} \, di]^{\frac{1}{1-\varepsilon}}$, show that around a zero inflation steady state the (log) price level will satisfy

$$p_t = \left(\frac{1}{N}\right) \sum_{k=0}^{N-1} p_{t-k}^*.$$

d) Consider the particular case of $N = 2$ and $\beta = 1$ and assume that the consumer's marginal rate of substitution between labor and consumption is given by $\sigma c_t + \varphi n_t$. Assume also that all output is consumed. Show that this case can be written as

$$p_t^* = \frac{1}{2} p_{t-1}^* + \frac{1}{2} E_t\{p_{t+1}^*\} + \delta \; (\tilde{y}_t + E_t\{\tilde{y}_{t+1}\})$$

where $\delta \equiv \sigma + \varphi$.

e) Assume that money demand takes the simple form $m_t - p_t = y_t$ and that both m_t and a_t follow (independent) random walks, with innovations ε_t^m and ε_t^a, respectively. Derive a closed-form expression for the output gap, employment, and the price level as a function of the exogenous shocks.

f) Discuss the influence of δ on the persistence of the effects of a monetary shock, and provide some intuition for that result.

3.6 The Mankiw–Reis Model: Inflation Dynamics under Predetermined Prices

Suppose that each period a fraction of firms $1 - \theta$ gets to choose *a path of future prices* for their respective goods (a "price plan"), while the remaining fraction θ keep their current price plans. Let $\{P_{t,t+k}\}_{k=0}^{\infty}$ denote the price plan chosen by firms that get to revise that plan in period t. Firm's technology is given by $Y_t(i) = \sqrt{A_t} \, N_t(i)$. Consumer's period utility is assumed to take the form $U(C_t, N_t) = C_t - \frac{N_t^2}{2}$, where $C_t \equiv [\int_0^1 C_t(i)^{1-\frac{1}{\varepsilon}} di]^{\frac{\varepsilon}{\varepsilon-1}}$. The demand for real balances is assumed to be given by $\frac{M_t}{P_t} = C_t$. All output is consumed.

a) Let $P_t \equiv [\int_0^1 P_t(i)^{1-\varepsilon} di]^{\frac{1}{1-\varepsilon}}$ denote the aggregate price index. Show that, up to a first-order approximation,

$$p_t = (1-\theta) \sum_{j=0}^{\infty} \theta^j \; p_{t-j,t}. \tag{36}$$

b) A firm i, revising its price plan in period t will seek to maximize

$$\sum_{k=0}^{\infty} \theta^k \, E_t \left\{ Q_{t,t+k} Y_{t+k}(i) \left(P_{t,t+k} - \frac{W_{t+k}}{\sqrt{A_{t+k}}} \right) \right\}.$$

Derive the first-order condition associated with that problem, and show that it implies the following approximate log-linear rule for the price plan

$$p_{t,t+k} = \mu + E_t\{\psi_{t+k}\} \tag{37}$$

for $k = 0, 1, 2, \ldots$ and where $\psi_t = w_t - \frac{1}{2}a_t$ is the nominal marginal cost.

c) Use the optimality conditions for the consumer's problem, and the labor market clearing condition to (i) show that the *natural* level of output satisfies $y_t^n = -\mu + a_t$, and (ii) the (log) real marginal cost (in deviation from its perfect foresight steady state value) equals the output gap, i.e.,

$$\widehat{mc}_t = \tilde{y}_t$$

for all t, where $\tilde{y}_t \equiv y_t - y_t^n$.

d) Using (36) and (37), show how one can derive the following equation for inflation

$$\pi_t = \frac{1-\theta}{\theta} \tilde{y}_t + \frac{1-\theta}{\theta} \sum_{j=1}^{\infty} \theta^j \, E_{t-j}\{\Delta\tilde{y}_t + \pi_t\}. \tag{38}$$

e) Suppose that the money supply follows a random walk process $m_t = m_{t-1} + u_t$, where $m_t \equiv \log M_t$ and $\{u_t\}$ is white noise. Determine the dynamic response of output, employment, and inflation to a money supply shock. Compare the implied response to one obtained under the standard New Keynesian Phillips curve, where $\pi_t = \beta \, E_t\{\pi_{t+1}\} + \kappa \, \tilde{y}_t$ (Hint: use the fact that in equilibrium $y_t = m_t - p_t$, substitute for $\tilde{y}_t$ in (38) in order to obtain a difference equation for the (log) price level).

f) Suppose that technology is described by the random walk process $a_t = a_{t-1} + \varepsilon_t$, where $a_t \equiv \log A_t$, and $\{\varepsilon_t\}$ is white noise. Determine the dynamic response of output, output gap, employment, and inflation to a technology shock. Compare the implied response to one obtained under the standard New Keynesian Phillips curve, where $\pi_t = \beta \, E_t\{\pi_{t+1}\} + \kappa \, \tilde{y}_t$ (Hint: same as (e) above).

4

Monetary Policy Design in the Basic New Keynesian Model

This chapter addresses the question of how monetary policy should be conducted, using as a reference framework the basic New Keynesian model developed in chapter 3. To start, that model's efficient allocation is characterized and shown to correspond to the equilibrium allocation of the decentralized economy under monopolistic competition and flexible prices once an appropriately chosen subsidy is in place. As it will be demonstrated, when prices are sticky, that allocation can be attained by means of a policy that fully stabilizes the price level.

The objectives of the optimal monetary policy are first determined, and then the issues pertaining to its implementation are addressed. Examples of interest rate rules that implement the optimal policy, i.e., optimal interest rate rules, are provided. But an argument is given that none of those rules seems a likely candidate to guide monetary policy in practice, for they all require that the central bank respond contemporaneously to changes in a variable—the natural rate of interest—that is not observable in actual economies. That observation motivates the introduction of rules that a central bank could arguably follow in practice (labeled as *simple rules*), and the development of a criterion to evaluate the relative desirability of those rules, based on their implied welfare effects. An illustration of that approach to policy evaluation is provided by analyzing the properties of two such simple rules: a Taylor rule and a constant money growth rule.

4.1   The Efficient Allocation

The efficient allocation associated with the model economy described in chapter 3 can be determined by solving the problem facing a benevolent social planner seeking to maximize the representative household's welfare, given technology and preferences. Thus, for each period the optimal allocation must maximize the household's utility

$$U\left(C_t, N_t\right)$$

where $C_t \equiv (\int_0^1 C_t(i)^{1-\frac{1}{\varepsilon}} \, di)^{\frac{\varepsilon}{\varepsilon-1}}$, subject to the resource constraints

$$C_t(i) = A_t \, N_t(i)^{1-\alpha}$$

for all $i \in [0, 1]$ and

$$N_t = \int_0^1 N_t(i) \, di.$$

The associated optimality conditions are

$$C_t(i) = C_t, \quad \text{all } i \in [0, 1] \tag{1}$$

$$N_t(i) = N_t, \quad \text{all } i \in [0, 1] \tag{2}$$

$$-\frac{U_{n,t}}{U_{c,t}} = MPN_t \tag{3}$$

where $MPN_t \equiv (1 - \alpha) \, A_t \, N_t^{-\alpha}$ denotes the economy's average marginal product of labor (which in the case of the symmetric allocation considered above also happens to coincide with the marginal product for each individual firm).

Thus, it is optimal to produce and consume the same quantity of all goods and to allocate the same amount of labor to all firms. That result is a consequence of all goods entering the utility function symmetrically, combined with concavity of utility and identical technologies to produce all goods. Once that symmetric allocation is imposed, the remaining condition defining the efficient allocation, equation (3), equates the marginal rate of substitution between consumption and work hours to the corresponding marginal rate of transformation (which in turn corresponds to the marginal product of labor). Note also that the latter condition coincides with the one determining the equilibrium allocation of the classical monetary model (with perfect competition and fully flexible prices) analyzed in chapter 2.

Next, the factors that make the equilibrium allocation in the baseline model suboptimal are discussed.

4.2 Sources of Suboptimality in the Basic New Keynesian Model

The basic New Keynesian model developed in chapter 3 is characterized by two distortions, whose implications are worth considering separately. The first distortion is the presence of market power in goods markets, exercised by monopolistically competitive firms. That distortion is unrelated to the presence of sticky prices, i.e., it would be effective even under the assumption of flexible prices. The second distortion results from the assumption of infrequent adjustment of prices by firms. Next, both types of distortions and their implications for the efficiency of equilibrium allocations are discussed.

4.2.1 Distortions Unrelated to Sticky Prices: Monopolistic Competition

The fact that each firm perceives the demand for its differentiated product to be imperfectly elastic endows it with some market power and leads to pricing-above-marginal cost policies. To isolate the role of monopolistic competition let us suppose for the time being that prices are fully flexible, i.e., each firm can adjust freely the price of its good each period. In that case, and under these assumptions, the profit maximizing price is identical across firms. In particular, under an isoelastic demand function (with price-elasticity ε), the optimal price-setting rule is given by

$$P_t = \mathcal{M} \frac{W_t}{MPN_t}$$

where $\mathcal{M} \equiv \frac{\varepsilon}{\varepsilon-1} > 1$ is the (gross) optimal markup chosen by firms and $\frac{W_t}{MPN_t}$ is the marginal cost. Accordingly,

$$-\frac{U_{n,t}}{U_{c,t}} = \frac{W_t}{P_t} = \frac{MPN_t}{\mathcal{M}} < MPN_t$$

where the first equality follows from the optimality conditions of the household. Hence, it is seen that the presence of a nontrivial price markup implies that condition (3) characterizing the efficient allocation is violated. Because, in equilibrium, the marginal rate of substitution $-U_{n,t}/U_{c,t}$ and the marginal product of labor are, respectively, increasing and decreasing (or nonincreasing) in hours, the presence of a markup distortion leads to an inefficiently low level of employment and output.

The above inefficiency resulting from the presence of market power can be eliminated through the suitable choice of an employment subsidy. Let τ denote the rate at which the cost of employment is subsidized, and assume that the outlays associated with the subsidy are financed by means of lump-sum taxes. Then, under flexible prices, $P_t = \mathcal{M} \frac{(1-\tau)W_t}{MPN_t}$. Accordingly,

$$-\frac{U_{n,t}}{U_{c,t}} = \frac{W_t}{P_t} = \frac{MPN_t}{\mathcal{M}(1-\tau)}.$$

Hence, the optimal allocation can be attained if $\mathcal{M}(1 - \tau) = 1$ or, equivalently, by setting $\tau = \frac{1}{\varepsilon}$. In much of the analysis below it is assumed that such an optimal subsidy is in place. By construction, the equilibrium under flexible prices is efficient in that case.

4.2.2 Distortions Associated with the Presence of Staggered Price Setting

The assumed constraints on the frequency of price adjustment constitute a source of inefficiency on two different grounds. First, the fact that firms do not adjust their prices continuously implies that the economy's average markup will vary over time in response to shocks, and will generally differ from the constant frictionless markup $\mathcal{M}$. Formally, and denoting the economy's average markup as $\mathcal{M}_t$ (defined as the ratio of average price to average marginal cost),

$$\mathcal{M}_t = \frac{P_t}{(1-\tau)(W_t/MPN_t)} = \frac{P_t \mathcal{M}}{W_t/MPN_t}$$

where the second equality follows from the assumption that the subsidy in place exactly offsets the monopolistic competition distortion, which allows the isolation of the role of sticky prices. In that case,

$$-\frac{U_{n,t}}{U_{c,t}} = \frac{W_t}{P_t} = MPN_t \, \frac{\mathcal{M}}{\mathcal{M}_t}$$

which violates efficiency condition (3) to the extent that $\mathcal{M}_t \neq \mathcal{M}$. The efficiency of the equilibrium allocation can only be restored if policy manages to stabilize the economy's average markup at its frictionless level.

In addition to the above inefficiency, which implies either too low or too high a level of aggregate employment and output, the presence of staggered price setting is a source of a second type of inefficiency. The latter has to do with the fact that the relative prices of different goods will vary in a way unwarranted by changes in preferences or technologies, as a result of the lack of synchronization in price adjustments. Thus, generally $P_t(i) \neq P_t(j)$ for any pair of goods (i, j) whose prices do not happen to have been adjusted in the same period. Such *relative price distortions* will lead, in turn, to different quantities of the different goods being produced and consumed, i.e., $C_t(i) \neq C_t(j)$, and, as a result, $N_t(i) \neq N_t(j)$ for some (i, j). That outcome violates efficiency conditions (1) and (2). Attaining the efficiency allocation requires that the quantities produced and consumed of all goods are equalized (and, hence, so are their prices and marginal costs). Accordingly, markups should be identical across firms and goods at all times, in addition to being constant (and equal to the frictionless markup) on average.

Next, the policy that will attain those objectives is characterized.

4.3   Optimal Monetary Policy in the Basic New Keynesian Model

In addition to assuming an optimal subsidy in place that exactly offsets the market power distortion, and in order to keep the analysis simple, the analysis is restricted to the case where there are no inherited relative price distortions, i.e., $P_{-1}(i) = P_{-1}$ for all $i \in [0, 1]$.[1] Under those assumptions, the efficient allocation can be attained by a policy that stabilizes marginal costs at a level consistent with firms'

---

[1] The case of a nondegenerate initial distribution of prices is analyzed in Yun (2005). In the latter case, the optimal monetary policy converges to the one described here after a transition period.

desired markup, *given the prices in place*. If that policy is expected to be in place indefinitely, no firm has an incentive to adjust its price, because it is currently charging its optimal markup and expects to keep doing so in the future without having to change its price. As a result, $P_t^* = P_{t-1}$ and, hence, $P_t = P_{t-1}$ for $t = 0, 1, 2, \ldots$ In other words, the aggregate price level is fully stabilized and no relative price distortions emerge. In addition, $\mathcal{M}_t = \mathcal{M}$ for all t, and output and employment match their counterparts in the flexible price equilibrium allocation (which, in turn, corresponds to the efficient allocation, given the subsidy in place).

Using the notation for the log-linearized model introduced in chapter 3, the optimal policy requires that for all t,

$$\widetilde{y}_t = 0$$
$$\pi_t = 0$$

i.e., the output gap is closed at all times, which (as implied by the New Keynesian Phillips curve) leads to zero inflation. The dynamic IS equation then implies

$$i_t = r_t^n$$

for all t, i.e., the equilibrium nominal interest rate (which equals the real rate, given zero inflation) must be equal to the natural interest rate.

Two features of the optimal policy are worth emphasizing. First, stabilizing output is not desirable in and of itself. Instead, output should vary one for one with the natural level of output, i.e., $y_t = y_t^n$ for all t. There is no reason, in principle, why the natural level of output should be constant or follow a smooth trend, because all kinds of real shocks will be a source of variations in its level. In that context, policies that stress output stability (possibly about a smooth trend) may generate potentially large deviations of output from its natural level and, thus, be suboptimal. This point is illustrated in section 4.3.1, in the context of a quantitative analysis of a simple policy rule.

Second, price stability emerges as a feature of the optimal policy even though, *a priori*, the policymaker does *not* attach any weight to such an objective. Instead, price stability is closely associated with the attainment of the efficient allocation (which is a more immediate policy objective). But the only way to replicate the (efficient) flexible price allocation when prices are sticky is by making all firms content with their existing prices, so that the assumed constraints on the adjustment of those prices are effectively nonbinding. Aggregate price stability then follows as a consequence of no firm willing to adjust its price.

4.3.1 Implementation: Optimal Interest Rate Rules

Next, some candidate rules for implementing the optimal policy are considered. All of them are consistent with the desired equilibrium outcome. Some, however, are *also* consistent with other suboptimal outcomes. In all cases, and in order to analyze its equilibrium implications, the candidate rule considered is embedded in the two equations describing the non-policy block of the basic New Keynesian model introduced in chapter 3. Those two key equations are shown here again for convenience

$$\widetilde{y}_t = E_t\{\widetilde{y}_{t+1}\} - \frac{1}{\sigma}\,(i_t - E_t\{\pi_{t+1}\} - r_t^n) \tag{4}$$

$$\pi_t = \beta\,E_t\{\pi_{t+1}\} + \kappa\,\widetilde{y}_t. \tag{5}$$

4.3.1.1 An Exogenous Interest Rate Rule

Consider the candidate interest rate rule

$$i_t = r_t^n \tag{6}$$

for all t. This is a rule that instructs the central bank to adjust the nominal rate one for one with variations in the natural rate (and only in response to variations in the latter). Such a rule would seem a natural candidate to implement the optimal policy since (6) was shown earlier to be always satisfied in an equilibrium that attains the optimal allocation.

Substituting (6) into (4) and rearranging terms represents the equilibrium conditions under rule (6) by means of the system

$$\begin{bmatrix} \widetilde{y}_t \\ \pi_t \end{bmatrix} = \mathbf{A_0} \begin{bmatrix} E_t\{\widetilde{y}_{t+1}\} \\ E_t\{\pi_{t+1}\} \end{bmatrix} \tag{7}$$

where

$$\mathbf{A_0} \equiv \begin{bmatrix} 1 & \frac{1}{\sigma} \\ \kappa & \beta + \frac{\kappa}{\sigma} \end{bmatrix}.$$

Note that $\widetilde{y}_t = \pi_t = 0$ for all t—the outcome associated with the optimal policy—is *one* solution to (7). That solution, however, is *not* unique: It can be shown that one of the two (real) eigenvalues of $\mathbf{A_0}$ always lies in the interval $(0, 1)$, while the second is strictly greater than unity. Given that both $\widetilde{y}_t$ and π_t are nonpredetermined, the existence of an eigenvalue outside the unit circle implies the existence of a multiplicity of equilibria in addition to $\widetilde{y}_t = \pi_t = 0$ for all t.[2] In that case nothing guarantees that the latter allocation will be precisely the one that will emerge as an equilibrium. That shortcoming leads to the consideration of alternative rules to (6).

---

[2] See, e.g., Blanchard and Kahn (1980).

4.3.1.2   An Interest Rate Rule with an Endogenous Component

Let us consider next the following interest rate rule

$$i_t = r_t^n + \phi_\pi \, \pi_t + \phi_y \, \tilde{y}_t \tag{8}$$

where ϕ_π and ϕ_y are non-negative coefficients determined by the central bank, that describe the strength of the interest rate response to deviations of inflation or the output gap from their target levels.

As above, substitute the nominal rate out using the assumed interest rate rule, and represent the equilibrium dynamics by means of a system of difference equations of the form

$$\begin{bmatrix} \tilde{y}_t \\ \pi_t \end{bmatrix} = \mathbf{A_T} \begin{bmatrix} E_t\{\tilde{y}_{t+1}\} \\ E_t\{\pi_{t+1}\} \end{bmatrix} \tag{9}$$

where

$$\mathbf{A_T} \equiv \Omega \begin{bmatrix} \sigma & 1 - \beta\phi_\pi \\ \sigma\kappa & \kappa + \beta(\sigma + \phi_y) \end{bmatrix}$$

and $\Omega \equiv \frac{1}{\sigma + \phi_y + \kappa\phi_\pi}$.

Once again, the desired outcome ($\tilde{y}_t = \pi_t = 0$ for all t) is always a solution to the dynamical system (9) and, hence, an equilibrium of the economy under rule (8). Yet, in order for that outcome to be the only (stationary) equilibrium, both eigenvalues of matrix $\mathbf{A_T}$ should lie within the unit circle. The size of those eigenvalues now depends on the policy coefficients (ϕ_π, ϕ_y), in addition to the non-policy parameters. Under the assumption of non-negative values for (ϕ_π, ϕ_y), a necessary and sufficient condition for $\mathbf{A_T}$ to have two eigenvalues within the unit circle and, hence, for the equilibrium to be unique, is given by[3]

$$\kappa \, (\phi_\pi - 1) + (1 - \beta) \, \phi_y > 0. \tag{10}$$

Thus, roughly speaking, the monetary authority should respond to deviations of inflation and the output gap from their target levels by adjusting the nominal rate with "sufficient strength." Figure 4.1 illustrates graphically the regions of parameter space for (ϕ_π, ϕ_y) associated with determinate and indeterminate equilibria, as implied by condition (10).

Interestingly, and somewhat paradoxically, if condition (10) is satisfied, both the output gap and inflation will be zero and, hence, $i_t = r_t^n$ for all t will hold ex-post. Thus, and in contrast with the case considered above (in which the equilibrium outcome $i_t = r_t^n$ was also taken to be the policy rule), it is the presence of a "threat" of a strong response by the monetary authority to an eventual deviation of

---

[3] See Bullard and Mitra (2002) for a proof.

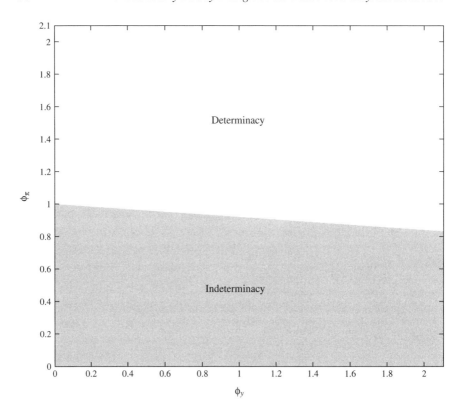

Figure 4.1 Determinacy and Indeterminacy Regions for a
Contemporaneous Interest Rate Rule

the output gap and inflation from target that suffices to rule out any such deviation
in equilibrium.

Some economic intuition for the form of condition (10) can be obtained by
considering the eventual implications of rule (8) for the nominal rate, were a
permanent increase in inflation of size $d\pi$ to occur (and assuming no permanent
changes in the natural rate)

$$di = \phi_\pi \, d\pi + \phi_y \, d\widetilde{y}$$
$$= \left(\phi_\pi + \frac{\phi_y \, (1 - \beta)}{\kappa} \right) d\pi \qquad (11)$$

where the second equality makes use of the long term relationship between inflation and the output gap implied by (5). Note that condition (10) is equivalent to
the term in brackets in (11) being greater than one. Thus, the equilibrium will
be unique under interest rate rule (8) whenever ϕ_π and ϕ_y are sufficiently large
enough to guarantee that the real rate eventually rises in the face of an increase in

inflation (thus tending to counteract that increase and acting as a stabilizing force). The previous property is often referred to as the *Taylor principle* and, to the extent that it prevents the emergence of multiple equilibria, it is naturally viewed as a desirable feature of any interest rate rule.[4]

4.3.1.3 A Forward-Looking Interest Rate Rule

In order to illustrate the existence of a multiplicity of policy rules capable of implementing the optimal policy, let us consider the following forward-looking rule

$$i_t = r_t^n + \phi_\pi E_t\{\pi_{t+1}\} + \phi_y E_t\{\widetilde{y}_{t+1}\} \tag{12}$$

which has the monetary authority to adjust the nominal rate in response to variations in *expected* inflation and the *expected* output gap, as opposed to their current values, as assumed in (8).

Under (12) the implied dynamics are described by the system

$$\begin{bmatrix} \widetilde{y}_t \\ \pi_t \end{bmatrix} = \mathbf{A_F} \begin{bmatrix} E_t\{\widetilde{y}_{t+1}\} \\ E_t\{\pi_{t+1}\} \end{bmatrix}$$

where

$$\mathbf{A_F} \equiv \begin{bmatrix} 1 - \sigma^{-1}\phi_y & -\sigma^{-1}(\phi_\pi - 1) \\ \kappa(1 - \sigma^{-1}\phi_y) & \beta - \kappa\sigma^{-1}(\phi_\pi - 1) \end{bmatrix}.$$

In this case, the conditions for a unique equilibrium (i.e., for both eigenvalues of $\mathbf{A_F}$ lying within the unit circle) are twofold and given by[5]

$$\kappa (\phi_\pi - 1) + (1 - \beta) \phi_y > 0 \tag{13}$$

$$\kappa (\phi_\pi - 1) + (1 + \beta) \phi_y < 2\sigma(1 + \beta). \tag{14}$$

Figure 4.2 represents the determinacy/indeterminacy regions in (ϕ_π, ϕ_y) space, under the baseline calibration for the remaining parameters. Note that in contrast with the "contemporaneous" rule considered in subsection 4.3.1.2, determinacy of equilibrium under the present forward-looking rule requires that the central bank reacts neither "too strongly" nor "too weakly" to deviations of inflation and/or the output gap from target. Yet, figure 4.2 suggests that the kind of overreaction that would be conducive to indeterminacy would require rather extreme values of the inflation and/or output gap coefficients, well above those characterizing empirical interest rate rules.

---

[4] See Woodford (2002) for a discussion.
[5] Bullard and Mitra (2002) list a third condition, given by the inequality $\phi_y < \sigma(1 + \beta^{-1})$, as necessary for uniqueness. But it can be easily checked that the latter condition is implied by the two conditions (13) and (14).

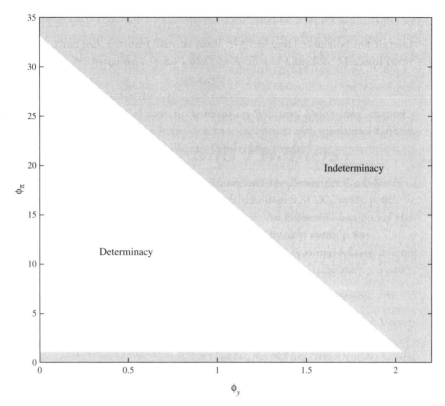

Figure 4.2   Determinacy and Indeterminacy Regions for a
Forward-Looking Interest Rate Rule

4.3.2   Practical Shortcomings of Optimal Policy Rules

Subsection 4.3.1 provided two examples of interest rate rules that implement the
optimal policy, thus guaranteeing that the efficient allocation is attained as the
unique equilibrium outcome. While such optimal interest rate rules appear to take
a relatively simple form, there exists an important reason why they are unlikely to
provide useful practical guidance for the conduct of monetary policy. The reason is
that they both require that the policy rate be adjusted one-for-one with the natural
rate of interest, thus implicitly assuming observability of the latter variable. That
assumption is plainly unrealistic because determination of the natural rate and its
movements requires an exact knowledge of (i) the economy's "true model," (ii)
the values taken by all its parameters, and (iii) the realized value (observed in real
time) of all the shocks impinging on the economy.

   Note that a similar requirement would have to be met if, as implied by (8) and
(12), the central bank should also adjust the nominal rate in response to deviations
of output from the natural level of output, because the latter is also unobservable.

That requirement, however, is not nearly as binding as the unobservability of the natural rate of interest, for nothing prevents the central bank from implementing the optimal policy by means of a rule that does not require a systematic response to changes in the output gap. Formally, ϕ_y in (8) or (12) could be set to zero, with uniqueness of equilibrium being still guaranteed by the choice of an inflation coefficient greater than unity (and no greater than $1 + 2\sigma(1+\beta)\kappa^{-1}$ in the case of the forward-looking rule).

The practical shortcomings of optimal interest rate rules discussed above have led many authors to propose a variety of "simple rules"—understood as rules that a central bank could arguably adopt in practice—and to analyze their properties.[6] In that context, an interest rate rule is generally considered "simple" if it makes the policy instrument a function of observable variables only, and does not require any precise knowledge of the exact model or the values taken by its parameters. The desirability of any given simple rule is thus given to a large extent by its robustness, i.e., its ability to yield a good performance across different models and parameter configurations.

In the following section, two such simple rules are analyzed—a simple Taylor-type rule and a constant money growth rule—and their performance is assessed in the context of the baseline New Keynesian model.

4.4 Two Simple Monetary Policy Rules

This section provides an illustration of how the basic New Keynesian model developed in chapter 3 can be used to assess the performance of two policy rules. A formal evaluation of the performance of a simple rule (relative, say, to the optimal rule or to an alternative simple rule) requires the use of some quantitative criterion. Following the seminal work of Rotemberg and Woodford (1999), much of the literature has adopted a welfare-based criterion, relying on a second-order approximation to the utility losses experienced by the representative consumer as a consequence of deviations from the efficient allocation. As shown in appendix 4.1, under the assumptions made in this chapter (which guarantee the optimality of the flexible price equilibrium), that approximation yields the following *welfare loss function*

$$\mathbb{W} = \frac{1}{2} E_0 \sum_{t=0}^{\infty} \beta^t \left[\left(\sigma + \frac{\varphi + \alpha}{1 - \alpha} \right) \tilde{y}_t^2 + \frac{\varepsilon}{\lambda} \pi_t^2 \right]$$

where welfare losses are expressed in terms of the equivalent permanent consumption decline, measured as a fraction of steady state consumption.

---

[6] The volume edited by John Taylor (1999) contains several important contributions in that regard.

The average welfare loss per period is thus given by the following linear combination of the variances of the output gap and inflation

$$\mathbb{L} = \frac{1}{2}\left[\left(\sigma + \frac{\varphi + \alpha}{1 - \alpha}\right)var(\tilde{y}_t) + \frac{\varepsilon}{\lambda}var(\pi_t)\right].$$

Note that the relative weight of output gap fluctuations in the loss function is increasing in σ, φ, and α. The reason is that larger values of those "curvature" parameters amplify the effect of any given deviation of output from its natural level on the size of the gap between the marginal rate of substitution and the marginal product of labor, which is a measure of the economy's aggregate inefficiency. On the other hand, the weight of inflation fluctuations is increasing in the elasticity of substitution among goods ε—because the latter amplifies the welfare losses caused by any given price dispersion—and the degree of price stickiness θ (which is inversely related to λ), which amplifies the degree of price dispersion resulting from any given deviation from zero inflation.

Given a policy rule and a calibration of the model's parameters, one can determine the implied variance of inflation and the output gap and the corresponding welfare losses associated with that rule (relative to the optimal allocation). That procedure is illustrated next through the analysis of two simple rules.

4.4.1   A Taylor-type Interest Rate Rule

Let us first consider the following interest rule, in the spirit of Taylor (1993)

$$i_t = \rho + \phi_\pi \, \pi_t + \phi_y \, \widehat{y}_t \tag{15}$$

where $\widehat{y}_t \equiv \log(Y_t/Y)$ denotes the log deviation of output from its steady state and where $\phi_\pi > 0$ and $\phi_y > 0$ are assumed to satisfy the determinacy condition (10). Again, the choice of intercept $\rho \equiv -\log \beta$ is consistent with a zero inflation steady state.

Note that (15) can be rewritten in terms of the output gap as

$$i_t = \rho + \phi_\pi \, \pi_t + \phi_y \, \tilde{y}_t + v_t \tag{16}$$

where $v_t \equiv \phi_y \, \widehat{y}_t^n$. The resulting equilibrium dynamics are thus identical to those of the interest rate rule analyzed in chapter 3, with v_t now reinterpreted as a driving force proportional to the deviations of natural output from steady state, instead of an exogenous monetary policy shock. Note that the variance of the "shock" v_t is no longer exogenous, but increasing in ϕ_y, the coefficient determining the response of the monetary authority to fluctuations in output. Formally, the equilibrium

Table 4.1 Evaluation of Simple Monetary Policy Rules

	Taylor Rule				Constant Money Growth	
ϕ_π	1.5	1.5	5	1.5	—	—
ϕ_y	0.125	0	0	1	—	—
$(\sigma_\zeta, \rho_\zeta)$	—	—	—	—	$(0, 0)$	$(0.0063, 0.6)$
$\sigma(\tilde{y})$	0.55	0.28	0.04	1.40	1.02	1.62
$\sigma(\pi)$	2.60	1.33	0.21	6.55	1.25	2.77
welfare loss	0.30	0.08	0.002	1.92	0.08	0.38

dynamics are described by the system

$$\begin{bmatrix} \tilde{y}_t \\ \pi_t \end{bmatrix} = \mathbf{A_T} \begin{bmatrix} E_t\{\tilde{y}_{t+1}\} \\ E_t\{\pi_{t+1}\} \end{bmatrix} + \mathbf{B_T}\,(\hat{r}_t^n - v_t)$$

where $\mathbf{A_T}$ and $\mathbf{B_T}$ are defined as in chapter 3. Assuming that variations in the technology parameter a_t represent the only driving force in the economy, and are described by a stationary AR(1) process with autoregressive coefficient ρ_a, the following equality holds:

$$\hat{r}_t^n - v_t = -\sigma \psi_{ya}^n (1 - \rho_a)\,a_t - \phi_y \psi_{ya}^n\,a_t$$
$$= -\psi_{ya}^n\,[\sigma(1 - \rho_a) + \phi_y]\,a_t$$

where, as in chapter 3, $\psi_{ya}^n \equiv \frac{1+\varphi}{\sigma+\varphi+\alpha(1-\sigma)} > 0$. From the analysis in chapter 3, the variance of the output gap and inflation under a rule of the form (16) is proportional to that of $\mathbf{B_T}\,(\hat{r}_t^n - v_t)$, which is strictly increasing in ϕ_y. Hence, a policy seeking to stabilize output by responding aggressively to deviations in that variable from steady state (or trend) is bound to lower the representative consumer's utility by increasing the variance of the output gap and inflation.[7]

The left panel of table 4.1 displays some statistics for four different calibrations of rule (15), corresponding to alternative configurations for ϕ_π and ϕ_y. The first column corresponds to the calibration proposed by Taylor (1993) as a good approximation to the interest rate policy of the Fed during the Greenspan years.[8] The second and third rules assume no response to output fluctuations with a very aggressive anti-inflation stance in the case of the third rule ($\phi_\pi = 5$). Finally, the fourth rule assumes a strong output-stabilization motive ($\phi_y = 1$). The remaining parameters are calibrated at their baseline values, as introduced in chapter 3.

For each version of the Taylor rule, table 4.1 shows the implied standard deviations of the output gap and (annualized) inflation, both expressed in percent

---

[7] Notice that in this simple example the optimal allocation can be attained by setting $\phi_y = -\sigma(1 - \rho_a)$. In that case, the simple rule is equivalent to the optimal rule $i_t = r_t^n + \phi_\pi \pi_t$.

[8] Taylor's proposed coefficient values were 1.5 for inflation and 0.5 for output, based on a specification with *annualized* inflation and interest rates. The choice of $\phi_y = 0.5/4$ is consistent with Taylor's proposed calibration because both i_t and π_t in the model are expressed in quarterly rates.

terms, as well as the welfare losses resulting from the associated deviations from the efficient allocation, expressed as a fraction of steady state consumption. Several results stand out. First, in a way consistent with the analysis above, versions of the rule that involve a systematic response to output variations generate larger fluctuations in the output gap and inflation and, hence, larger welfare losses. Those losses are moderate (0.3 percent of steady state consumption) under Taylor's original calibration, but they become substantial (close to 2 percent of steady state consumption) when the output coefficient ϕ_y is set to unity. Second, the smallest welfare losses are attained when the monetary authority responds to changes in inflation only. Furthermore, those losses (as well as the underlying fluctuations in the output gap and inflation) become smaller as the strength of that response increases. Hence, and at least in the context of the basic New Keynesian model considered here, a simple Taylor-type rule that responds aggressively to movements in inflation can approximate arbitrarily well the optimal policy.

4.4.2   A Constant Money Growth Rule

Next, a simple rule consisting of a constant growth rate for the money supply is considered, which is a rule generally associated with Friedman (1960). Without loss of generality, a zero rate of growth of the money supply is assumed, which is consistent with zero inflation in the steady state (given the absence of secular growth). Formally,

$$\Delta m_t = 0$$

for all t.

Once again, the assumption of a monetary rule requires that equilibrium conditions (4) and (5) be supplemented with a money market clearing condition. Take the latter to be of the form

$$l_t = y_t - \eta\, i_t - \zeta_t$$

where $l_t \equiv m_t - p_t$ denotes (log) real balances and ζ_t is an exogenous money demand shock following the process

$$\Delta \zeta_t = \rho_\zeta\, \Delta \zeta_{t-1} + \varepsilon_t^\zeta$$

where $\rho_\zeta \in [0, 1)$.

It is convenient to rewrite the money market equilibrium condition in terms of deviations from steady state as

$$\widehat{l_t} = \tilde{y}_t + \widehat{y}_t^n - \eta\, \widehat{i}_t - \zeta_t.$$

Letting $l_t^+ \equiv l_t + \zeta_t$ denote (log) real balances adjusted by the exogenous component of money demand,

$$\widehat{i}_t = \frac{1}{\eta}\, (\tilde{y}_t + \widehat{y}_t^n - \widehat{l_t^+}).$$

In addition, using the definition of l_t^+ together with the assumed rule $\Delta m_t = 0$,

$$\widehat{l}_{t-1}^+ = \widehat{l}_t^+ + \pi_t - \Delta \zeta_t.$$

Combining the previous two equations with (4) and (5) to substitute out the nominal rate, the equilibrium dynamics under a constant money growth rule can be summarized by the system

$$\mathbf{A}_{M,0} \begin{bmatrix} \widetilde{y}_t \\ \pi_t \\ \widehat{l}_{t-1}^+ \end{bmatrix} = \mathbf{A}_{M,1} \begin{bmatrix} E_t\{\widetilde{y}_{t+1}\} \\ E_t\{\pi_{t+1}\} \\ \widehat{l}_t^+ \end{bmatrix} + \mathbf{B}_M \begin{bmatrix} \widehat{r}_t^n \\ \widehat{y}_t^n \\ \Delta \zeta_t \end{bmatrix}$$

where $\mathbf{A}_{M,0}$, $\mathbf{A}_{M,1}$, and $\mathbf{B}_M$ are defined as in chapter 3.

The right panel of table 4.1 reports the standard deviation of the output gap and inflation, as well as the implied welfare losses, under a constant money growth rule. Two cases are considered, depending on whether money demand is assumed to be subject to exogenous disturbances. In both cases the natural output and the natural rate of interest vary in response to technology shocks (according to the baseline calibration of the latter introduced in chapter 3). When money demand shocks are allowed for, the corresponding process for $\Delta \zeta$ is calibrated by estimating an AR(1) process for the (first-differenced) residual of a money demand function for the period 1989:I–2004:IV—a period characterized by substantial stability in the demand for money—computed using an interest rate semi-elasticity of $\eta = 4$ (see discussion in chapter 3). The estimated standard deviation for the residual of the AR(1) process is $\sigma_\zeta = 0.0063$ while the estimated AR(1) coefficient is $\rho_\zeta = 0.6$.

Notice that in the absence of money demand shocks, a constant money growth rule delivers a performance comparable, in terms of welfare losses, to a Taylor rule with coefficients $\phi_\pi = 1.5$ and $\phi_y = 0$. Yet, when the calibrated money demand shock is introduced, the performance of a constant money growth rule deteriorates considerably, with the volatility of both the output gap and inflation rising to a level associated with welfare losses above those of the baseline Taylor rule. Thus, and not surprisingly, the degree of stability of money demand is a key element in determining the desirability of a rule that focuses on the control of a monetary aggregate.

4.5 Notes on the Literature

An early detailed discussion of the case for price stability in the basic New Keynesian model can be found in Goodfriend and King (1997). Svensson (1997) contains an analysis of the desirability of inflation targeting strategies, using a not-fully-microfounded model.

When deriving the optimal policy no inherited dispersion of prices across firms was assumed. A rigorous analysis of the optimal monetary policy in the case of an initial nondegenerate price distribution can be found in Yun (2005).

Taylor (1993) introduced the simple formula commonly known as the *Taylor rule*, as providing a good approximation to Fed policy in the early Greenspan years. Judd and Rudebusch (1998) and Clarida, Galí, and Gertler (2000) estimate alternative versions of the Taylor rule, and examine its (in)stability over the postwar period. Taylor (1999) uses the rule calibrated for the Greenspan years as a benchmark for the evaluation of monetary policy during other episodes over the postwar period. Orphanides (2003) argues that the bulk of the deviations from the baseline Taylor rule observed in the pre-Volcker era may have been the result of large biases in real time measures of the output gap.

Key contributions to the literature on the properties of alternative simple rules can be found in the papers contained in the volume edited by Taylor (1999). In particular, the paper by Rotemberg and Woodford (1999) derives a second-order approximation to the utility of the representative consumer. Chapter 6 in Woodford (2003) provides a detailed discussion of welfare-based evaluations of policy rules.

Appendix: A Second-Order Approximation to a Household's Welfare: The Case of an Undistorted Steady State

This appendix derives a second-order approximation to the utility of the representative consumer when the economy remains in a neighborhood of an efficient steady state, in a way consistent with the assumptions made in this chapter. The generalization to the case of a distorted steady state is left for chapter 5.

A second-order approximation of utility is derived around a given steady state allocation. Frequent use is made of the following second-order approximation of relative deviations in terms of log deviations

$$\frac{Z_t - Z}{Z} \simeq \widehat{z}_t + \frac{1}{2} \widehat{z}_t^2$$

where $\widehat{z}_t \equiv z_t - z$ is the log deviation from steady state for a generic variable z_t. All along it is assumed that utility is separable in consumption and hours (i.e., $U_{cn} = 0$). In order to lighten the notation, define $U_t \equiv U(C_t, N_t)$, $U_t^n \equiv U(C_t^n, N_t^n)$, and $U \equiv U(C, N)$.

The second-order Taylor expansion of U_t around a steady state (C, N) yields

$$U_t - U \simeq U_c C \left(\frac{C_t - C}{C} \right) + U_n N \left(\frac{N_t - N}{N} \right) + \frac{1}{2} U_{cc} C^2 \left(\frac{C_t - C}{C} \right)^2$$
$$+ \frac{1}{2} U_{nn} N^2 \left(\frac{N_t - N}{N} \right)^2$$

In terms of log deviations,

$$U_t - U \simeq U_c C \left(\widehat{y}_t + \frac{1-\sigma}{2} \widehat{y}_t^2 \right) + U_n N \left(\widehat{n}_t + \frac{1+\varphi}{2} \widehat{n}_t^2 \right)$$

where $\sigma \equiv -\frac{U_{cc}}{U_c} C$ and $\varphi \equiv \frac{U_{nn}}{U_n} N$, and where use of the market clearing condition $\widehat{c}_t = \widehat{y}_t$ has been made.

The next step consists in rewriting $\widehat{n}_t$ in terms of output. Using the fact that $N_t = (\frac{Y_t}{A_t})^{\frac{1}{1-\alpha}} \int_0^1 (\frac{P_t(i)}{P_t})^{-\frac{\varepsilon}{1-\alpha}} di$,

$$(1 - \alpha) \widehat{n}_t = \widehat{y}_t - a_t + d_t$$

where $d_t \equiv (1 - \alpha) \log \int_0^1 (\frac{P_t(i)}{P_t})^{-\frac{\varepsilon}{1-\alpha}} di$. The following lemma shows that d_t is proportional to the cross-sectional variance of relative prices.

Lemma 1: In a neighborhood of a symmetric steady state, and up to a second-order approximation, $d_t = \frac{\varepsilon}{2} var_i \{ p_t(i) \}$.

Proof: Let $\widehat{p}_t(i) \equiv p_t(i) - p_t$. Notice that

$$\left(\frac{P_t(i)}{P_t} \right)^{1-\varepsilon} = \exp \left[(1 - \varepsilon) \widehat{p}_t(i) \right]$$

$$= 1 + (1 - \varepsilon) \widehat{p}_t(i) + \frac{(1 - \varepsilon)^2}{2} \widehat{p}_t(i)^2.$$

Note that from the definition of P_t, $1 = \int_0^1 (\frac{P_t(i)}{P_t})^{1-\varepsilon} di$. A second-order approximation to this expression thus implies

$$E_i \{ \widehat{p}_t(i) \} = \frac{(\varepsilon - 1)}{2} E_i \{ \widehat{p}_t(i)^2 \}.$$

In addition, a second-order approximation to $(\frac{P_t(i)}{P_t})^{-\frac{\varepsilon}{1-\alpha}}$ yields

$$\left(\frac{P_t(i)}{P_t} \right)^{-\frac{\varepsilon}{1-\alpha}} = 1 - \frac{\varepsilon}{1-\alpha} \widehat{p}_t(i) + \frac{1}{2} \left(\frac{\varepsilon}{1-\alpha} \right)^2 \widehat{p}_t(i)^2.$$

Combining the two previous results, it follows that

$$\int_0^1 \left(\frac{P_t(i)}{P_t} \right)^{-\frac{\varepsilon}{1-\alpha}} di = 1 + \frac{1}{2} \left(\frac{\varepsilon}{1-\alpha} \right) \frac{1}{\Theta} E_i \{ \widehat{p}_t(i)^2 \}$$

$$= 1 + \frac{1}{2} \left(\frac{\varepsilon}{1-\alpha} \right) \frac{1}{\Theta} var_i \{ p_t(i) \}$$

where $\Theta \equiv \frac{1-\alpha}{1-\alpha+\alpha\varepsilon}$, and where the last equality follows from the observation that, up to second order,

$$\int_0^1 (p_t(i) - p_t)^2 \, di \simeq \int_0^1 (p_t(i) - E_i\{p_t(i)\})^2 \, di$$
$$\equiv var_i\{p_t(i)\}.$$

Finally, using the definition of d_t and up to a second-order approximation,

$$d_t \equiv (1-\alpha)\log \int_0^1 \left(\frac{P_t(i)}{P_t}\right)^{-\frac{\varepsilon}{1-\alpha}} di \simeq \frac{\varepsilon}{2\Theta} \, var_i\{p_t(i)\}$$

QED.

Now, the period t utility can be rewritten as

$$U_t - U = U_c C \left(\widehat{y}_t + \frac{1-\sigma}{2}\, \widehat{y}_t^2\right)$$
$$+ \frac{U_n N}{1-\alpha}\left(\widehat{y}_t + \frac{\varepsilon}{2\Theta}\, var_i\{p_t(i)\} + \frac{1+\varphi}{2(1-\alpha)}\, (\widehat{y}_t - a_t)^2\right) + t.i.p.$$

where $t.i.p.$ stands for *terms independent of policy*.

Efficiency of the steady state implies $-\frac{U_n}{U_c} = MPN$. Thus, and using the fact that $MPN = (1-\alpha)(Y/N)$ and $Y = C$,

$$\frac{U_t - U}{U_c C} \simeq -\frac{1}{2}\left[\frac{\varepsilon}{\Theta}\, var_i\{p_t(i)\} - (1-\sigma)\, \widehat{y}_t^2 + \frac{1+\varphi}{1-\alpha}\, (\widehat{y}_t - a_t)^2\right] + t.i.p.$$
$$= -\frac{1}{2}\left[\frac{\varepsilon}{\Theta}\, var_i\{p_t(i)\} + \left(\sigma + \frac{\varphi+\alpha}{1-\alpha}\right)\, \widehat{y}_t^2 - 2\left(\frac{1+\varphi}{1-\alpha}\right)\, \widehat{y}_t a_t\right] + t.i.p.$$
$$= -\frac{1}{2}\left[\frac{\varepsilon}{\Theta}\, var_i\{p_t(i)\} + \left(\sigma + \frac{\varphi+\alpha}{1-\alpha}\right)\, (\widehat{y}_t^2 - 2\widehat{y}_t\, \widehat{y}_t^n)\right] + t.i.p.$$
$$= -\frac{1}{2}\left[\frac{\varepsilon}{\Theta}\, var_i\{p_t(i)\} + \left(\sigma + \frac{\varphi+\alpha}{1-\alpha}\right)\, \widetilde{y}_t^2\right] + t.i.p.$$

where $\widehat{y}_t^n \equiv y_t^n - y^n$, and where the fact was used that $\widehat{y}_t^n = \frac{1+\varphi}{\sigma(1-\alpha)+\varphi+\alpha}\, a_t$ and $\widehat{y}_t - \widehat{y}_t^n = \widetilde{y}_t$.

Accordingly, a second-order approximation to the consumer's welfare losses can be written and expressed as a fraction of steady state consumption (and up to additive terms independent of policy) as

$$\mathbb{W} = E_0 \sum_{t=0}^{\infty} \beta^t \left(\frac{U_t - U}{U_c C} \right)$$

$$= -\frac{1}{2} E_0 \sum_{t=0}^{\infty} \beta^t \left(\frac{\varepsilon}{\Theta} var_i\{p_t(i)\} + \left(\sigma + \frac{\varphi + \alpha}{1 - \alpha} \right) \tilde{y}_t^2 \right).$$

The final step consists in rewriting the terms involving the price dispersion variable as a function of inflation. In order to do so, make use of the following lemma

Lemma 2: $\sum_{t=0}^{\infty} \beta^t var_i\{p_t(i)\} = \frac{\theta}{(1-\beta\theta)(1-\theta)} \sum_{t=0}^{\infty} \beta^t \pi_t^2$

Proof: Woodford (2003, chapter 6)

Using the fact that $\lambda \equiv \frac{(1-\theta)(1-\beta\theta)}{\theta} \Theta$, the previous lemma can be combined with the expression for the welfare losses above to obtain

$$\mathbb{W} = -\frac{1}{2} E_0 \sum_{t=0}^{\infty} \beta^t \left[\left(\frac{\varepsilon}{\lambda} \right) \pi_t^2 + \left(\sigma + \frac{\varphi + \alpha}{1 - \alpha} \right) \tilde{y}_t^2 \right].$$

References

Blanchard, Olivier J., and Charles Kahn (1980): "The Solution of Linear Difference Equations under Rational Expectations," *Econometrica* 48, no. 5, 1305–1311.

Bullard, James, and Kaushik Mitra (2002): "Learning About Monetary Policy Rules," *Journal of Monetary Economics* 49, no. 6, 1105–1130.

Clarida, Richard, Jordi Galí, and Mark Gertler (2000): "Monetary Policy Rules and Macroeconomic Stability: Evidence and Some Theory," *Quarterly Journal of Economics* 105, no. 1, 147–180.

Friedman, Milton (1960): *A Program for Monetary Stability*, Fordham University Press, New York.

Goodfriend, Marvin, and Robert G. King (1997): "The New Neoclassical Synthesis," *NBER Macroeconomics Annual 1997*, 231–282.

Judd, John P., and Glenn Rudebusch (1998): "Taylor's Rule and the Fed: A Tale of Three Chairmen," *FRBSF* [Federal Reserve Bank of San Francisco] *Economic Review*, no. 3, 3–16.

Orphanides, Athanasios (2003): "The Quest for Prosperity Without Inflation," *Journal of Monetary Economics* 50, no. 3, 633–663.

Rotemberg, Julio, and Michael Woodford (1999): "Interest Rate Rules in an Estimated Sticky Price Model," in J. B. Taylor (ed.), *Monetary Policy Rules*, University of Chicago Press, Chicago, IL.

Svensson, Lars E. O. (1997) "Inflation Forecast Targeting: Implementing and Monitoring Inflation Targets," *European Economic Review* 41, no. 6, 1111–1147.

Taylor, John B. (1993): "Discretion versus Policy Rules in Practice," *Carnegie-Rochester Series on Public Policy* 39, 195–214.

Taylor, John B., ed. (1999): "An Historical Analysis of Monetary Policy Rules," in J. B. Taylor (ed.), *Monetary Policy Rules*, University of Chicago Press, Chicago, IL.

Taylor, John B. (1999): *Monetary Policy Rules*, University of Chicago Press, Chicago, IL.

Woodford, Michael (2001): "The Taylor Rule and Optimal Monetary Policy," *American Economic Review* 91, no. 2, 232–237.

Woodford, Michael (2003): *Interest and Prices: Foundations of a Theory of Monetary Policy*, Princeton University Press, Princeton, NJ.

Yun, Tack (2005): "Optimal Monetary Policy with Relative Price Distortions," *American Economic Review* 95, no. 1, 89–109.

Exercises

4.1   Inflation Targeting with Noisy Data

Consider a model economy whose output gap and inflation dynamics are described by the system

$$\pi_t = \beta E_t\{\pi_{t+1}\} + \kappa \, \tilde{y}_t \tag{17}$$

$$\tilde{y}_t = -\frac{1}{\sigma} \, (i_t - E_t\{\pi_{t+1}\} - r_t^n) + E_t\{\tilde{y}_{t+1}\} \tag{18}$$

where all variables are defined as in the text. The natural rate r_t^n is assumed to follow the exogenous process

$$r_t^n - \rho = \rho_r \, (r_{t-1}^n - \rho) + \varepsilon_t$$

where $\{\varepsilon_t\}$ is a white-noise process and $\rho_r \in [0, 1)$.

Suppose that inflation is measured with some *i.i.d.* error ξ_i, i.e., $\pi_t^o = \pi_t + \xi_t$ where π_t^o denotes measured inflation. Assume that the central bank follows the rule

$$i_t = \rho + \phi_\pi \, \pi_t^o. \tag{19}$$

a) Solve for the equilibrium processes for inflation and the output gap under the rule (19). (Hint: you may want to start analyzing the simple case of $\rho_r = 0$.)

b) Describe the behavior of inflation, the output gap, and the nominal rate when ϕ_π approaches infinity.

c) Determine the size of the inflation coefficient that minimizes the variance of actual inflation.

4.2   Monetary Policy and the Effects of Technology Shocks

Consider a New Keynesian economy with equilibrium conditions

$$y_t = E_t\{y_{t+1}\} - \frac{1}{\sigma} (i_t - E_t\{\pi_{t+1}\} - \rho) \tag{20}$$

$$\pi_t = \beta \ E_t\{\pi_{t+1}\} + \kappa \ (y_t - y_t^n) \tag{21}$$

where all variables are defined as in the text.

Monetary policy is described by a simple rule of the form

$$i_t = \rho + \phi_\pi \ \pi_t$$

where $\phi_\pi > 1$. Labor productivity is given by

$$y_t - n_t = a_t$$

where a_t is an exogenous technology parameter that evolves according to

$$a_t = \rho_a \ a_{t-1} + \varepsilon_t$$

where $\rho_a \in [0, 1)$ and $\{\varepsilon_t\}$ is an i.i.d. process.

The underlying RBC model is assumed to imply a natural level of output proportional to technology

$$y_t^n = \psi_y \ a_t$$

where $\psi_y > 1$.

a) Describe in words where (20) and (21) come from.

b) Determine the equilibrium response of output, employment, and inflation to a technology shock. (Hint: guess that each endogenous variable will be proportional to the contemporaneous value of technology.)

c) Describe how those responses depend on the value of ϕ_π and κ. Provide some intuition. What happens when $\phi_\pi \to \infty$? What happens as the degree of price rigidities changes?

d) Analyze the joint response of employment and output to a technology shock and discuss briefly the implications for assessment of the role of technology as a source of business cycles.

4.3   Interest Rate versus Money Supply Rules

Consider an economy described by the equilibrium conditions

$$\tilde{y}_t = E_t\{\tilde{y}_{t+1}\} - \frac{1}{\sigma} (i_t - E_t\{\pi_{t+1}\} - r_t^n)$$

$$\pi_t = \beta \ E_t\{\pi_{t+1}\} + \kappa \ \tilde{y}_t$$

$$m_t - p_t = y_t - \eta \ i_t$$

where all variables are defined as in the text. Both y_t^n and r_t^n evolve exogenously, independent of monetary policy.

The central bank seeks to minimize a loss function of the form

$$\alpha \, var(\tilde{y}_t) + var(\pi_t).$$

a) Show how the optimal policy could be implemented by means of an interest rate rule.

b) Show that a rule requiring a constant money supply will generally be suboptimal. Explain. (Hint: derive the path of money under the optimal policy.)

c) Derive a money supply rule that would implement the optimal policy.

4.4 Optimal Monetary Policy with Price Setting in Advance

Consider an economy where the representative consumer maximizes

$$E_0 \sum_{t=0}^{\infty} \beta^t \, U\left(C_t, \frac{M_t}{P_t}, N_t\right)$$

subject to a sequence of dynamic budget constraints

$$P_t \, C_t + M_t + Q_t B_t \le M_{t-1} + B_{t-1} + W_t \, N_t + T_t$$

and where all variables are defined as in the text.

Assume that period utility is given by

$$U\left(C_t, \frac{M_t}{P_t}, N_t\right) = \log C_t + \log \frac{M_t}{P_t} - \frac{N_t^{1+\varphi}}{1+\varphi}. \tag{22}$$

Firms are monopolistically competitive, each producing a differentiated good whose demand is given by $Y_t(i) = (\frac{P_t(i)}{P_t})^{-\varepsilon} Y_t$. Each firm has access to the linear production function

$$Y_t(i) = A_t \, N_t(i) \tag{23}$$

where productivity evolves according to

$$\frac{A_t}{A_{t-1}} = (1+\gamma_a) \, \exp\{\varepsilon_t\}$$

with $\{\varepsilon_t\}$ being an i.i.d. normally distributed process with mean zero and variance σ_ε^2.

The money supply varies exogenously according to the process

$$\frac{M_t}{M_{t-1}} = (1+\gamma_m) \, \exp\{u_t\} \tag{24}$$

where $\{u_t\}$ is an i.i.d. normally distributed process with mean zero and variance σ_u^2.

Finally, assume that all output is consumed, so that in equilibrium $Y_t = C_t$ for all t.

a) Derive the optimality conditions for the problem facing the representative consumer.

b) Assume that firms are monopolistically competitive, each producing a differentiated good. For each period, after observing the shocks, firms set the price of their good in order to maximize current profit

$$Y_t(i) \left(P_t(i) - \frac{W_t}{A_t} \right)$$

subject to the demand schedule above. Derive the optimality condition associated with the firm's problem.

c) Show that the equilibrium levels of aggregate employment, output, and inflation are given by

$$N_t = \left(1 - \frac{1}{\varepsilon} \right)^{\frac{1}{1+\varphi}} \equiv \Theta$$

$$Y_t = \Theta A_t$$

$$\pi_t = (\gamma_m - \gamma_a) + u_t - \varepsilon_t.$$

d) Discuss how utility depends on the two parameters describing monetary policy, γ_m and σ_u^2 (recall that the nominal interest rate is constrained to be non-negative, i.e., $i_t \geq 0$ for all t). Show that the optimal policy must satisfy the Friedman rule and discuss alternative ways of supporting that rule in equilibrium.

e) Next, assume that for each period firms have to set the price in advance, i.e., before the realization of the shocks. In that case they will choose a price in order to maximize the discounted profit

$$E_{t-1} \left\{ Q_{t-1,t} Y_t(i) \left(P_t(i) - \frac{W_t}{A_t} \right) \right\}$$

subject to the demand schedule $Y_t(i) = (\frac{P_t(i)}{P_t})^{-\varepsilon} Y_t$, where $Q_{t-1,t} \equiv \beta \frac{C_{t-1}}{C_t} \frac{P_{t-1}}{P_t}$ is the stochastic discount factor. Derive the first-order condition of the firm's problem and solve (exactly) for the equilibrium levels of employment, output, and real balances.

f) Evaluate expected utility at the equilibrium values of output, real balances, and employment.

g) Consider the class of money supply rules of the form (24) such that $u_t = \phi_\varepsilon \, \varepsilon_t + \phi_v \, v_t$, where $\{v_t\}$ is a normally distributed i.i.d. process with zero mean and unit variance, and independent of $\{\varepsilon_t\}$ at all leads and lags. Notice that within that family of rules, monetary policy is fully described by three parameters: γ_m, ϕ_ε, and ϕ_v. Determine the values of those parameters that maximize expected utility, subject to the constraint of a non-negative nominal interest rate. Show that the resulting equilibrium under the optimal policy replicates the flexible price equilibrium analyzed above.

4.5   A Price Level Based Interest Rate Rule

Consider an economy described by the equilibrium conditions

$$\tilde{y}_t = E_t\{\tilde{y}_{t+1}\} - \frac{1}{\sigma}\left(i_t - E_t\{\pi_{t+1}\} - r_t^n\right)$$

$$\pi_t = \beta \, E_t\{\pi_{t+1}\} + \kappa \, \tilde{y}_t.$$

Show that the interest rate rule

$$i_t = r_t^n + \phi_p \, \widehat{p}_t$$

where $\widehat{p}_t \equiv p_t - p^*$, where p^* is a price level target, generates a unique stationary equilibrium, if and only if, $\phi_p > 0$.

5

Monetary Policy Tradeoffs:
Discretion versus Commitment

In chapter 4 the optimal monetary policy problem was analyzed in the context of a baseline model in which the presence of staggered price setting was the only relevant distortion that the central bank had to confront. It was shown that a policy that seeks to replicate the flexible price equilibrium allocation is both feasible and optimal in that context. That policy requires that the central bank responds to shocks so that the price level is fully stabilized. The rationale for such a policy is easy to summarize: With zero inflation output equals its natural level, which in turn, under the assumptions made in chapter 4, is also the efficient level. Thus, in the environment analyzed in chapter 4, the central bank does not face a meaningful policy tradeoff and "strict inflation targeting" emerges as the optimal policy.

The analysis of such an environment and its implications for the design of monetary policy is useful from a pedagogical point of view, but is not realistic. The reason is that, in practice, central banks view themselves as facing significant tradeoffs, at least in the short run. As a result, even central banks that call themselves "inflation targeters" do not claim to be seeking to stabilize inflation completely in the short run, independently of the consequences that this would entail for the evolution of real variables like output and employment. Instead, the presence of short run tradeoffs have led inflation targeting central banks to pursue a policy that allows for a partial accommodation of inflationary pressures in the short run. This is in order to avoid a too-large instability of output and employment while remaining committed to a medium term inflation target. A policy of that kind is often referred to in the literature as *flexible inflation targeting*.[1]

In this chapter, a policy tradeoff is introduced, and then the problem of optimal monetary policy is revisited. As shown below, the existence of such a policy

---

Much of the material in this chapter is based on my paper "The Science of Monetary Policy: A New Keynesian Perspective," coauthored with Richard Clarida and Mark Gertler, and published in the *Journal of Economic Literature*, 1999.

[1] The term *flexible inflation targeting* was coined by Lars Svensson to refer to the kind of optimal monetary policies that result from the minimization of a central bank loss function that attaches a nonzero penalty to output gap fluctuations. This is in addition to inflation fluctuations, whenever there is a tradeoff between the stabilization of both variables.

tradeoff, combined with the forward-looking nature of inflation, makes it desirable for the central bank to be able to commit to a state-contingent policy plan (as opposed to pursuing a policy characterized by sequential, or period-by-period, optimization).

5.1 The Monetary Policy Problem: The Case of an Efficient Steady State

When nominal rigidities coexist with *real* imperfections, the flexible price equilibrium allocation is generally inefficient. In that case, it is no longer optimal for the central bank to seek to replicate that allocation. On the other hand, any deviation of economic activity from its natural (i.e., flexible price) level generates variations in inflation, with consequent relative price distortions.

A special case of interest arises when the possible inefficiencies associated with the flexible price equilibrium do not affect the steady state, which remains efficient. This section analyzes the optimal monetary policy problem under that assumption. In contrast with the analysis in chapter 4, however, here *short run* deviations are allowed for between the natural and efficients levels of output. More precisely, the gap between the two is assumed to follow a stationary process with a zero mean. Implicitly, the presence of some real imperfections that generate a time-varying gap between output and its efficient counterpart, are assumed even in the absence of price rigidities.

In that case, and as shown in appendix 5.1, the welfare losses experienced by the representative household are, up to a second-order approximation, proportional to

$$E_0 \left\{ \sum_{t=0}^{\infty} \beta^t \left(\pi_t^2 + \alpha_x\, x_t^2 \right) \right\} \tag{1}$$

where $x_t = y_t \quad y_t^e$ denotes the *welfare-relevant output gap*, i.e., the deviation between (log) output y_t and its efficient level y_t^e. As before, $\pi_t \equiv p_t - p_{t-1}$ denotes the rate of inflation between periods $t - 1$ and t. Coefficient α_x represents the weight of output gap fluctuations (relative to inflation) in the loss function, and is given by $\alpha_x = \frac{\kappa}{\varepsilon}$ where κ is the coefficient on x_t in the New Keynesian Phillips curve, and ε is the elasticity of substitution between goods. More generally, and stepping beyond the welfare-theoretic justification for (1), one can interpret α_x as the weight attached by the central bank to deviations of output from its efficient level (relative to price stability) in its own loss function, which does not necessarily have to coincide with the household's.

A structural equation relating inflation and the welfare-relevant output gap can be derived by using the identity $\widetilde{y}_t \equiv x_t + (y_t^e - y_t^n)$ to substitute for the output gap $\tilde{y}_t$ in the NKPC relationship derived in chapter 3. This yields the following structural equation for inflation

$$\pi_t = \beta E_t\{\pi_{t+1}\} + \kappa \, x_t + u_t \tag{2}$$

where $u_t \equiv \kappa (y_t^e - y_t^n)$.

Hence, the central bank will seek to minimize (1) subject to the sequence of constraints given by (2). Two features of that problem are worth stressing. First, note that, under the previous assumptions, the disturbance u_t is exogenous with respect to monetary policy, because the latter can influence neither the natural nor the efficient level of output. As a result, the central bank will take the current and anticipated values of u_t as given when solving its policy problem.

Second, and most important, time variations in the gap between the efficient and natural levels of output—reflected in fluctuations in u_t—generate a tradeoff for the monetary authority, because they make it impossible to attain simultaneously zero inflation and an efficient level of activity. This is a key difference from the model analyzed in chapter 4, where $y_t^n = y_t^e$ for all t, thus implying $u_t = 0$ for all t. In appendix 5.2 several potential sources of variation in the gap between the efficient and natural levels of output are discussed, including exogenous changes in desired price or wage markups, as well as fluctuations in labor income taxes. Nevertheless, at least for the purposes of the analysis in this chapter, knowledge of the specific source of that gap is not important.

Following much of the literature, the disturbance u_t in (2) is referred to as a *cost-push shock*. Also, and for the remainder of this chapter, assume that u_t follows the exogenous AR(1) process

$$u_t = \rho_u u_{t-1} + \varepsilon_t^u \tag{3}$$

where $\rho_u \in [0, 1)$, and $\{\varepsilon_t^u\}$ is a white-noise process with constant variance σ_u^2.

While (2) is the only constraint needed in order to determine the equilibrium path for output and inflation under the optimal policy, implementation of that policy requires the use of an additional condition linking those variables with the monetary policy instrument, i.e., the interest rate. That condition can be obtained by rewriting the dynamic IS equation first derived in chapter 3 in terms of the welfare-relevant output gap

$$x_t = -\frac{1}{\sigma} (i_t - E_t\{\pi_{t+1}\} - r_t^e) + E_t\{x_{t+1}\} \tag{4}$$

where $r_t^e \equiv \rho + \sigma E_t\{\Delta y_{t+1}^e\}$ is the interest rate that supports the efficient allocation, and which is invariant to monetary policy. Henceforth, r_t^e is referred to as the *efficient interest rate*.

The forward-looking nature of constraint (2) in the policy problem requires the specification of the extent to which the central bank can credibly commit in advance to future policy actions. As will be clear below, the reason is that by committing to some future policies the central bank is able to influence expectations in a way that improves its short-run tradeoffs. Sections 5.1.1 and 5.1.2 characterize the optimal monetary policy under two alternative (and extreme) assumptions regarding the central bank's ability to commit to future policies.

5.1.1   Optimal Discretionary Policy

Start by considering a case in which the central bank treats the problem described above as one of sequential optimization, i.e., it makes whatever decision is optimal each period without committing itself to any future actions. That case is often referred to in the literature as *optimal policy under discretion*.

More specifically, each period the monetary authority is assumed to choose (x_t, π_t) in order to minimize the period losses

$$\pi_t^2 + \alpha_x \, x_t^2$$

subject to the constraint

$$\pi_t = \kappa \, x_t + v_t$$

where the term $v_t \equiv \beta E_t\{\pi_{t+1}\} + u_t$ is taken as given by the monetary authority, because u_t is exogenous and $E_t\{\pi_{t+1}\}$ is a function of expectations about *future* output gaps (as well as future u_t's) which, by assumption, cannot be currently influenced by the policymaker.[2]

The optimality condition for the problem above is given by

$$x_t = -\frac{\kappa}{\alpha_x} \pi_t \tag{5}$$

for $t = 0, 1, 2, \ldots$ The previous condition has a simple interpretation: In the face of inflationary pressures resulting from a cost-push shock the central bank must respond by driving output below its efficient level, thus creating a negative output gap, with the objective of dampening the rise in inflation. The central bank carries out such a "leaning against the wind" policy up to the point where condition (5) is satisfied. Thus, one can view (5) as a relation between target variables that the discretionary central bank will seek to maintain at all times and it is in that sense that it may be labeled a "targeting rule."[3]

---

[2] To be precise, the term $E_t\{\pi_{t+1}\}$ can be treated as given by the central bank because there are no endogenous state variables (e.g., past inflation) affecting current inflation. Otherwise the central bank would have to take into account the influence that its current actions, through their impact on those state variables, would have on future inflation.

[3] See, e.g., Svensson (1999) and Svensson and Woodford (2005) for a discussion of "targeting" versus "instrument" rules as alternative approaches to implementation of inflation targeting policies.

Using (5) to substitute for x_t in (2) yields the following difference equation for inflation

$$\pi_t = \frac{\alpha_x \beta}{\alpha_x + \kappa^2} E_t\{\pi_{t+1}\} + \frac{\alpha_x}{\alpha_x + \kappa^2} u_t.$$

Iterating the previous equation forward, an expression is obtained for equilibrium inflation under the optimal discretionary policy

$$\pi_t = \alpha_x \Psi\, u_t \qquad (6)$$

where $\Psi \equiv \frac{1}{\kappa^2 + \alpha_x(1-\beta\rho_u)}$. Combining (5) and (6) obtains an analogous expression for the output gap

$$x_t = -\kappa \Psi\, u_t. \qquad (7)$$

Thus, under the optimal discretionary policy, the central bank lets the output gap and inflation deviate from their targets in proportion to the current value of the cost-push shock. This is illustrated graphically by the circled lines in figures 5.1 and 5.2, which represent the responses under the optimal discretionary policy of the output gap, inflation, and the price level to a one-percent increase in u_t. In figure 5.1, the cost-push shock is assumed to be purely transitory ($\rho_u = 0$),

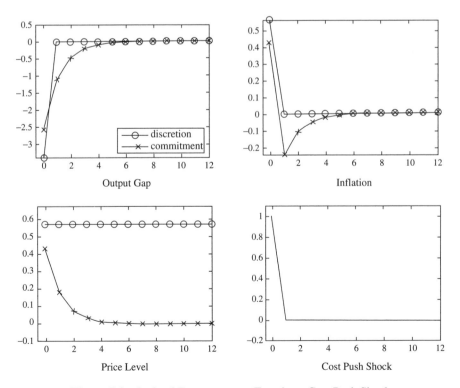

Figure 5.1 Optimal Responses to a Transitory Cost Push Shock

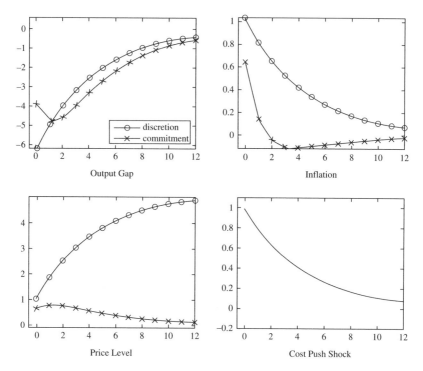

Figure 5.2   Optimal Responses to a Persistent Cost Push Shock

whereas in figure 5.2 it is assumed to have a positive autocorrelation ($\rho_u = 0.5$). The remaining parameters are set at the values assumed in the baseline calibration of chapter 3.

The path of the cost-push shock u_t, after a one percent increase, is displayed in the bottom-right plot of figures 5.1 and 5.2. In both cases the central bank finds it optimal to accommodate partly the inflationary pressures resulting from the cost-push shock, and thus let inflation rise. Note, however, that the increase in inflation is smaller than the increase that would be obtained if the output gap remained unchanged. In the latter case it is easy to check that inflation would be given by

$$\pi_t = \frac{1}{1 - \beta\rho_u} u_t$$

thus implying a larger response of inflation (in absolute value) at all horizons in response to the cost-push shock. Instead, under the optimal discretionary policy, the impact on inflation is dampened by the negative response of the output gap, also displayed in figures 5.1 and 5.2. Finally, it is seen that the implied response of inflation leads naturally to a permanent change in the price level, whose size is increasing in the persistence of the shock.

The analysis above implicitly assumes that the monetary authority can choose its desired level of inflation and the output gap at each point in time. Of course, in practice, a central bank cannot directly set either variable. One possible approach to implementing that policy is to adopt an interest rate rule that guarantees that the desired outcome is attained. Before deriving the form that such a rule may take it is convenient to determine the *equilibrium* interest rate under the optimal discretionary policy as a function of the exogenous driving forces. Thus, combining (6) and (7) with (4) yields:

$$i_t = r_t^e + \Psi_i \, u_t \tag{8}$$

where $\Psi_i \equiv \Psi \left[\kappa\sigma(1 - \rho_u) + \alpha_x\rho_u \right]$.

Applying the arguments of chapter 3, it is easy to see that (8) cannot be viewed as a desirable interest rate rule, for it does not guarantee a unique equilibrium and, hence, the attainment of the desired outcome. In particular, if "rule" (8) is used to eliminate the nominal rate in (4), the resulting equilibrium dynamics are represented by the system

$$\begin{bmatrix} x_t \\ \pi_t \end{bmatrix} = \mathbf{A_0} \begin{bmatrix} E_t\{x_{t+1}\} \\ E_t\{\pi_{t+1}\} \end{bmatrix} + \mathbf{B_0} \, u_t \tag{9}$$

where

$$\mathbf{A_0} \equiv \begin{bmatrix} 1 & \frac{1}{\sigma} \\ \kappa & \beta + \frac{\kappa}{\sigma} \end{bmatrix}; \quad \mathbf{B_0} \equiv \begin{bmatrix} -\frac{\Psi_i}{\sigma} \\ 1 - \frac{\kappa\Psi_i}{\sigma} \end{bmatrix}.$$

As argued in chapter 4, matrix $\mathbf{A_0}$ has always one eigenvalue outside the unit circle, thus implying that (9) has a multiplicity of solutions, only one of which corresponds to the desired outcome given by (6) and (7).

Consider instead the rule

$$i_t = r_t^e + \phi_\pi \, \pi_t \tag{10}$$

where $\phi_\pi \equiv (1 - \rho_u)\frac{\kappa\sigma}{\alpha_x} + \rho_u$, which can be obtained by combining (6) and (8) in a way that makes the nominal rate a function of inflation, an endogenous variable. It is easy to check that the previous rule is always consistent with the desired outcome of the policy problem under consideration here. Furthermore, using the arguments of chapter 4, it is known that a rule of the form (10) leads to a determinate equilibrium (corresponding to the desired outcome), if and only if, the inflation coefficient is greater than one or equivalently, if and only if, $\kappa\sigma > \alpha_x$, a condition that may or may not be satisfied.

In the context of the model, one can always derive a rule that guarantees equilibrium uniqueness (independent of parameter values). The rule can be derived by appending to the expression for the equilibrium nominal rate under the optimal discretionary policy (given by (8)), a term proportional to the deviation between inflation and the equilibrium value of the latter under that policy, with the coefficient of proportionality being greater than one (in order to satisfy the Taylor principle). Formally,

$$i_t = r_t^e + \Psi_i\, u_t + \phi_\pi\, (\pi_t - \alpha_x \Psi\, u_t) \tag{11}$$
$$= r_t^e + \Theta_i\, u_t + \phi_\pi\, \pi_t$$

where $\Theta_i \equiv \Psi\, [\kappa\sigma(1 - \rho_u) - \alpha_x(\phi_\pi - \rho_u)]$ for an arbitrary inflation coefficient satisfying $\phi_\pi > 1$.

In practice, interest rate rules like (10) and (11) are not easy to implement, for the reasons spelled out in chapter 4: They require knowledge of the model's parameters and real-time observation of variations in the cost-push shock and the efficient interest rate. Those difficulties have led some authors to emphasize "targeting rules" like (5) as practical guides for monetary policy, as opposed to "instrument rules" like (10) and (11). Under a targeting rule, the central bank would adjust its instrument until a certain optimal relation between target variables is satisfied. In the aforementioned example, however, following such a targeting rule requires that the efficient level of output y_t^e be observed in real time in order to determine the output gap x_t.

5.1.2 Optimal Policy under Commitment

After having analyzed the optimal policy under discretion, next is the case of a central bank that is assumed to be able to commit, with full credibility, to a *policy plan*. In the context of the model, such a plan consists of a specification of the desired levels of inflation and the output gap at all possible dates and states of nature, current and future. More specifically, the monetary authority is assumed to choose a state-contingent sequence $\{x_t, \pi_t\}_{t=0}^{\infty}$ that minimizes

$$\frac{1}{2}\, E_0 \sum_{t=0}^{\infty} \beta^t\, (\pi_t^2 + \alpha_x\, x_t^2)$$

subject to the sequence of constraints

$$\pi_t = \beta\, E_t\{\pi_{t+1}\} + \kappa\, x_t + u_t$$

and where, as in section 5.1.1, $\{u_t\}$ follows the exogenous process (3).

In order to solve the previous problem it is useful to write down the associated Lagrangian, which is given by

$$\mathcal{L} = E_0 \sum_{t=0}^{\infty} \beta^t \left[\frac{1}{2}\, (\pi_t^2 + \alpha_x\, x_t^2) + \gamma_t\, (\pi_t - \kappa\, x_t - \beta\, \pi_{t+1}) \right]$$

where $\{\gamma_t\}_{t=0}^{\infty}$ is a sequence of Lagrange multipliers, and where the law of iterated expectations has been used to eliminate the conditional expectation that appeared in each constraint.

Differentiating the Lagrangian with respect to x_t and π_t yields the optimality conditions

$$\alpha_x \, x_t - \kappa \, \gamma_t = 0$$
$$\pi_t + \gamma_t - \gamma_{t-1} = 0$$

that must hold for $t = 0, 1, 2, \dots$ and where $\gamma_{-1} = 0$, because the inflation equation corresponding to period -1 is not an effective constraint for the central bank choosing its optimal plan in period 0.

Combining the two optimality conditions to eliminate the Lagrange multipliers yields

$$x_0 = -\frac{\kappa}{\alpha_x} \, \pi_0 \tag{12}$$

and

$$x_t = x_{t-1} - \frac{\kappa}{\alpha_x} \, \pi_t \tag{13}$$

for $t = 1, 2, 3, \dots$.

Note that (12) and (13) can be jointly represented by the single equation in "levels"

$$x_t = -\frac{\kappa}{\alpha_x} \, \widehat{p}_t \tag{14}$$

for $t = 0, 1, 2, \dots$ where $\widehat{p}_t \equiv p_t - p_{-1}$ is the (log) deviation between the price level and an "implicit target" given by the price level prevailing one period before the central bank chooses its optimal plan. Thus, (14) can be viewed as a "targeting rule" that the central bank must follow period by period in order to implement the optimal policy under commitment.

It is worth pointing out the difference between (14) and the corresponding targeting rule for the discretionary case given by (5). Thus, the optimal discretionary policy requires that the central bank keeps output below (above) its efficient level as long as inflation is positive (negative). By way of contrast, under the optimal policy with commitment the central bank sets the sign and size of the output gap in proportion to the deviations of the price *level* from its implicit target. As is discussed next, this has important consequences for the economy's equilibrium response to a cost push shock.

By combining optimality condition (14) with (2), after rewriting the latter in terms of the price level, the stochastic difference equation satisfied by $\widehat{p}_t$ under the optimal policy is derived

$$\widehat{p}_t = a\, \widehat{p}_{t-1} + a\beta\, E_t\{\widehat{p}_{t+1}\} + a\, u_t$$

for $t = 0, 1, 2, \ldots$ where $a \equiv \frac{\alpha_x}{\alpha_x(1+\beta)+\kappa^2}$.

The stationary solution to the previous difference equation is given by

$$\widehat{p}_t = \delta\, \widehat{p}_{t-1} + \frac{\delta}{(1 - \delta\beta\rho_u)}\, u_t \qquad (15)$$

for $t = 0, 1, 2, \ldots$ where $\delta \equiv \frac{1-\sqrt{1-4\beta a^2}}{2a\beta} \in (0, 1)$. Then (14) is used to derive the equilibrium process for the output gap

$$x_t = \delta\, x_{t-1} - \frac{\kappa\delta}{\alpha_x(1 - \delta\beta\rho_u)}\, u_t \qquad (16)$$

for $t = 1, 2, 3, \ldots$ with the response at the time of the shock ($t = 0$) being given by

$$x_0 = -\frac{\kappa\delta}{\alpha_x(1 - \delta\beta\rho_u)}\, u_0.$$

The lines with crosses in figure 5.1 show the equilibrium responses of the output gap, inflation, and the price level to a one percent transitory cost-push shock. Analogous responses for the case of a persistence cost-push shock are displayed in figure 5.2. In both cases those responses are shown side by side with the responses implied by the optimal discretionary policy (represented by the circled lines described earlier), thus facilitating comparison of the two regimes' outcomes.

A look at the case of a transitory cost-push shock illustrates the difference most clearly. In the case of discretionary policy, both the output gap and inflation return to their zero initial value once the shock has vanished (i.e., one period after the shock). By contrast, and as implied by (15) and (16), under the optimal policy with commitment the deviations in the output gap and inflation from target persist well beyond the life of the shock, i.e., they display endogenous or intrinsic persistence. Given that a zero inflation, zero output gap outcome is feasible once the shock has vanished, why does the central bank find it optimal to maintain a persistently negative output gap and inflation? The reason is simple: By committing to such a response, the central bank manages to improve the output gap/inflation tradeoff in the period when the shock occurs. In the case illustrated in figure 5.1 it lowers the initial impact of the cost-push shock on inflation (relative to the discretionary case), while incurring smaller output gap losses in the same period. This is possible because of the forward-looking nature of inflation, which can be highlighted by iterating (2) forward to yield

$$\pi_t = \kappa \, x_t + \kappa \sum_{k=1}^{\infty} \beta^k \, E_t\{x_{t+k}\} + u_t.$$

Hence, it is seen that the central bank can offset the inflationary impact of a cost push shock by lowering the current output gap x_t, but also by committing to lower future output gaps (or, equivalently, future reductions in the price level). If credible, such "promises" will bring about a downward adjustment in the sequence of expectations $E_t\{x_{t+k}\}$ for $k = 1, 2, 3, \ldots$. As a result, and in response to a positive realization of the cost-push shock u_t, the central bank may achieve any given level of current inflation π_t with a smaller decline in the current output gap x_t. That is the sense in which the output gap/inflation tradeoff is improved by the possibility of commitment. Given the convexity of the loss function in inflation and output gap deviations, the dampening of those deviations in the period of the shock brings about an improvement in overall welfare relative to the case of discretion, because the implied benefits are not offset by the (relatively small) losses generated by the deviations in subsequent periods (and which are absent in the discretionary case).

Figure 5.2 displays analogous impulse responses under the assumption that $\rho_u = 0.8$. Note that in this case the economy reverts back to the initial position only asymptotically, even under the optimal discretionary policy (because the inflationary pressures generated by the shock remain effective at all horizons, albeit with a declining influence). Yet, some of the key qualitative features emphasized above are still present: In particular, the optimal policy with commitment manages once again to attain both lower inflation and a smaller output gap (in absolute value) at the time of the shock, relative to the optimal discretionary policy. Note also that under the optimal policy with commitment the price level reverts back to its original level, albeit at a slower rate than in the case of a transitory shock. As a result inflation displays some positive short run autocorrelation, illustrating the fact that the strong negative short run autocorrelation observed in the case of a purely transitory shock is not a necessary implication of the policy with commitment.

In all cases, a feature of the economy's response under discretionary policy is the attempt to stabilize the output gap in the medium term more than the optimal policy under commitment calls for, without internalizing the benefits in terms of short term stability that result from allowing larger deviations of the output gap at future horizons. This characteristic, which is most clearly illustrated by the example of a purely transitory cost-push shock represented in figure 5.1, is often referred to as the *stabilization bias* associated with the discretionary policy.[4]

---

[4] The stabilization bias must be distinguished from the inflation bias that arises when the zero inflation steady state is associated with an inefficiently low level of activity. The stabilization bias is obtained independent of the degree of inefficiency of the steady state, as discussed below.

As in the case of discretion, one might be interested in deriving an interest rate rule that would bring about the paths of output gap and inflation implied by the optimal policy under commitment. Next, such a rule is derived for the special case of serially uncorrelated cost push shocks ($\rho_u = 0$). In that case, combining (4), (15), and (16) yields the process describing the equilibrium nominal rate under the optimal policy with commitment

$$i_t = r_t^e - (1 - \delta)\left(1 - \frac{\sigma\kappa}{\alpha_x}\right)\widehat{p}_t$$

$$= r_t^e - (1 - \delta)\left(1 - \frac{\sigma\kappa}{\alpha_x}\right)\sum_{k=0}^{t}\delta^{k+1}\,u_{t-k}.$$

Thus, one possible rule that would bring about the desired allocation as the unique equilibrium is given by

$$i_t = r_t^e - \left[\phi_p + (1 - \delta)\left(1 - \frac{\sigma\kappa}{\alpha_x}\right)\right]\sum_{k=0}^{t}\delta^{k+1}\,u_{t-k} + \phi_p\,\widehat{p}_t$$

for any $\phi_p > 0$. Note that under the previous formulation the central bank stands ready to respond to any deviation of the price level from the path prescribed by (15), though this will not be necessary in equilibrium.[5]

5.2   The Monetary Policy Problem: The Case of a Distorted Steady State

Next, consider the case in which the presence of uncorrected real imperfections generate a permanent gap between the natural and the efficient levels of output, which is reflected in an inefficient steady state. The size of the steady state distortion is measured by a parameter Φ representing the wedge between the marginal product of labor and the marginal rate of substitution between consumption and hours, both evaluated at the steady state. Formally, Φ is defined by

$$-\frac{U_n}{U_c} = MPN\,(1 - \Phi).$$

Below, it is assumed $\Phi > 0$, which implies that the steady state levels of output and employment are below their respective efficient levels. The presence of firms' market power in the goods market as assumed in the basic model of chapter 3 constitutes an example of the kind of distortion that, if uncorrected through an appropriate subsidy, would generate an inefficiently low level of activity. In that case, and as implied by the analysis of chapter 4, $\Phi \equiv 1 - \frac{1}{\mathcal{M}} > 0$, where $\mathcal{M}$ is the steady state gross markup.

---

[5] An interest rate rule that displays a positive response to the price level can be shown to generate a unique equilibrium in the basic New Keynesian model. See exercise 4.5 in chapter 4.

Under the assumption of a "small" steady state distortion (i.e., when Φ has the same order of magnitude as fluctuations in the output gap or inflation), and as shown in appendixes 5.1 and 5.2, the component of the welfare losses experienced by the representative household that can be affected by policy is approximately proportional, in a neighborhood of the zero inflation steady state, to the expression

$$E_0 \sum_{t=0}^{\infty} \beta^t \left[\frac{1}{2} (\pi_t^2 + \alpha_x \, \widehat{x}_t^2) - \Lambda \, \widehat{x}_t \right] \tag{17}$$

where $\Lambda \equiv \Phi \frac{\lambda}{\varepsilon} > 0$ and $\widehat{x}_t = x_t - x$ represents the deviation of the welfare-relevant output gap from its value $x < 0$ in the zero inflation steady state. Note that the linear term $\widehat{x}_t$ captures the fact that any marginal increase in output has a positive effect on welfare (thus decreasing welfare losses), because output is assumed to be below its efficient level.

Similarly, the inflation equation can be written in terms of $\widehat{x}_t$ as

$$\pi_t = \beta E_t \{\pi_{t+1}\} + \kappa \, \widehat{x}_t + u_t \tag{18}$$

where now $u_t \equiv \kappa (\widehat{y}_t^e - \widehat{y}_t^n)$. Thus, the monetary authority will seek to minimize (17) subject to the sequence of constraints given by (18) for $t = 0, 1, 2, \ldots$

Note that under the assumption of the "small" steady state distortion made above, the linear term $\Lambda \, \widehat{x}_t$ is already of second order, thus giving the central bank's problem the convenient linear–quadratic format.[6]

As in section 5.1, the solution is characterized to the central bank's problem under discretion, before turning to the optimal policy with commitment.

5.2.1 Optimal Discretionary Policy

In the absence of a commitment technology, the monetary authority chooses (x_t, π_t) in order to minimize the period losses

$$\frac{1}{2} (\pi_t^2 + \alpha_x \, \widehat{x}_t^2) - \Lambda \, \widehat{x}_t$$

subject to the constraint

$$\pi_t = \kappa \, \widehat{x}_t + v_t$$

where, once again, $v_t \equiv \beta E_t \{\pi_{t+1}\} + u_t$ is taken as given by the policymaker.

---

[6] In the presence of a large distortion, the presence of a linear term in (17) would require the use of a second-order approximation to the equilibrium condition connecting output gap and inflation.

The associated optimality condition is

$$\widehat{x}_t = \frac{\Lambda}{\alpha_x} - \frac{\kappa}{\alpha_x} \pi_t. \tag{19}$$

Note that (19) implies, for any given level of inflation, a more expansionary policy than that given in the absence of a steady state distortion. This is a consequence of the desire by the central bank to partly correct for the inefficiently low average level of activity.

Plugging (19) into (18) and solving the resulting difference equation yields the following expression for equilibrium inflation

$$\pi_t = \frac{\Lambda\kappa}{\kappa^2 + \alpha_x(1-\beta)} + \alpha_x \Psi \, u_t. \tag{20}$$

Combining (20) and (19) yields the corresponding expression for the equilibrium output gap

$$\widehat{x}_t = \frac{\Lambda(1-\beta)}{\kappa^2 + \alpha_x(1-\beta)} - \kappa \Psi \, u_t.$$

Thus, it is seen that the presence of a distorted steady state does not affect the response of the output gap and inflation to shocks under the optimal policy. It has, however, an effect on the average levels of inflation and the output gap around which the economy fluctuates. In particular, when the natural level of output and employment are inefficiently low ($\Lambda > 0$), the optimal discretionary policy leads to positive average inflation as a consequence of the central bank's incentive to push output above its natural steady state level.[7] That incentive increases with the degree of inefficiency of the natural steady state, which explains the fact that the average inflation is increasing in Λ (and hence in Φ), giving rise to the *classical inflation bias* phenomenon.

5.2.2   Optimal Policy under Commitment

As in the case of an efficient steady state, the optimal policy under commitment is solved by setting up the Lagrangean corresponding to the central bank's problem, which in this case is given by

$$\mathcal{L} = E_0 \sum_{t=0}^{\infty} \beta^t \left[\frac{1}{2}(\pi_t^2 + \alpha_x \, \widehat{x}_t^2) - \Lambda \, \widehat{x}_t + \gamma_t \, (\pi_t - \kappa \, \widehat{x}_t - \beta \, \pi_{t+1}) \right]$$

where $\{\gamma_t\}$ are the Lagrange multipliers associated with the sequence of constraints (18), for $t = 0, 1, 2, \ldots$

---

[7] Notice that in the steady state, $\widehat{x} = y - y^n$.

The corresponding optimality conditions are given by

$$\alpha_x \, \widehat{x}_t - \kappa \, \gamma_t - \Lambda = 0$$
$$\pi_t + \gamma_t - \gamma_{t-1} = 0$$

which must hold for $t = 0, 1, 2, \ldots$ and where $\gamma_{-1} = 0$. The previous conditions can be combined to yield the following difference equation for the (log) price level

$$\widehat{p}_t = a \, \widehat{p}_{t-1} + a\beta \, E_t\{\widehat{p}_{t+1}\} + \alpha\kappa \Lambda + a \, u_t$$

for $t = 0, 1, 2, \ldots$ where, as above, $\widehat{p}_t \equiv p_t - p_{-1}$ and $a \equiv \frac{\alpha_x}{\alpha_x(1+\beta)+\kappa^2}$.

The stationary solution to the previous difference equation describes the evolution of the equilibrium price level under the optimal policy with commitment. It takes the form

$$\widehat{p}_t = \delta \, \widehat{p}_{t-1} + \frac{\delta}{1 - \delta\beta\rho_u} \, u_t + \frac{\delta\kappa \Lambda}{1 - \delta\beta}$$

where $\delta \equiv \frac{1-\sqrt{1-4\beta a^2}}{2a\beta} \in (0, 1)$. The corresponding path for the output gap is given by

$$\widehat{x}_t = \delta \, \widehat{x}_{t-1} - \frac{\kappa\delta}{\alpha_x(1 - \delta\beta\rho_u)} \, u_t + \Lambda \left[1 - \delta \left(1 + \frac{\kappa^2}{\alpha_x(1 - \delta\beta)} \right) \right].$$

Thus, as was the case under the discretionary policy, the response to a cost-push shock under the optimal policy with commitment is not affected by the presence of a distorted steady state. Hence, the impulse responses displayed in figures 5.1 and 5.2 illustrating the economy's response to a cost-push shock under discretion and under commitment remain valid in the present context. In particular, the optimal policy under discretion is characterized by an identical stabilization bias.

In the presence of a distorted steady state, an additional difference arises between the discretionary and commitment policies, unrelated to the response to shocks: it has to do with the deterministic component of inflation and its evolution over time. As shown above, in the case of discretion that component takes the form a constant positive mean, resulting from the period-by-period incentive to close the gap between output and its efficient level, which results in inflation. In the case of commitment, however, it is seen that the price level converges asymptotically to a constant, given by $\lim_{T\to\infty} p_T = p_{-1} + \frac{\delta\kappa \Lambda}{(1-\delta\beta)(1-\delta)}$. Hence, after displaying a positive value at the beginning of the optimal plan's implementation, the deterministic component of inflation (around which actual inflation fluctuates in response to shocks) declines gradually over time, following the path $\frac{\delta^{t+1}\kappa \Lambda}{1-\delta\beta}$. Hence, under the optimal plan the economy eventually converges to an equilibrium characterized by zero average inflation, and in that sense observationally equivalent to that of an economy with an efficient steady state. The desirability of such a policy is justified by the benefits arising from its anticipation by the public, which improves the short run tradeoff facing the central bank, allowing it to raise output above its natural level (with the consequent welfare improvement) with more subdued effects on inflation (because the public anticipates a gradual return of output to its natural level). Thus, the central bank's ability to commit avoids (at least asymptotically) the inflation bias that characterizes the outcome of the discretionary policy.

5.3   Notes on the Literature

This chapter follows closely Clarida, Galí, and Gertler (1999), where the optimal monetary policy in the context of the basic New Keynesian model augmented with an ad-hoc cost-push shock is analyzed, and where the outcomes under discretion and commitment are compared. That paper also contains a discussion of the classical inflation bias, whose ultimate source is modelled as a positive target for the output gap in the policymaker's loss function. The original treatment of the inflation bias and the gains from commitment, in the context of a new classical model with a Lucas supply curve, can be found in Kydland and Prescott (1980) and Barro and Gordon (1983).

Woodford (2003a) discusses a source of monetary policy tradeoffs different from cost-push shocks: that created by the presence of transaction frictions that lead to an indirect utility function in which real balances are one of the arguments, as in the model at the end of chapter 2. In that context, and in addition to variations in inflation and the output gap, variations in the nominal rate (which acts as a tax on money holdings) are a source of welfare losses. As a result, a policy that fully stabilizes the output gap and inflation by making the interest rate move one for one with the natural rate, while feasible, is no longer optimal because it implies excessive interest rate volatility. The optimal policy, as shown by Woodford, smoothens the fluctuations in the nominal rate, at the cost of some variations in inflation and output gap.

The approximation to welfare in the presence of "small" steady state distortions presented here follows the analysis in Woodford (2003b). The analysis of optimal policy in the presence of "large" steady state distortions lies beyond the scope of this book. The main difficulty in that case arises from the presence of a linear term in the second-order approximation to the welfare loss function. In that context, the use of a log-linear (i.e., first-order) approximation to the equilibrium conditions to describe the evolution of endogenous variables leads to second-order terms potentially relevant to welfare being ignored (e.g., the losses associated with steady state effects of different degrees of volatility).

Several approaches to overcoming that problem are found in the literature. A first approach consists of solving for the evolution of the endogenous variables using a second-order (or higher) approximation to the equilibrium conditions under a given policy rule, and evaluating the latter using the original second-order approximation to the welfare losses. An application of that approach to the monetary policy problem can be found in Schmitt-Grohé and Uribe (2004), among others.

The second approach, due to Benigno and Woodford (2005), makes use of a second-order approximation to the structural equations of the model in order to replace the linear terms appearing in the welfare loss function and rewriting those losses as a function of quadratic terms only. The resulting quadratic loss function can then be minimized subject to the constraints provided by log-linearized equilibrium conditions. That approach allows one to preserve the convenient structure and properties of linear–quadratic problems, including the linearity of their implied optimal policy rules.

A third approach, illustrated in Khan, King, and Wolman (2003), requires that the optimal policy be determined in a first stage using the exact structural equations and utility function, and log-linearizing the resulting equilibrium conditions (embedding the optimal policy) in order to characterize the optimal responses to shocks.

Appendix

5.1 A Second-Order Approximation to Welfare Losses: The Case of a Small Steady State Distortion

As shown in appendix 4.1 of chapter 4, a second-order Taylor expansion to period t utility, combined with a goods market clearing condition, yields

$$U_t - U = U_c C \left(\widehat{y}_t + \frac{1-\sigma}{2} \widehat{y}_t^2 \right)$$
$$+ \frac{U_n N}{1-\alpha} \left(\widehat{y}_t + \frac{\varepsilon}{2\Theta} var_i\{p_t(i)\} + \frac{1+\varphi}{2(1-\alpha)} (\widehat{y}_t - a_t)^2 \right) + t.i.p.$$

where $t.i.p.$ stands for *terms independent of policy*.

Let Φ denote the size of the steady state distortion, implicitly defined by $-\frac{U_n}{U_c} = MPN (1 - \Phi)$. Using the fact that $MPN = (1-\alpha)(Y/N)$,

$$\frac{U_t - U}{U_c C} = \widehat{y}_t + \frac{1-\sigma}{2} \widehat{y}_t^2 - (1 - \Phi)$$
$$\times \left(\widehat{y}_t + \frac{\varepsilon}{2\Theta} var_i\{p_t(i)\} + \frac{1+\varphi}{2(1-\alpha)} (\widehat{y}_t - a_t)^2 \right) + t.i.p.$$

Under the "small distortion" assumption (so that the product of Φ with a second-order term can be ignored as negligible),

$$\frac{U_t - U}{U_c C} = \Phi \, \widehat{y}_t - \frac{1}{2} \left[\frac{\varepsilon}{\Theta} \, var_i\{p_t(i)\} - (1-\sigma) \, \widehat{y}_t^2 + \frac{1+\varphi}{1-\alpha} \, (\widehat{y}_t - a_t)^2 \right] + t.i.p.$$

$$= \Phi \, \widetilde{y}_t - \frac{1}{2} \left[\frac{\varepsilon}{\Theta} \, var_i\{p_t(i)\} + \left(\sigma + \frac{\varphi+\alpha}{1-\alpha} \right) \widehat{y}_t^2 - 2 \left(\frac{1+\varphi}{1-\alpha} \right) \widehat{y}_t a_t \right] + t.i.p.$$

$$= \Phi \, \widetilde{y}_t - \frac{1}{2} \left[\frac{\varepsilon}{\Theta} \, var_i\{p_t(i)\} + \left(\sigma + \frac{\varphi+\alpha}{1-\alpha} \right) (\widehat{y}_t^2 - 2\widehat{y}_t \, \widehat{y}_t^e) \right] + t.i.p.$$

$$= \Phi \, \widehat{x}_t - \frac{1}{2} \left[\frac{\varepsilon}{\Theta} \, var_i\{p_t(i)\} + \left(\sigma + \frac{\varphi+\alpha}{1-\alpha} \right) \widehat{x}_t^2 \right] + t.i.p.$$

where $\widehat{y}_t^e \equiv y_t^e - y^e$, and where the fact was used that $\widehat{y}_t^e = \frac{1+\varphi}{\sigma(1-\alpha)+\varphi+\alpha} \, a_t$ and $\widehat{y}_t - \widehat{y}_t^e = x_t - (y - y^e) = x_t - x \equiv \widehat{x}_t$.

Accordingly, a second-order approximation can be written to the consumer's welfare losses (up to additive terms independent of policy), and expressed as a fraction of steady state consumption as

$$\mathbb{W} = E_0 \sum_{t=0}^{\infty} \beta^t \left(\frac{U_t - U}{U_c C} \right)$$

$$= E_0 \sum_{t=0}^{\infty} \beta^t \left[\Phi \, \widehat{x}_t - \frac{1}{2} \left(\frac{\varepsilon}{\Theta} \, var_i\{p_t(i)\} + \left(\sigma + \frac{\varphi+\alpha}{1-\alpha} \right) \widehat{x}_t^2 \right) \right] + t.i.p.$$

Using Lemma 2 in appendix 4.1 of chapter 4, the welfare losses can be rewritten as

$$\mathbb{W} = E_0 \sum_{t=0}^{\infty} \beta^t \left[\Phi \, \widehat{x}_t - \frac{1}{2} \left(\frac{\varepsilon}{\lambda} \right) \pi_t^2 + \left(\sigma + \frac{\varphi+\alpha}{1-\alpha} \right) \widehat{x}_t^2 \right] + t.i.p.$$

Note that in the particular case of an efficient steady state $\Phi = 0$ and $\widehat{x}_t = x_t$. Moreover, if as in chapter 4 the model satisfies $y_t^n - y_t^e$ for all t, then $\widehat{x}_t - x_t - \widetilde{y}_t$ with the implied loss function taking the form used in that chapter.

5.2   Sources of Cost-Push Shocks

This appendix describes two possible sources of cost-push shocks, variations in desired price markups, and exogenous variations in wage markups.

a) *Variations in desired price markups.*

Assume that the elasticity of substitution among goods varies over time according to some stationary stochastic process $\{\varepsilon_t\}$. Let the associated desired markup be given by $\mu_t^n \equiv \frac{\varepsilon_t}{\varepsilon_t - 1}$. The log-linearized price-setting rule is then given by

$$p_t^* = (1 - \beta\theta) \sum_{k=1}^{\infty} (\beta\theta)^k \ E_t\{\mu_{t+k}^n + mc_{t+k} + p_{t+k}\}$$

$$= (1 - \beta\theta) \sum_{k=1}^{\infty} (\beta\theta)^k E_t\{\widetilde{mc}_{t+k} + p_{t+k}\}$$

where $\widetilde{mc}_t \equiv mc_t + \mu_t^n$. The resulting inflation equation then becomes

$$\pi_t = \beta E_t\{\pi_{t+1}\} + \lambda \ \widetilde{mc}_t$$
$$= \beta E_t\{\pi_{t+1}\} + \lambda \ \widehat{mc}_t + \lambda(\mu_t^n - \mu)$$
$$= \beta E_t\{\pi_{t+1}\} + \kappa \ (y_t - \overline{y}_t^n) + \lambda(\mu_t^n - \mu)$$

where $\overline{y}_t^n$ denotes the equilibrium level of output under flexible prices *and* a constant price markup μ. Letting $x_t \equiv y_t - \overline{y}_t^n$ and $u_t \equiv \lambda(\mu_t^n - \mu)$ yields the formulation used in the main text.

b) *Exogenous Variations in Wage Markups*

In that case, $\pi_t = \beta E_t\{\pi_{t+1}\} + \lambda \ \widehat{mc}_t$, though now

$$mc_t = w_t - a_t$$
$$= \mu_{w,t} + mrs_t - a_t$$
$$= \mu_{w,t} + (\sigma + \varphi) \ y_t - (1 + \varphi) \ a_t$$

where $\mu_{w,t}$ represents a time-varying, exogenous wage markup. Under flexible prices and a constant wage markup (at its steady state level μ_w),

$$mc = \mu_w + (\sigma + \varphi) \ \overline{y}_t^n - (1 + \varphi) \ a_t$$

where $\overline{y}_t^n$ denotes the equilibrium level of output under a constant price and wage markup.

The difference between the two previous expressions is thus given by

$$\widehat{mc}_t = (\sigma + \varphi) \ (y_t - \overline{y}_t^n) + (\mu_{w,t} - \mu_w)$$

which can be plugged into the inflation equation to yield

$$\pi_t = \beta E_t\{\pi_{t+1}\} + \kappa x_t + u_t$$

where $x_t \equiv y_t - \overline{y}_t^n$ and $u_t \equiv \lambda(\mu_{w,t} - \mu_w)$.

References

Barro, Robert J., and David Gordon (1983): "A Positive Theory of Monetary Policy in a Natural Rate Model," *Journal of Political Economy* 91, no. 4, 589–610.

Benigno, Pierpaolo, and Michael Woodford (2005): "Inflation Stabilization and Welfare: The Case of a Distorted Steady State," *Journal of the European Economic Association* 3, no. 6, 1185–1236.

Clarida, Richard, Jordi Galí, and Mark Gertler (1999): "The Science of Monetary Policy: A New Keynesian Perspective," *Journal of Economic Literature* 37, 1661–1707.

Khan, Aubhik, Robert G. King, and Alexander L. Wolman (2003): "Optimal Monetary Policy," *Review of Economic Studies*, 825–860.

Kydland, Finn E., and Edward C. Prescott (1980): "Rules Rather than Discretion: The Inconsistency of Optimal Plans," *Journal of Political Economy* 85, no. 3, 473–492.

Schmitt-Grohé, Stephanie, and Martin Uribe (2004): "Optimal Fiscal and Monetary Policy under Sticky Prices," *Journal of Economic Theory* 114, 198–230.

Steinsson, Jón (2003): "Optimal Monetary Policy in an Economy with Inflation Persistence," *Journal of Monetary Economics* 50, no. 7, 1425–1456.

Svensson, Lars (1999): "Inflation Targeting as a Monetary Policy Rule," *Journal of Monetary Economics* 43, no. 9, 607–654.

Svensson, Lars, and Michael Woodford (2005): "Implementing Optimal Monetary Policy through Inflation-Forecast Targeting," in B. S. Bernanke and M. Woodford (eds.), *The Inflation Targeting Debate*, University of Chicago Press, Chicago, IL.

Woodford, Michael (2003a): "Optimal Interest Rate Smoothing," *Review of Economic Studies* 70, no. 4, 861–886.

Woodford, Michael (2003b): *Interest and Prices: Foundations of a Theory of Monetary Policy*, Princeton University Press, Princeton, NJ.

Exercises

5.1   An Optimal Taylor Rule

Consider an economy with Calvo-type staggered price setting whose equilibrium dynamics are described by the system

$$x_t = E_t\{x_{t+1}\} - \frac{1}{\sigma}\,(i_t - E_t\{\pi_{t+1}\} - \rho) + \varepsilon_t$$

$$\pi_t = \beta\,E_t\{\pi_{t+1}\} + \kappa\,x_t + u_t$$

where $\{\varepsilon_t\}$ and $\{u_t\}$ are i.i.d., mutually uncorrelated, demand and supply disturbances with variances given by σ_ε^2 and σ_u^2 respectively.

Assume that the monetary authority adopts a simple Taylor rule of the form

$$i_t = \rho + \phi_\pi\,\pi_t.$$

a) Solve for the equilibrium processes for the output gap and inflation, as a function of the exogenous supply and demand shocks.

b) Determine the value of the inflation coefficient ϕ_π that minimizes the central bank's loss function

$$\alpha_x \ var(x_t) + var(\pi_t).$$

c) Discuss and provide intuition for the dependence of the optimal inflation coefficient on the weight α_x and the variance ratio $\frac{var(\varepsilon)}{var(u)}$. What assumptions on parameter values would warrant an aggressive response to inflation implemented through a large ϕ_π? Explain.

5.2 Optimal Markovian Policy

Consider an economy where inflation is described by the augmented NKPC

$$\pi_t = \beta \ E_t\{\pi_{t+1}\} + \kappa \ x_t + u_t$$

where $\{u_t\}$ is an exogenous cost-push shock following a stationary AR(1) process

$$u_t = \rho_u \ u_{t-1} + \varepsilon_t^u.$$

In period 0, the central bank chooses once and for all its policy among the class of Markovian policies of the form $x_t = \psi_x u_t$ and $\pi_t = \psi_\pi u_t$ for all t, in order to minimize the loss function

$$E_0 \sum_{t=0}^{\infty} \beta^t \left(\pi_t^2 + \alpha_x \ x_t^2\right)$$

subject to the sequence of constraints describing the evolution of inflation.

a) Determine the optimal values of ψ_x and ψ_π.

b) Compare the resulting optimal policy to the optimal discretionary policy analyzed in this chapter. Which one is more desirable from a welfare point of view? Explain.

c) Compare the resulting optimal policy to the optimal policy under commitment analyzed in this chapter. Which one is more desirable from a welfare point of view? Explain.

5.3 Optimal Monetary Policy in the Presence of Transaction Frictions

As shown in Woodford (2003a), in the presence of real balances as a source of indirect utility in an otherwise standard New Keynesian model, a second-order approximation to the representative household's welfare is proportional to

$$-\frac{1}{2} \ E_0 \sum_{t=0}^{\infty} \beta^t \left(\pi_t^2 + \alpha_x \ x_t^2 + \alpha_i \ i_t^2\right).$$

Consider the problem of choosing the state-contingent policy $\{x_t, \pi_t\}_{t=0}^{\infty}$ that maximizes welfare subject to the sequence of constraints

$$\pi_t = \beta E_t\{\pi_{t+1}\} + \kappa\, x_t$$

$$x_t = -\frac{1}{\sigma}\,(i_t - E_t\{\pi_{t+1}\} - r_t^n) + E_t\{x_{t+1}\}$$

for $t = 0, 1, 2, \ldots$ where the natural rate r_t^n is assumed to follow an exogenous process.

a) Determine the optimality conditions for the problem described above.

b) Show that the implied optimal policy can be implemented by means of an interest rate rule of the form

$$i_t = \left(1 + \frac{\kappa}{\sigma\beta}\right) i_{t-1} + \frac{1}{\beta}\, \Delta i_{t-1} + \frac{\kappa}{\alpha_i \sigma}\, \pi_t + \frac{\alpha_x}{\alpha_i \sigma}\, \Delta x_t$$

that is independent of r_t^n and its properties.

5.4 Inflation Persistence and Monetary Policy

As shown in Steinsson (2003), in the presence of partial price indexation by firms the second-order approximation to the household's welfare losses takes the form

$$\frac{1}{2}\, E_0 \sum_{t=0}^{\infty} \beta^t [\alpha_x\, x_t^2 + (\pi_t - \gamma\, \pi_{t-1})^2]$$

where γ denotes the degree of price indexation to past inflation. The equation describing the evolution of inflation is now given by

$$\pi_t - \gamma\, \pi_{t-1} = \kappa\, x_t + \beta E_t\{(\pi_{t+1} - \gamma\, \pi_t)\} + u_t$$

where u_t represents an exogenous i.i.d. cost-push shock.

a) Determine the optimal policy under discretion.

b) Determine the optimal policy under commitment.

c) Discuss how the degree of indexation γ affects the optimal responses to a transitory cost-push shock under the previous two scenarios.

5.5 Monetary Policy, Optimal Steady State Inflation, and the Zero Lower Bound

Consider a New Keynesian model with equilibrium conditions given by

$$x_t = E_t\{x_{t+1}\} - \frac{1}{\sigma}\,(i_t - E_t\{\pi_{t+1}\} - \rho) + \varepsilon_t$$

and

$$\pi_t - \pi = \beta \ E_t\{(\pi_{t+1} - \pi)\} + \kappa \ x_t + u_t$$

where x_t is the (welfare-relevant) output gap, π_t denotes inflation, i_t is the nominal rate, and π is steady state inflation. The disturbances ε_t and u_t represent demand and cost-push shocks, and are assumed to follow independent and serially uncorrelated normal distributions with zero mean and variances σ_ε^2 and σ_u^2 respectively.

Assume that the loss function for the monetary authority is given by

$$\Theta \pi + E_0 \sum_{t=0}^{\infty} \beta^t \left[\alpha_x \ x_t^2 + (\pi_t - \pi)^2 \right]$$

where the first term is assumed to capture the costs of steady state inflation.

a) Derive the optimal policy under discretion (i.e., the time-consistent policy resulting from period-by-period maximization), including the choice of steady state inflation π subject to the constraint that the interest rate hits the zero-bound constraint with only a 5 percent probability.

b) Derive an interest rate rule that would implement the optimal allocation derived in (a) as the unique equilibrium.

6

A Model with Sticky Wages and Prices

Throughout the previous chapters the labor market has been modelled as a perfectly competitive market, in which households and firms take the wage as given. This chapter departs from that assumption by introducing some imperfections in the labor market and analyzing their consequences for monetary policy. In particular, it is assumed that households/workers have some monopoly power, which allows them to set the wage for the differentiated labor services they supply. Furthermore, as was done with the price-setting firms in chapter 3, the assumption here is that workers face Calvo-type constraints on the frequency with which they can adjust wages.

A key result emerges from the analysis of the model with sticky wages and prices: fully stabilizing price inflation is no longer optimal. Instead, the central bank should be concerned about both price and wage stability, because fluctuations in both price and wage inflation, as well as in the output gap, are a source of inefficiencies in the allocation of resources that result in welfare losses for households. Accordingly, the optimal policy seeks to strike a balance between three different objectives, with the relative weights attached to them being a function of the underlying parameter values.

This chapter is organized as follows. Section 6.1 describes a benchmark model in which both sticky wages and sticky prices coexist. Section 6.2 derives the model's log-linearized equilibrium conditions. Section 6.3 discusses the relevant central bank's objective function and analyzes the limiting cases of full price flexibility and full wage flexibility. Section 6.4 derives and characterizes the optimal monetary policy, while section 6.5 studies the performance of alternative simple rules and their merits as an approximation to the optimal policy. Section 6.6 concludes with some bibliographical notes.

6.1 A Model with Staggered Wage and Price Setting

This section lays out a model of an economy in which nominal wages, as well as prices, are sticky. Following Erceg, Henderson, and Levin (2000), wage stickiness is introduced in a way analogous to price stickiness, as modelled in chapter 3. In particular, a continuum of differentiated labor services is assumed, all of which are used by each firm. Each household is specialized in one type of labor, which it supplies monopolistically.[1] Each period only a (constant) fraction of household/labor types, drawn randomly from the population, can adjust their posted nominal wage. As a result, the aggregate nominal wage responds sluggishly to shocks, generating inefficient variations in the wage markup. In addition, wage inflation, combined with the staggering of wage adjustments, brings about relative wage distortions and an inefficient allocation of labor in a way symmetric to the relative price distortions generated by price inflation in the presence of staggered price setting.

Next, the problem facing firms and households in this environment is described.

6.1.1 Firms

As in chapter 3, a continuum of firms is assumed, indexed by $i \in [0, 1]$, each of which produces a differentiated good with a technology represented by the production function

$$Y_t(i) = A_t \, N_t(i)^{1-\alpha} \tag{1}$$

where $Y_t(i)$ denotes the output of good i, A_t is an exogenous technology parameter common to all firms, and $N_t(i)$ is an index of labor input used by firm i and defined by

$$N_t(i) \equiv \left[\int_0^1 N_t(i, j)^{1 - \frac{1}{\varepsilon_w}} \, dj \right]^{\frac{\varepsilon_w}{\varepsilon_w - 1}} \tag{2}$$

where $N_t(i, j)$ denotes the quantity of type-j labor employed by firm i in period t. Note that parameter ε_w represents the elasticity of substitution among labor varieties. Note also the assumption of a continuum of labor types, indexed by $j \in [0, 1]$.

Let $W_t(j)$ denote the nominal wage for type-j labor effective in period t, for all $j \in [0, 1]$. As discussed below, wages are set by workers of each type (or a union representing them) and taken as given by firms. Given the wages effective at any point in time for the different types of labor services, cost minimization yields a corresponding set of demand schedules for each firm i and labor type j, given the firm's total employment $N_t(i)$

$$N_t(i, j) = \left(\frac{W_t(j)}{W_t} \right)^{-\varepsilon_w} N_t(i) \tag{3}$$

for all $i, j \in [0, 1]$, where

$$W_t \equiv \left[\int_0^1 W_t(j)^{1-\varepsilon_w} \, dj \right]^{\frac{1}{1-\varepsilon_w}} \tag{4}$$

---

[1] Equivalently, one can think of a continuum of unions, each of which represents a set of households/workers specialized in a given labor service, and sets the wage on their behalf.

is an aggregate wage index. Substituting (3) into the definition of $N_t(i)$, one can obtain the convenient aggregation result

$$\int_0^1 W_t(j) N_t(i, j) \, dj = W_t \, N_t(i)$$

i.e., the wage bill of any given firm can be expressed as the product of the wage index W_t and that firm's employment index $N_t(i)$.

Hence, and conditional on an optimal allocation of the wage bill among the different types of labor implied by (3), a firm adjusting its price in period t will solve the following problem, which is identical to the one analyzed in chapter 3

$$\max_{P_t^*} \sum_{k=0}^{\infty} \theta_p^k E_t \left\{ Q_{t,t+k} \left(P_t^* \, Y_{t+k|t} - \Psi_{t+k}(Y_{t+k|t}) \right) \right\}$$

subject to the sequence of demand constraints

$$Y_{t+k|t} = \left(\frac{P_t^*}{P_{t+k}} \right)^{-\varepsilon_p} C_{t+k}$$

for $k = 0, 1, 2, \ldots$ where $Q_{t,t+k} \equiv \beta^k \, (C_{t+k}/C_t)^{-\sigma} \, (P_t/P_{t+k})$ is the stochastic discount factor for nominal payoffs, $\Psi_{t+k}(\cdot)$ is the cost function, and $Y_{t+k|t}$ denotes output in period $t+k$ for a firm that last reset its price in period t. Notice that a subscript p has been added to parameters θ and ε for symmetry with their labor market counterparts.

As shown in chapter 3, the aggregation of the resulting price-setting rules yields, to a first-order approximation and in a neighborhood of the zero inflation steady state, the following equation for price inflation π_t^p

$$\pi_t^p = \beta E_t \{\pi_{t+1}^p\} - \lambda_p \, \widehat{\mu}_t^p \tag{5}$$

where $\widehat{\mu}_t^p \equiv \mu_t^p - \mu^p = -\widehat{mc}_t$ and $\lambda_p \equiv \frac{(1-\theta_p)(1-\beta\theta_p)}{\theta_p} \frac{1-\alpha}{1-\alpha+\alpha\varepsilon_p}$. Note that, for the sake of symmetry with the wage-inflation equation derived below, the inflation equation is written as a function of the (log) deviation of the average price markup from its desired (or steady state) value, instead of the (log) marginal cost. Hence, and as discussed in chapter 3, the presence (or anticipation) of average price markups below their desired levels leads firms that are adjusting prices to raise the latter, thus generating positive inflation.

6.1.2 Households

Assume a continuum of households indexed by $j \in [0, 1]$. As in the basic model of chapter 3, a typical household seeks to maximize

$$E_0 \left\{ \sum_{t=0}^{\infty} \beta^t \, U(C_t(j), N_t(j)) \right\}$$

subject to a sequence of budget constraints (to be specified below), where $N_t(j)$ is the quantity of labor supplied, and

$$C_t(j) \equiv \left(\int_0^1 C_t(i, j)^{1-\frac{1}{\varepsilon_p}} \, di \right)^{\frac{\varepsilon_p}{\varepsilon_p - 1}} \qquad (6)$$

is a consumption index analogous to the one used in chapter 3, where $i \in [0, 1]$ indexes the type of good. The main difference relative to the baseline model of chapter 3 is that now each household is assumed to specialize in the supply of a different type of labor, also indexed by $j \in [0, 1]$. Furthermore, each household has some monopoly power in the labor market, and posts the (nominal) wage at which it is willing to supply specialized labor services to firms that demand them. Alternatively, think of many households specializing in the same type of labor (with their joint mass remaining infinitesimal), and delegating their wage decision to a trade union that acts in their interest.

In a way analogous to the assumptions on the price-setting constraints facing firms, assume that for each period only a fraction $1 - \theta_w$ of households/unions, drawn randomly from the population, reoptimize their posted nominal wage. Under the assumption of full consumption risk sharing across households, all households/unions resetting their wage in any given period will choose the same wage, because they face an identical problem.[2] Next, the problem facing households will be formalized and solved.

6.1.2.1 Optimal Wage Setting

Let us first consider how households choose the wage for their labor type when allowed to reoptimize that wage. Consider a household resetting its wage in period t, and let W_t^* denote the newly set wage. The household will choose W_t^* in order to maximize

$$E_t \left\{ \sum_{k=0}^{\infty} (\beta \theta_w)^k \, U(C_{t+k|t}, N_{t+k|t}) \right\} \qquad (7)$$

where $C_{t+k|t}$ and $N_{t+k|t}$ respectively denote the consumption and labor supply in period $t + k$ of a household that last reset its wage in period t. Thus, expression (7) can be interpreted as the expected discounted sum of utilities generated over the (uncertain) period during which the wage remains unchanged at the level W_t^* set in the current period. Note that the utility generated under any other wage set in the future is irrelevant from the point of view of the optimal setting of the current wage, and thus can be ignored in (7).

---

[2] The existence of a complete set of securities markets is assumed, which will guarantee that in equilibrium the marginal utility of consumption is equalized across households at all times (assuming identical initial conditions).

Maximization of (7) is subject to the sequence of labor demand schedules and flow budget constraints that are effective while W_t^* remains in place, i.e.,

$$N_{t+k|t} = \left(\frac{W_t^*}{W_{t+k}}\right)^{-\varepsilon_w} N_{t+k}$$

$$P_{t+k} C_{t+k|t} + E_{t+k}\{Q_{t+k,t+k+1} D_{t+k+1|t}\} \leq D_{t+k|t} + W_t^* N_{t+k|t} - T_{t+k}$$

for $k = 0, 1, 2, \ldots$ where $N_{t+k} \equiv \int_0^1 N_{t+k}(i) \, di$ denotes aggregate employment in period $t + k$, $D_{t+k|t}$ is the market value in period $t + k$ of the portfolio of securities held at the beginning of that period by households that last reoptimized their wage in period t, while $E_{t+k}\{Q_{t+k,t+k+1} D_{t+k+1|t}\}$ is the corresponding market value as of period $t + k$ of the portfolio purchased in that period, which yields a random payoff $D_{t+k+1|t}$. The remaining variables are defined as in chapter 3.

The first-order condition associated with the problem above is given by

$$\sum_{k=0}^{\infty} (\beta\theta_w)^k E_t \left\{ N_{t+k|t} U_c(C_{t+k|t}, N_{t+k|t}) \frac{W_t^*}{P_{t+k}} + \mathcal{M}_w U_n(C_{t+k|t}, N_{t+k|t}) \right\} = 0$$

where $\mathcal{M}_w \equiv \frac{\varepsilon_w}{\varepsilon_w - 1}$.

Letting $MRS_{t+k|t} \equiv -\frac{U_n(C_{t+k|t}, N_{t+k|t})}{U_c(C_{t+k|t}, N_{t+k|t})}$ denote the marginal rate of substitution between consumption and hours in period $t + k$ for the household resetting the wage in period t, the optimality condition above can be rewritten as

$$\sum_{k=0}^{\infty} (\beta\theta_w)^k E_t \left\{ N_{t+k|t} U_c(C_{t+k|t}, N_{t+k|t}) \left(\frac{W_t^*}{P_{t+k}} - \mathcal{M}_w MRS_{t+k|t}\right) \right\} = 0. \quad (8)$$

Note that in the limiting case of full wage flexibility ($\theta_w = 0$),

$$\frac{W_t^*}{P_t} = \frac{W_t}{P_t} = \mathcal{M}_w MRS_{t|t}$$

for all t. Thus, $\mathcal{M}_w$ is the wedge between the real wage and the marginal rate of substitution that prevails in the absence of wage rigidities, i.e., the *desired* gross wage markup.

Note also that in a perfect foresight zero inflation steady state

$$\frac{W^*}{P} = \frac{W}{P} = \mathcal{M}_w MRS.$$

Log-linearizing (8) around that steady state yields, after some algebraic manipulation, the following approximate wage setting rule

$$w_t^* = \mu^w + (1 - \beta\theta_w) \sum_{k=0}^{\infty} (\beta\theta_w)^k E_t \{mrs_{t+k|t} + p_{t+k}\} \quad (9)$$

where $\mu^w \equiv \log \mathcal{M}_w$.

The intuition behind wage setting rule (9) is straightforward. First, w_t^* is increasing in expected future prices, because households care about the purchasing power of their nominal wage. Second, w_t^* is increasing in the expected average marginal disutilities of labor (in terms of goods) over the life of the wage, because households want to adjust their expected average real wage accordingly, given expected future prices.

As in previous chapters, the utility function is specialized to be of the form

$$U(C, N) = \frac{C^{1-\sigma}}{1-\sigma} - \frac{N^{1+\varphi}}{1+\varphi}.$$

The assumed separability between consumption and hours, combined with the assumption of complete asset markets, implies that consumption is independent of the wage history of a household, i.e., $C_{t+k|t} = C_{t+k}$ for $k = 0, 1, 2, \ldots$, a result that is invoked in what follows. Thus, the (log) marginal rate of substitution in period $t + k$ for a household that last reset its wage in period t can be written as $mrs_{t+k|t} = \sigma c_{t+k} + \varphi n_{t+k|t}$.

Letting $mrs_{t+k} \equiv \sigma c_{t+k} + \varphi n_{t+k}$ define the economy's *average* marginal rate of substitution,

$$mrs_{t+k|t} = mrs_{t+k} + \varphi \left(n_{t+k|t} - n_{t+k} \right)$$
$$= mrs_{t+k} - \varepsilon_w \varphi \left(w_t^* - w_{t+k} \right)$$

Hence, (9) can be rewritten as

$$w_t^* = \frac{1-\beta\theta_w}{1+\varepsilon_w\varphi} \sum_{k=0}^{\infty} (\beta\theta_w)^k \ E_t \left\{ \mu_w + mrs_{t+k} + \varepsilon_w\varphi \ w_{t+k} + p_{t+k} \right\}$$
$$= \frac{1-\beta\theta_w}{1+\varepsilon_w\varphi} \sum_{k=0}^{\infty} (\beta\theta_w)^k \ E_t \left\{ (1 + \varepsilon_w\varphi) \ w_{t+k} - \widehat{\mu}_{t+k}^w \right\}$$
$$= \beta\theta_w \ E_t\{w_{t+1}^*\} + (1 - \beta\theta_w) \left(w_t - (1 + \varepsilon_w\varphi)^{-1} \ \widehat{\mu}_t^w \right) \qquad (10)$$

where $\widehat{\mu}_t^w \equiv \mu_t^w - \mu^w$ denotes the deviations of the economy's (log) average wage markup as $\mu_t^w \equiv (w_t - p_t) - mrs_t$ from its steady state level μ^w.

6.1.2.2 Wage Inflation Dynamics

Given the assumed wage setting structure, the evolution of the aggregate wage index (4) is given by

$$W_t = \left[\theta_w W_{t-1}^{1-\varepsilon_w} + (1 - \theta_w)(W_t^*)^{1-\varepsilon_w} \right]^{\frac{1}{1-\varepsilon_w}} .$$

The previous equation can be log-linearized around the zero (wage) inflation steady state to yield

$$w_t = \theta_w \ w_{t-1} + (1 - \theta_w) \ w_t^*. \qquad (11)$$

Combining (10) and (11) and letting $\pi_t^w = w_t - w_{t-1}$ denote wage inflation yields, after some manipulation, the baseline wage inflation equation

$$\pi_t^w = \beta E_t\{\pi_{t+1}^w\} - \lambda_w \, \widehat{\mu}_t^w \qquad (12)$$

where $\lambda_w \equiv \frac{(1-\theta_w)(1-\beta\theta_w)}{\theta_w(1+\varepsilon_w\varphi)}$. Note that this wage inflation equation has a form analogous to (5), the equation describing the dynamics of price inflation. The intuition behind it is identical: When the average wage in the economy is below the level consistent with maintaining (on average) the desired markup, households readjusting their nominal wage will tend to increase the latter, thus generating positive wage inflation.

In this model wage inflation equation (12) replaces condition $w_t - p_t = mrs_t$, one of the optimality conditions associated with the household's problem used extensively in previous chapters. The imperfect adjustment of nominal wages will generally drive a wedge between the real wage and the marginal rate of substitution of each household and, as a result, between the average real wage and the average marginal rate of substitution, leading to variations in the average wage markup and, given (12), also in wage inflation.

6.1.2.3 Other Optimality Conditions

In addition to the optimal wage setting condition (8), the solution to the above household's problem also yields a conventional Euler equation as an optimality condition, as derived in chapter 2 using a simple variational argument

$$\frac{Q_t}{P_t} U_c(C_t, N_{t|t-k}) = \beta E_t \left\{ \frac{U_c(C_{t+1}, N_{t+1|t-k})}{P_{t+1}} \right\}$$

where, as in previous chapters, Q_t is the price in period t of a one-period riskless discount bond paying one unit of currency in $t+1$. The left side of the above equation represents the loss in utility resulting from the reduction in consumption required to purchase one such bond (for a household that last reset its wage in period $t-k$), while the right side reflects the expected utility gains from consuming the associated one period ahead payoff.

Under the utility function assumed above, that optimality condition can be log-linearized to yield

$$c_t = E_t\{c_{t+1}\} - \frac{1}{\sigma}(i_t - E_t\{\pi_{t+1}^p\} - \rho) \qquad (13)$$

where $i_t \equiv -\log Q_t$ is the nominal yield on the one-period bond. Note that the previous Euler equation takes the same form as those used in earlier chapters, thus being independent of the presence (or nonpresence) of wage rigidities.

6.2   Equilibrium

The analysis of the model's equilibrium starts by deriving a version of the equations for price and wage inflation in terms of the output gap $\tilde{y}_t \equiv y_t - y_t^n$. Importantly, the concept of natural output y_t^n used in this chapter is to be understood as referring to the equilibrium level of output in the absence of *both* price and wage rigidities. A new variable, the *real wage gap*, is introduced and denoted by $\tilde{\omega}_t$ and formally defined as

$$\tilde{\omega}_t \equiv \omega_t - \omega_t^n$$

where $\omega_t \equiv w_t - p_t$ denotes the real wage, and where ω_t^n is the *natural real wage*, i.e., the real wage that would prevail in the absence of nominal rigidities, and which is given by

$$\omega_t^n = \log(1-\alpha) + (y_t^n - n_t^n) - \mu^p$$
$$= \log(1-\alpha) + \psi_{wa}^n \, a_t - \mu^p$$

where $\psi_{wa}^n \equiv \frac{1-\alpha\psi_{ya}^n}{1-\alpha} > 0$ and $\psi_{ya}^n \equiv \frac{1+\varphi}{\sigma(1-\alpha)+\varphi+\alpha}$ (with the latter as derived in chapter 3).

First, relate the average price markup to the output and real wage gaps. Using the fact that $\mu_t^p = mpn_t - \omega_t$,

$$\widehat{\mu}_t^p = (mpn_t - \omega_t) - \mu^p$$
$$= (\tilde{y}_t - \tilde{n}_t) - \tilde{\omega}_t$$
$$= -\frac{\alpha}{1-\alpha}\,\tilde{y}_t - \tilde{\omega}_t. \tag{14}$$

Hence, combining (5) and (14) yields the following equation for price inflation as a function of the output and real wage gaps

$$\pi_t^p = \beta E_t\{\pi_{t+1}^p\} + \kappa_p\,\tilde{y}_t + \lambda_p\,\tilde{\omega}_t \tag{15}$$

where $\kappa_p \equiv \frac{\alpha\lambda_p}{1-\alpha}$.

Similarly,

$$\widehat{\mu}_t^w = \omega_t - mrs_t - \mu^w$$
$$= \tilde{\omega}_t - (\sigma\,\tilde{y}_t + \varphi\,\tilde{n}_t)$$
$$= \tilde{\omega}_t - \left(\sigma + \frac{\varphi}{1-\alpha}\right)\tilde{y}_t. \tag{16}$$

Combining (12) and (16) yields an analogous version of the wage inflation equation in terms of the output and real wage gaps

$$\pi_t^w = \beta E_t\{\pi_{t+1}^w\} + \kappa_w\,\tilde{y}_t - \lambda_w\,\tilde{\omega}_t \tag{17}$$

where $\kappa_w \equiv \lambda_w\left(\sigma + \frac{\varphi}{1-\alpha}\right)$.

In addition, there is an identity relating the changes in the wage gap to price inflation, wage inflation, and the natural wage

$$\tilde{\omega}_t \equiv \tilde{\omega}_{t-1} + \pi_t^w - \pi_t^p - \Delta\omega_t^n. \tag{18}$$

In order to complete the non-policy block of the model, equilibrium conditions (15), (17), and (18) must be supplemented with a dynamic IS equation familiar from earlier chapters, which can be derived by combining the goods market clearing condition $y_t = c_t$ with Euler equation (13). The resulting expression is rewritten in terms of the output gap as

$$\tilde{y}_t = -\frac{1}{\sigma} (i_t - E_t\{\pi_{t+1}^p\} - r_t^n) + E_t\{\tilde{y}_{t+1}\} \tag{19}$$

where the natural interest rate $r_t^n \equiv \rho + \sigma E_t\{\Delta y_t^n\}$ should now be understood as the prevailing rate in an equilibrium with flexible wages and prices.

Finally, and in order to close the model, how the interest rate is determined must be specified. This is done by postulating an interest rate rule of the form

$$i_t = \rho + \phi_p \pi_t^p + \phi_w \pi_t^w + \phi_y \tilde{y}_t + v_t \tag{20}$$

where v_t is an exogenous component, possibly a function of r_t^n and $\Delta\omega_t^n$ (or their leads and lags), and normalized to have zero mean.

Plugging (20) into (19) to eliminate the interest rate and collecting the remaining conditions (15), (17), (18), (19), and (20) can represent the equilibrium dynamics by means of a system of the form

$$\mathbf{A}_{w,0} \mathbf{x}_t = \mathbf{A}_{w,1} E_t\{\mathbf{x}_{t+1}\} + \mathbf{B}_w \mathbf{z}_t \tag{21}$$

where $\mathbf{x}_t \equiv [\tilde{y}_t, \pi_t^p, \pi_t^w, \tilde{\omega}_{t-1}]'$, $\mathbf{z}_t \equiv [\hat{r}_t^n - v_t, \Delta\omega_t^n]'$,

$$\mathbf{A}_{w,0} \equiv \begin{bmatrix} \sigma + \phi_y & \phi_p & \phi_w & 0 \\ -\kappa_p & 1 & 0 & 0 \\ -\kappa_w & 0 & 1 & 0 \\ 0 & -1 & 1 & 1 \end{bmatrix}$$

$$\mathbf{A}_{w,1} \equiv \begin{bmatrix} \sigma & 1 & 0 & 0 \\ 0 & \beta & 0 & \lambda_p \\ 0 & 0 & \beta & -\lambda_w \\ 0 & 0 & 0 & 1 \end{bmatrix}; \quad \mathbf{B}_w \equiv \begin{bmatrix} 1 & 0 \\ 0 & 0 \\ 0 & 0 \\ 0 & 1 \end{bmatrix}$$

and where $\{\mathbf{z}_t\}$ follows a given exogenous process.

An important property of (21) is worth emphasizing at this point: In general, the system does *not* have a solution satisfying $\tilde{y}_t = \pi_t^p = \pi_t^w = 0$ for all t, not even under the assumption that the intercept of the interest rate rule adjusts one-for-one to variations in the natural rate of interest ($v_t = \widehat{r}_t^n$, for all t). An implication of that result is that the allocation associated with the equilibrium with flexible prices and wages cannot be attained in the presence of nominal rigidities in both goods and labor markets. The intuition for the previous result rests on the idea that in order for the constraints on price and wage setting not to be binding (and hence, not to distort the equilibrium allocation) all firms and workers should view their current prices and wages as the desired ones. This makes any adjustment unnecessary and leads to constant aggregate price and wage levels, i.e., zero inflation in both markets. Note, however, that such an outcome implies a constant real wage, which will generally be inconsistent with the flexible price/flexible wage allocation. Only when the natural wage is constant (so that $\Delta \omega_t^n = 0$ for all t) and as long as the central bank adjusts the nominal rate one for one with changes in the natural rate (i.e., $v_t = \widehat{r}_t^n$ for all t) the outcome $\widetilde{y}_t = \pi_t^p = \pi_t^w = 0$ for all t is a solution to (21) and, hence, is consistent with equilibrium.

A second question of interest relates to the conditions that the rule (20) must satisfy to guarantee a unique stationary equilibrium or, equivalently, a unique stationary solution to the system of difference equations (21). Given that vector $\mathbf{x}_t$ contains three non-predetermined variables and one predetermined variable, (local) uniqueness requires that three eigenvalues of $\mathbf{A}_w$ lie inside, and one outside, the unit circle.

Figure 6.1 displays the configurations of coefficients ϕ_p and ϕ_w associated with a unique equilibrium, as well as the region of indeterminacy, under the assumption that $\phi_y = 0$. As before, the analysis is restricted to non-negative values for those coefficients. The condition for uniqueness implied by the numerical analysis underlying figure 6.1 is given by

$$\phi_p + \phi_w > 1$$

or, what is equivalent, the central bank must adjust the nominal rate more than one-for-one in response to variations in any arbitrary weighted average of price and wage inflation. The previous condition can be viewed as extending the Taylor principle requirement discussed in earlier chapters to the case where the central bank is allowed to respond to wage inflation in addition to price inflation. Figure 6.2 shows how the region consistent with a determinate equilibrium in the (ϕ_p, ϕ_w) parameter space becomes larger as the coefficient on the output gap ϕ_y increases.

6.2.1 Dynamic Responses to a Monetary Policy Shock

Not surprisingly, the presence of staggered wage setting influences the economy's equilibrium response to different shocks. Figure 6.3 illustrates this point by displaying the responses of output, price inflation, wage inflation, and real wages to a monetary policy shock. Both the policy intervention (a persistent increase in the

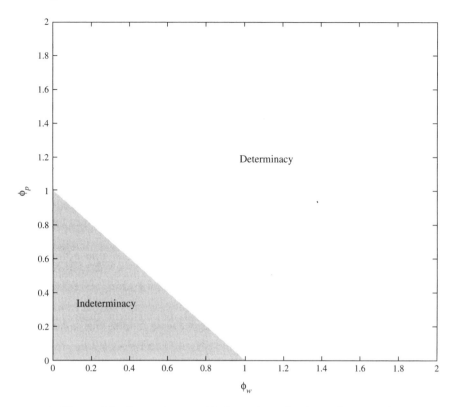

Figure 6.1 Determinacy and Indeterminacy Regions when $\phi_y \geq 0$

interest rate rule shifter v_t) and the model's calibration are identical to the analogous experiment carried out in chapter 3. In particular, a simple policy rule of the form (20) is assumed with $\phi_p = 1.5$ and $\phi_y = \phi_w = 0$. The only difference here is to allow for sticky wages, introduced as described above. In order to disentangle the role played by each type of rigidity, results are shown for three alternative calibrations of θ_p and θ_w. The first calibration corresponds to an economy in which price and wage rigidities coexist. As in the baseline model of chapter 3, it is assumed that $\theta_p = 2/3$. In addition, $\theta_w = 3/4$ is set, which implies an average duration of wage spells of four quarters. The latter assumption seems to accord with the empirical evidence (e.g., Taylor 1999). The second calibration assumes sticky prices and flexible wages ($\theta_p = 2/3$, $\theta_w = 0$) and, hence, corresponds to the basic model introduced in chapter 3. Finally, the third calibration corresponds to an economy with flexible prices and sticky wages ($\theta_p = 0$, $\theta_w = 3/4$). The intervention consists of an increase of 0.25 percentage points in the exogenous component of the interest rate rule. That change would lead, in the absence of an endogenous component in the interest rate rule, to an impact increase of one percentage point in the (annualized) nominal interest rate. As in the analogous

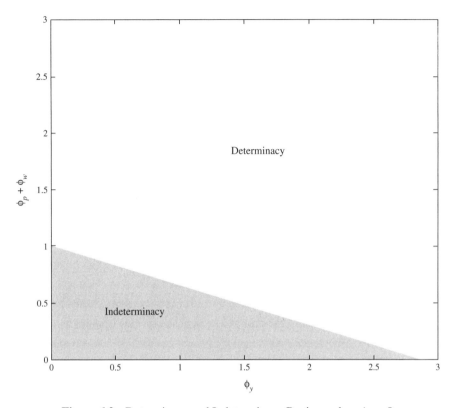

Figure 6.2 Determinacy and Indeterminacy Regions when $\phi_y = 0$

experiment of chapter 3, assume an autoregressive coefficient of 0.5 in the AR(1) process followed by the interest rate rule shifter.

In order to interpret the results shown in figure 6.3, it is useful to take the responses under sticky prices and flexible wages—already discussed in chapter 3 and represented here by the dashed lines—as a benchmark. The presence of both sticky wages and prices (responses shown by the solid lines) generates, not surprisingly, a more muted response of wage inflation. The latter partly explains the sluggish response of the real wage, which in turn reduces the impact of the decline in activity on the real marginal cost and, hence, the limited size of the inflation response. As a result, there is only a moderate endogenous response of the monetary authority to the lower inflation, thus implying persistently higher interest rates, which in turn account for the larger decline in output. By contrast, in the flexible wage economy the decline in activity leads to an (implausibly) large and persistent reduction in the real wage, which amplifies the size of the price inflation drop and the endogenous reaction of the monetary authority, leading to an overall more muted response of output.

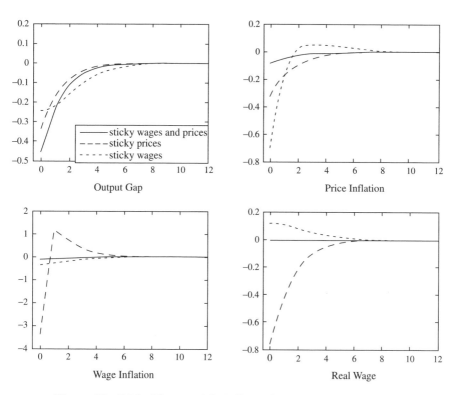

Figure 6.3 Sticky Wages and the Effects of a Monetary Policy Shock

Consider next the consequences of assuming the presence of sticky wages and flexible prices (impulse responses represented by the dotted lines). Again, the presence of sticky wages dampens the response of wage inflation to the contractionary monetary policy shock. But now, and given the absence of constraints on price adjustment, price inflation falls considerably in response to the decline in activity and the ensuing lower marginal costs. The large decline in prices in turn leads to a rise in the average real wage that, in turn, dampens (and eventually overturns) the effects of the activity decline on price inflation.

Neither the large negative response of wage inflation and the real wage in the sticky price/flexible wage model, nor the rapid fall in price inflation and the resulting large increase in the real wage in the sticky wage/flexible price model, appear to be consistent with existing estimates of the dynamic effects of exogenous monetary policy shocks. The latter estimates, and in particular those of the response of real wages to a monetary policy shock, are instead more in line with the predictions of the model with both sticky prices and wages.[3]

---

[3] See, e.g., Christiano, Eichenbaum, and Evans (2005).

6.3   Monetary Policy Design with Sticky Wages and Prices

This section explores some of the normative implications of the coexistence of sticky prices and sticky wages, as modelled in the framework above, for the conduct of monetary policy. In so doing, and in order to keep the analysis as simple as possible, necessary assumptions are made to guarantee that the *natural allocation*, i.e., the equilibrium allocation in the absence of nominal rigidities, is also the efficient allocation. Given the absence of mechanisms (e.g., capital accumulation) for the economy as a whole to transfer resources across periods, the efficient allocation corresponds to the solution of a sequence of static social planner problems of the form

$$\max \int_0^1 U(C_t(j), N_t(j))\, dj$$

subject to (1), (2), and (6), as well as the usual market clearing conditions. The optimality conditions for that problem are given by

$$C_t(i, j) = C_t, \quad \text{all } i, j \in [0, 1] \tag{22}$$

$$N_t(i, j) = N_t(j) = N_t(i) = N_t, \quad \text{all } i, j \in [0, 1] \tag{23}$$

$$-\frac{U_{n,t}}{U_{c,t}} = MPN_t \tag{24}$$

where $MPN_t \equiv (1 - \alpha) A_t N_t^{1-\alpha}$. Note that, under the assumptions, if *all* firms and households reoptimize their prices each period they will all choose the same prices and wages and, hence, (22) and (23) will be satisfied. On the other hand, optimal price and wage setting implies

$$\frac{W_t}{P_t} = -\frac{U_{n,t}}{U_{c,t}} \mathcal{M}_w$$

and

$$P_t = \mathcal{M}_p \frac{(1 - \tau) W_t}{MPN_t}$$

where τ is an employment subsidy, funded through lump sum taxes. Note that by setting $\tau = 1 - \frac{1}{\mathcal{M}_p \mathcal{M}_w}$, condition (24) is also satisfied, thus guaranteeing the efficiency of the flexible price/flexible wage equilibrium allocation. The latter property is assumed to hold for the remainder of this chapter.

Appendix 6.1 derives a second-order approximation to the average welfare losses experienced by households in the economy with sticky wages and prices, resulting from fluctuations around a steady state with zero wage and price inflation. When the latter is efficient, as is the case under the optimal subsidy derived above, those welfare losses, expressed as a fraction of steady state consumption, are given by

$$\mathbb{W} = \frac{1}{2} E_0 \sum_{t=0}^{\infty} \beta^t \left(\left(\sigma + \frac{\varphi + \alpha}{1 - \alpha} \right) \widetilde{y}_t^2 + \frac{\varepsilon_p}{\lambda_p} (\pi_t^p)^2 + \frac{\varepsilon_w(1 - \alpha)}{\lambda_w} (\pi_t^w)^2 \right) + t.i.p.$$

(25)

where $t.i.p.$ collects various terms that are independent of policy. Thus, by ignoring the latter terms, the average period welfare loss can be written as a linear combination of the variances of the output gap, price inflation, and wage inflation given by

$$\mathbb{L} = \left(\sigma + \frac{\varphi + \alpha}{1 - \alpha} \right) var(\widetilde{y}_t) + \frac{\varepsilon_p}{\lambda_p} var(\pi_t^p) + \frac{\varepsilon_w(1 - \alpha)}{\lambda_w} var(\pi_t^w).$$

(26)

Note that the relative weight of each of the variances is a function of the underlying parameter values. The weights associated with output gap and price inflation fluctuations are identical to those derived and discussed in chapter 4 for a version of the model economy with sticky prices and flexible wages. The presence of sticky wages implies an additional source of welfare losses, associated with wage inflation fluctuations. The contribution of wage inflation volatility to the welfare losses is increasing in (i) the elasticity of substitution among labor types (ε_w), (ii) the elasticity of output with respect to labor input $1 - \alpha$, and (iii) the degree of wage stickiness θ_w (which is inversely related to λ_w). Note that (i) and (ii) amplify the negative effect on aggregate productivity of any given dispersion of wages across labor types, while (iii) raises the degree of wage dispersion resulting from any given rate of wage inflation different from zero.

In general, and as argued above, the lower bound of zero welfare losses that characterizes an allocation where $\widetilde{y}_t = \pi_t^p = \pi_t^w = 0$ for all t is not attainable. The optimal policy will thus have to strike a balance in stabilizing the three abovementioned variables.

In the limiting case of flexible wages, $\lambda_w \to +\infty$, and the term in the loss function associated with wage inflation volatility vanishes (i.e., wage inflation is no longer costly). Note that in that case the wage markup is constant and hence,

$$\widetilde{\omega}_t = \sigma \, \widetilde{c}_t + \varphi \, \widetilde{n}_t$$

$$= \left(\sigma + \frac{\varphi}{1 - \alpha} \right) \widetilde{y}_t$$

which, substituted into (17), yields a New Keynesian Phillips curve identical to that derived in chapter 3, namely,

$$\pi_t^p = \beta E_t\{\pi_{t+1}^p\} + \kappa_p \, \widetilde{y}_t$$

where $\kappa_p \equiv \lambda_p \left(\sigma + \frac{\varphi+\alpha}{1-\alpha} \right)$. Accordingly, and as shown in chapter 3, there is no longer a tradeoff between stabilization of price inflation and stabilization of the output gap with the optimal policy requiring that $\pi_t^p = \widetilde{y}_t = 0$ for all t.

Similarly, in the limiting case of flexible prices (but sticky wages), $\lambda_p \to +\infty$ so that only the terms associated with fluctuations in the output gap and wage inflation remain a source of welfare losses. In that case, and using the fact that price markups will be constant,

$$\widetilde{\omega}_t = \widetilde{y}_t - \widetilde{n}_t$$
$$= -\frac{\alpha}{1-\alpha} \, \widetilde{y}_t$$

which, substituted into (17), yields the wage-inflation equation

$$\pi_t^w = \beta E_t\{\pi_{t+1}^w\} + \kappa_w \, \widetilde{y}_t$$

where $\kappa_w \equiv \lambda_w \left(\sigma + \frac{\varphi+\alpha}{1-\alpha} \right)$. In that case, the optimal policy will attain the zero lower bound for the welfare losses by fully stabilizing the output gap and wage inflation, i.e., $\pi_t^w = \widetilde{y}_t = 0$ for all t.

Thus, with the exception of the limiting case of full wage flexibility, a policy that seeks to stabilize price inflation completely (i.e., a strict price inflation targeting policy) will be suboptimal. The same is true for a strict wage inflation targeting policy, with the exception of an economy with fully flexible prices.

6.4 Optimal Monetary Policy

Next, the optimal monetary policy is characterized in the economy in which both prices and wages are sticky. For concreteness, the case will be restricted to one of full commitment. The central bank will seek to maximize (25) subject to (15), (17), and (18) for $t = 0, 1, 2, \ldots$. Let $\{\xi_{1,t}\}$, $\{\xi_{2,t}\}$ and $\{\xi_{3,t}\}$ denote the sequence of Lagrange multipliers associated with the previous constraints, respectively. The optimality conditions for the optimal policy problem are thus given by

$$\left(\sigma + \frac{\varphi + \alpha}{1-\alpha} \right) \widetilde{y}_t + \kappa_p \, \xi_{1,t} + \kappa_w \, \xi_{2,t} = 0 \tag{27}$$

$$\frac{\varepsilon_p}{\lambda_p} \, \pi_t^p - \Delta\xi_{1,t} + \xi_{3,t} = 0 \tag{28}$$

$$\frac{\varepsilon_w(1-\alpha)}{\lambda_w} \, \pi_t^w - \Delta\xi_{2,t} - \xi_{3,t} = 0 \tag{29}$$

$$\lambda_p \, \xi_{1,t} - \lambda_w \, \xi_{2,t} + \xi_{3,t} - \beta E_t\{\xi_{3,t+1}\} = 0 \tag{30}$$

for $t = 0, 1, 2, \ldots$ which, together with the constraints (15), (17), and (18) given $\xi_{1,-1} = \xi_{2,-1} = 0$ and an initial condition for $\widetilde{\omega}_{-1}$, characterize the solution to the

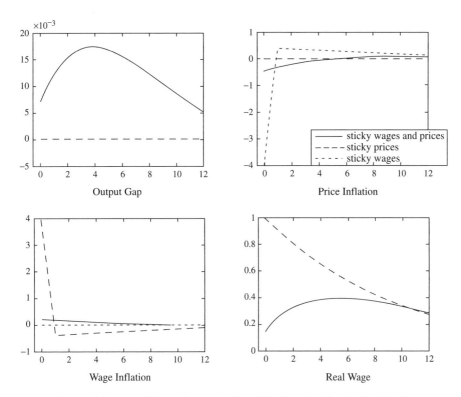

Figure 6.4 The Effects of a Technology Shock under the Optimal Policy

optimal policy problem. The equilibrium is represented in a compact way under the optimal policy as the stationary solution to the dynamical system

$$\mathbf{A}_0^* \, \mathbf{x}_t = \mathbf{A}_1^* \, E_t\{\mathbf{x}_{t+1}\} + \mathbf{B}^* \, \Delta a_t$$

where $\mathbf{x}_t \equiv [\widetilde{y}_t, \, \pi_t^p, \, \pi_t^w, \, \widetilde{\omega}_{t-1}, \, \xi_{1,t-1}, \, \xi_{2,t-1}, \, \xi_{3,t}]'$ and where $\mathbf{A}_0^*$, $\mathbf{A}_1^*$, and $\mathbf{B}^*$ are defined in appendix 6.2.

Figure 6.4 displays the responses of the output gap, price and wage inflation, and the real wage to a positive technology shock under the optimal policy for the three parameter calibrations considered earlier. Note that, as shown in chapter 4, when only prices are sticky (dashed lines) the optimal policy implies full stabilization of the price level and no effect on inflation. Because that policy replicates the flexible price/flexible wage equilibrium allocation the responses of both output and the real wage correspond to their natural counterparts, with the necessary adjustment of the real wage attained through large and persistent wage inflation that, given the assumed flexibility of wages, causes no distortions.

When only wages are sticky (dotted lines), and in a way consistent with the discussion in section 6.3, the natural allocation can also be attained, though now it requires full stabilization of nominal wages and, hence, zero wage inflation. The latter requirement in turn implies that the adjustment in the real wage be achieved through negative price inflation that, given the assumption of flexible prices, is no longer costly in terms of welfare.

When both prices and wages are sticky the natural allocation can no longer be attained. In that case, the optimal policy strikes a balance between attaining the output and real wage adjustments warranted by the rise in productivity and, on the other hand, keeping wage and price inflation close to zero to avoid the distortions associated with nominal instability. As a result, and in response to a positive technology shock, the real wage rises but not as much as the natural wage (note that the latter coincides with the response under the two previous calibrations). Given the convexity of welfare losses in price and wage inflation, it is optimal to raise the real wage smoothly, through a mix of negative price inflation and positive wage inflation. The implied sluggishness of the real wage, combined with the improvement in technology, accounts for the observed overshooting of output, which rises above its natural level, generating a positive output gap.

Next, a particular configuration of parameter values is examined for which the optimal policy takes a simple form that can be characterized analytically.

6.4.1 A Special Case with an Analytical Solution

Let us assume $\kappa_p = \kappa_w$ and $\varepsilon_p = \varepsilon_w (1 - \alpha) \equiv \varepsilon$. Note that in that case optimality conditions (27), (28), and (29) in the monetary policy problem simplify to a single condition relating price and wage inflation to the output gap, given by

$$\lambda_w \, \pi_t^p + \lambda_p \, \pi_t^w = -\frac{\lambda_p}{\varepsilon} \, \Delta \tilde{y}_t$$

for $t = 1, 2, 3, \ldots$ and $\lambda_w \, \pi_0^p + \lambda_p \, \pi_0^w = -\frac{\lambda_p}{\varepsilon} \, \tilde{y}_0$ for period 0. Let us define the following weighted average of price and wage inflation as

$$\pi_t \equiv (1 - \vartheta) \, \pi_t^p + \vartheta \, \pi_t^w \tag{31}$$

where $\vartheta \equiv \frac{\lambda_p}{\lambda_p + \lambda_w} \in [0, 1]$ is increasing (decreasing) in the degree of wage (price) rigidities.

Thus, the above optimality condition can be written in terms of the composite inflation measure

$$\pi_t = -\frac{\vartheta}{\varepsilon} \, \Delta \tilde{y}_t$$

for $t = 1, 2, 3, \ldots$ and $\pi_0 = -\frac{\vartheta}{\varepsilon} \, \tilde{y}_0$ in period 0. Equivalently, the optimal policy must meet the following target criterion for $t = 0, 1, 2, \ldots$

$$\hat{q}_t = -\frac{\vartheta}{\varepsilon} \, \tilde{y}_t \tag{32}$$

where $\widehat{q}_t \equiv q_t - q_{-1}$ and $q_t \equiv (1 - \vartheta) \, p_t + \vartheta \, w_t$ is a weighted average of the (log) price and wage levels.

Note that, independent of parameter values, one can always combine the wage and price inflation equations (15) and (17) to obtain the following version of the New Keynesian Phillips curve in terms of composite inflation

$$\pi_t = \beta E_t\{\pi_{t+1}\} + \kappa \, \widetilde{y}_t \tag{33}$$

where now $\kappa \equiv \frac{\lambda_p \lambda_w}{\lambda_p + \lambda_w} \left(\sigma + \frac{\varphi + \alpha}{1 - \alpha}\right)$. Thus, (33) implies that there is no tradeoff between stabilization of the output gap and stabilization of the particular composite measure of inflation introduced above.

Using (32) to substitute $\widetilde{y}_t$ out in (33) and rewriting the latter in terms of levels (using $\pi_t \equiv \widehat{q}_t - \widehat{q}_{t-1}$) obtains the following second-order difference for the composite price level

$$\widehat{q}_t = a \, \widehat{q}_{t-1} + a\beta \, E_t\{\widehat{q}_{t+1}\} = 0$$

for $t = 0, 1, 2, \ldots$ where $a \equiv \frac{\vartheta}{\vartheta(1+\beta)+\kappa\varepsilon}$. The only stationary solution to the previous difference equation must satisfy $\widehat{q}_t = \delta \, \widehat{q}_{t-1}$ where $\delta \equiv \frac{1-\sqrt{1-4\beta a^2}}{2a\beta} \in (0, 1)$ for $t = 0, 1, 2, \ldots$ Given that $\widehat{q}_{-1} = 0$, it follows that the optimal policy requires stabilizing the composite price level at its inherited value, or equivalently,

$$\pi_t = 0$$

and, as a result,

$$\widetilde{y}_t = 0$$

for $t = 0, 1, 2, \ldots$

Thus, in the particular case considered here, the optimal policy takes a simple form: The central bank should focus uniquely on targeting and fully stabilizing a weighted average of price and wage inflation, with the weights determined by underlying parameters. In particular, the relative weight of price (wage) inflation is increasing in the degree of price (wage) stickiness.

A nice feature of the optimal policy in the particular case analyzed above is that its implementation by the monetary authority does not rely on the output gap being observable: It suffices that the monetary authority keeps track of the composite-inflation measure, and responds (aggressively) to any deviation from zero of that measure. Of course, and as seen above for the general case, the optimal policy does not have such a simple characterization, requiring instead that the central bank follow a much more complicated target rule satisfying (15), (17), (27), (28), (29), and (30) simultaneously. In that context, it is of interest to know to what extent different simple monetary policy rules may be able to approximate the optimal policy, an issue that is attended to in the following section.

6.5   Evaluation of Simple Rules under Sticky Wages and Prices

This section considers a number of simple monetary policy rules and provides a quantitative evaluation of their impact on welfare. Given a parameter calibration, that evaluation is based on the unconditional period losses implied by each simple rule, given by (26). In the simulation underlying that exercise, variations in the technology parameter a_t are assumed to be the only source of fluctuations. That parameter follows an AR(1) process with an autoregressive coefficient $\rho_a = 0.9$ and a standard deviation for its innovation of 0.01. The remaining parameters (other than the stickiness parameters θ_p and θ_w) are set at their baseline values. For θ_p and θ_w, three alternative calibrations are considered, as discussed below.

Six different simple rules are analyzed. The first rule, which is referred to as *strict price inflation targeting*, requires that price inflation be zero at all times ($\pi_t^p = 0$ for all t). Also assumed is an analogous rule for wage inflation, i.e., a *strict wage-inflation targeting* rule. The third rule stabilizes the weighted average of price and wage inflation given by (31). That rule is referred to as a *strict composite inflation targeting* rule. As shown in section 6.4.1, that rule is optimal whenever some specific conditions on the model's parameters are satisfied (which is not the case for the baseline calibration). But even when those conditions are not satisfied, that rule has a special interest because, as implied by (33), it is equivalent to a rule that fully stabilizes the output gap.

The remaining three rules considered take the form of a simple interest rate rule

$$i_t = \rho + 1.5\,\pi_t$$

where π_t refers, respectively, to price inflation, wage inflation, or composite inflation (31). These rules are referred to as *flexible (price, wage, or composite) inflation targeting* rules.

Table 6.1 reports the main findings of that exercise. For each simple rule, the implied standard deviation of (annualized) price inflation, (annualized) wage inflation, and the output gap is reported, as well as the corresponding average period welfare loss. In addition to the simple rules, the table also reports the corresponding statistics for the optimal policy, which provides a useful benchmark. The top panel reports statistics corresponding to the calibration of the wage and price stickiness parameters used earlier in this chapter, namely, $\theta_p = 2/3$ and $\theta_w = 3/4$. Relative to that benchmark, the second panel assumes a lower degree of wage rigidity ($\theta_w = 1/4$), while the third panel reports results for a lower degree of price rigidity ($\theta_p = 1/3$).

For the baseline calibration (top panel), the optimal policy implies near-constancy of the output gap, and a standard deviation of wage inflation that is one-third that of price inflation. The implied welfare losses (relative to the unattainable first–best allocation) are very small, less than 1/40 of a percent of

Table 6.1 Evaluation of Simple Rules

		Optimal Policy	Strict Rules			Flexible Rules		
			Price	Wage	Composite	Price	Wage	Composite
$\theta_p = \frac{2}{3}$	$\theta_w = \frac{3}{4}$							
	$\sigma(\pi^P)$	0.64	0	0.82	0.66	1.50	1.08	1.12
	$\sigma(\pi^w)$	0.22	0.98	0	0.19	1.05	0.30	0.42
	$\sigma(\tilde{y})$	0.04	2.38	0.52	0	0.75	1.16	0.01
	$\mathbb{L}$	0.023	0.184	0.034	0.023	0.221	0.081	0.089
$\theta_p = \frac{2}{3}$	$\theta_w = \frac{1}{4}$							
	$\sigma(\pi^P)$	0.29	0	0.82	0.21	1.40	1.45	1.30
	$\sigma(\pi^w)$	1.24	2.91	0	1.63	1.49	0.98	1.25
	$\sigma(\tilde{y})$	0.19	0.61	0.52	0	0.29	0.68	0.32
	$\mathbb{L}$	0.010	0.038	0.034	0.012	0.097	0.104	0.083
$\theta_p = \frac{1}{3}$	$\theta_w = \frac{3}{4}$							
	$\sigma(\pi^P)$	1.64	0	1.91	1.75	2.58	2.10	2.10
	$\sigma(\pi^w)$	0.11	0.98	0	0.06	1.47	0.07	0.10
	$\sigma(\tilde{y})$	0.17	2.38	0.27	0	0.87	0.60	0.58
	$\mathbb{L}$	0.016	0.184	0.021	0.017	0.271	0.030	0.031

steady state consumption. Among the simple rules, the one that targets composite inflation does, for practical purposes, as well as the optimal policy, generating a very similar pattern of volatilities of the three welfare-relevant variables. Given that wage inflation has a weight of 0.77 in composite inflation, it is perhaps not surprising that a strict wage inflation targeting ranks second among the simple rules considered, with implied losses only slightly above those of the optimal policy. Interestingly, under this baseline calibration, price inflation targeting rules are the worst, largely due to the large fluctuations in wage inflation and the output gap that result from following those rules.

When considering the second calibration (with lower wage rigidity), the ranking among strict targeting policies is not affected, even though the relative losses from targeting price inflation now decline considerably and are almost identical to those resulting from strict wage inflation targeting. In fact, when looking at flexible targeting rules, price inflation targeting appears as slightly more desirable than wage inflation targeting, though still less so than targeting composite inflation.

Finally, under the third calibration (associated with a lower degree of price rigidity), the relative desirability of wage inflation targeting increases, even though targeting composite inflation is still the most desirable strict targeting policy. That relative ranking is reversed when considering flexible targeting rules, with wage inflation targeting being now the most desirable, as was the case under the baseline calibration. Finally, it is worth noting that the losses associated with price inflation targeting are again one order of magnitude above the losses resulting from the rules that seek to stabilize wage inflation.

Overall, the message conveyed by the exercise of this section can be viewed as twofold. First, in the presence of sticky wages (coexisting with sticky prices), policies that focus exclusively on stabilizing price inflation are clearly suboptimal. Second, and in the absence of further imperfections, a policy that responds aggressively to an appropriate weighted average of price and wage inflation emerges as a most desirable one. Of course, choosing the appropriate weights remains a challenge. This quantitative analysis, based on calibrations that are likely to span the range of plausible parameters, suggests that a policy that gives a dominant weight to wage inflation in the definition of that composite generates small additional losses relative to the optimal policy. Interestingly, that conclusion appears at odds with the practice of most central banks, which seem to attach little weight to wage inflation as a target variable, with the interest in that variable often limited to its ability to influence (and thus help predict) current and future price inflation developments.

6.6 Notes on the Literature

Early examples of nonoptimizing rational expectations modelled with nominal wage rigidities can be found in the work of Fischer (1977) and Taylor (1980). Cooley and Cho (1995) and Bénassy (1995) were among the first papers that embedded the assumption of sticky nominal wages in a dynamic stochastic general equilibrium model, and examined its implications for the properties of a number of variables in the presence of both real and monetary shocks.

Erceg, Henderson, and Levin (2000) developed the New Keynesian model with both staggered price and staggered wage contracts à la Calvo that has become the framework of reference in the literature, and on which much of this chapter builds. The focus of their paper was, like this chapter, on the derivation of the implications for monetary policy. A similar focus, including a discussion of the special case in which targeting a weighted average of wage and price inflation is optimal, can be found in Woodford (2003, chapter 6) and Giannoni and Woodford (2003). Other work has focused instead on the impact of staggered wage setting on the persistence of the effects of monetary policy shocks. See, e.g., Huang and Liu (2002) and, especially, Woodford (2003, chapter 3) for a detailed discussion of the role of wage stickiness in that regard.

Staggered wage setting is also a common feature of medium-scale models like those of Kim (2000), Smets and Wouters (2003), and Christiano, Eichenbaum, and Evans (2005). An analysis of the optimal implementable rules in such a model can be found in Schmitt-Grohé and Uribe (2006), which also includes a numerical analysis of the requirements that the coefficients of the interest rate rule must satisfy to guarantee uniqueness of the equilibrium.

Appendix

6.1 A Second-Order Approximation to Welfare Losses with Price and Wage Stickiness

Using a second-order Taylor expansion to household j's period t utility around the steady state, combined with a goods market clearing condition and integrating across households yields

$$\int_0^1 (U_t(j) - U) \, dj \simeq U_c C \left(\hat{y}_t + \frac{1-\sigma}{2} \hat{y}_t^2 \right)$$

$$- U_n N \left(\int_0^1 \hat{n}_t(j) \, dj + \frac{1+\varphi}{2} \int_0^1 \hat{n}_t(j)^2 \, dj \right)$$

where $\sigma \equiv -\frac{U_{cc}}{U_c} C$ and $\varphi \equiv \frac{U_{nn}}{U_n} N$, and where use of the market clearing condition $\hat{c}_t = \hat{y}_t$ was made.

Define aggregate employment as $N_t \equiv \int_0^1 N_t(j) \, dj$, or, in terms of log deviations from steady state and up to a second-order approximation

$$\hat{n}_t + \frac{1}{2} \hat{n}_t^2 \simeq \int_0^1 \hat{n}_t(j) \, dj + \frac{1}{2} \int_0^1 \hat{n}_t(j)^2 \, dj.$$

Note also that

$$\int_0^1 \hat{n}_t(j)^2 dj = \int_0^1 (\hat{n}_t(j) - \hat{n}_t + \hat{n}_t)^2 dj$$

$$= \hat{n}_t^2 - 2\hat{n}_t \varepsilon_w \int_0^1 \hat{w}_t(j) \, dj + \varepsilon_w^2 \int_0^1 \hat{w}_t(j)^2 \, dj$$

$$\simeq \hat{n}_t^2 + \varepsilon_w^2 \, var_j \{w_t(j)\}$$

where use of the labor demand equation $\hat{n}_t(j) - \hat{n}_t = -\varepsilon_w \hat{w}_t(j)$ has been made and the fact that $\int_0^1 \hat{w}_t(j) \, dj = \frac{(\varepsilon_w - 1)}{2} var_i\{w_t(i)\}$ is of second order, a result analogous to that obtained for prices.

Thus, it can be written

$$\int_0^1 (U_t(j) - U) \, dj \simeq U_c C \left(\hat{y}_t + \frac{1-\sigma}{2} \hat{y}_t^2 \right)$$

$$- U_n N \left(\hat{n}_t + \frac{1+\varphi}{2} \hat{n}_t^2 + \frac{\varepsilon_w^2 \varphi}{2} var_j \{w_t(j)\} \right).$$

Next, derive a relationship between aggregate employment and output

$$N_t = \int_0^1 \int_0^1 N_t(i, j) \, dj \, di$$

$$= \int_0^1 N_t(i) \int_0^1 \frac{N_t(i, j)}{N_t(i)} \, dj \, di$$

$$= \Delta_{w,t} \int_0^1 N_t(i) \, di$$

$$= \Delta_{w,t} \left(\frac{Y_t}{A_t}\right)^{\frac{1}{1-\alpha}} \int_0^1 \left(\frac{Y_t(i)}{Y_t}\right)^{\frac{1}{1-\alpha}} \, di$$

$$= \Delta_{w,t} \, \Delta_{p,t} \left(\frac{Y_t}{A_t}\right)^{\frac{1}{1-\alpha}}$$

where $\Delta_{w,t} \equiv \int_0^1 \left(\frac{W_t(j)}{W_t}\right)^{-\varepsilon_w} dj$ and $\Delta_{p,t} \equiv \int_0^1 \left(\frac{P_t(i)}{P_t}\right)^{\frac{-\varepsilon_p}{1-\alpha}} di$.

Thus, the following second-order approximation to the relation between (log) aggregate output and (log) aggregate employment holds

$$(1 - \alpha) \, \widehat{n}_t = \widehat{y}_t - a_t + d_{w,t} + d_{p,t}$$

where $d_{w,t} \equiv (1 - \alpha) \log \int_0^1 \left(\frac{W_t(j)}{W_t}\right)^{-\varepsilon_w} dj$ and $d_{p,t} \equiv (1 - \alpha) \log \int_0^1 \left(\frac{P_t(i)}{P_t}\right)^{\frac{-\varepsilon_p}{1-\alpha}} di$.

As shown in appendix 4.1 of chapter 4, $d_{p,t} \simeq \frac{\varepsilon_p}{2\Theta} \, var_i\{p_t(i)\}$. Using an analogous derivation, one can show $d_{w,t} \simeq \frac{(1-\alpha)\varepsilon_w}{2} \, var_j\{w_t(j)\}$.

Hence, aggregate welfare can be rewritten as

$$\int_0^1 (U_t(j) - U) \, dj \simeq U_c C \left(\widehat{y}_t + \frac{1-\sigma}{2} \, \widehat{y}_t^2\right) - \frac{U_n N}{(1-\alpha)} \left(\widehat{y}_t + \frac{\varepsilon_p}{2\Theta} \, var_i\{p_t(i)\}\right.$$
$$\left. + \frac{\Upsilon}{2} \, var_j\{w_t(j)\} + \frac{1+\varphi}{2(1-\alpha)} \int_0^1 (\widehat{y}_t - a_t)^2 \, dj\right) + t.i.p.$$

where $\Upsilon \equiv \varepsilon_w(1-\alpha)(1+\varepsilon_w\varphi)$ and where *t.i.p.* stands for *terms independent of policy.*

Let Φ denote the size of the steady state distortion, implicitly defined by $-\frac{U_n}{U_c} = MPN(1-\Phi)$. Using the fact that $MPN = (1-\alpha)(Y/N)$,

$$\int_0^1 \frac{U_t(j) - U}{U_c C} \, dj = \widehat{y}_t + \frac{1-\sigma}{2} \, \widehat{y}_t^2 - (1-\Phi) \left(\widehat{y}_t + \frac{\varepsilon_p}{2\Theta} \, var_i\{p_t(i)\}\right.$$
$$\left. + \frac{\Upsilon}{2} \, var_j\{w_t(j)\} + \frac{1+\varphi}{2(1-\alpha)} \, (\widehat{y}_t - a_t)^2\right) + t.i.p.$$

Under the "small distortion" assumption (so that the product of Φ with a second-order term can be ignored as negligible) and ignoring the *t.i.p.* terms,

$$\int_0^1 \frac{U_t(j) - U}{U_c C} \, dj = \Phi \, \widehat{y}_t - \frac{1}{2} \left(\frac{\varepsilon_p}{\Theta} \, var_i\{p_t(i)\} + \Upsilon var_j\{w_t(j)\} - (1 - \sigma) \, \widehat{y}_t^2 \right.$$
$$\left. + \frac{1 + \varphi}{1 - \alpha} \, (\widehat{y}_t - a_t)^2 \right)$$

$$= \Phi \, \widehat{y}_t - \frac{1}{2} \left(\frac{\varepsilon_p}{\Theta} \, var_i\{p_t(i)\} + \Upsilon var_j\{w_t(j)\} \right.$$
$$\left. + \left(\sigma + \frac{\varphi + \alpha}{1 - \alpha} \right) \widehat{y}_t^2 - 2 \left(\frac{1 + \varphi}{1 - \alpha} \right) \widehat{y}_t a_t \right)$$

$$= \Phi \, \widehat{y}_t - \frac{1}{2} \left(\frac{\varepsilon_p}{\Theta} \, var_i\{p_t(i)\} + \Upsilon var_j\{w_t(j)\} \right.$$
$$\left. + \left(\sigma + \frac{\varphi + \alpha}{1 - \alpha} \right) (\widehat{y}_t^2 - 2\widehat{y}_t \, \widehat{y}_t^e) \right)$$

$$= \Phi \, \widehat{x}_t - \frac{1}{2} \left(\frac{\varepsilon_p}{\Theta} \, var_i\{p_t(i)\} + \Upsilon var_j\{w_t(j)\} \right.$$
$$\left. + \left(\sigma + \frac{\varphi + \alpha}{1 - \alpha} \right) \widehat{x}_t^2 \right)$$

where $\widehat{y}_t^e \equiv y_t^e - y^e$, and where the fact that $\widehat{y}_t^e = \frac{1 + \varphi}{\sigma(1 - \alpha) + \varphi + \alpha} a_t$ and $\widehat{y}_t - \widehat{y}_t^e = x_t - (y - y^e) = x_t - x \equiv \widehat{x}_t$.

Accordingly, a second-order approximation to the consumer's discounted utility can be written as follows (expressed as a fraction of steady state consumption and up to additive terms independent of policy):

$$\mathbb{W} = E_0 \sum_{t=0}^\infty \beta^t \left(\frac{U_t - U}{U_c C} \right)$$

$$= E_0 \sum_{t=0}^\infty \beta^t \left[\Phi \, \widehat{x}_t - \frac{1}{2} \left(\frac{\varepsilon_p}{\Theta} \, var_i\{p_t(i)\} + \Upsilon var_j\{w_t(j)\} + \left(\sigma + \frac{\varphi + \alpha}{1 - \alpha} \right) \widehat{x}_t^2 \right) \right]$$

Using Lemma 2 in appendix 4.1 of chapter 4, rewrite the welfare losses as

$$\mathbb{W} = E_0 \sum_{t=0}^\infty \beta^t \left[\Phi \, \widehat{x}_t - \frac{1}{2} \left(\frac{\varepsilon_p}{\lambda_p} \, (\pi_t^p)^2 + \frac{\varepsilon_w (1 - \alpha)}{\lambda_w} \, (\pi_t^w)^2 + \left(\sigma + \frac{\varphi + \alpha}{1 - \alpha} \right) \widehat{x}_t^2 \right) \right].$$

Note that in the particular case of an efficient steady state $\Phi = 0$ and $\widehat{x}_t = x_t$. Moreover, if the optimal subsidy discussed in the text is in place, the steady state is efficient and $\Phi = 0$ and $\widehat{x}_t = x_t$. In addition, the model satisfies $y_t^n = y_t^e$ for all t, thus $\widehat{x}_t = x_t = \widetilde{y}_t$.

6.2   Definitions of $\mathbf{A}_0^*$, $\mathbf{A}_1^*$, and $\mathbf{B}^*$

$$
\mathbf{A}_0^* \equiv
\begin{bmatrix}
-\frac{\alpha \lambda_p}{1-\alpha} & 1 & 0 & 0 & 0 & 0 & 0 \\
-\lambda_w\left(\sigma + \frac{\varphi}{1-\alpha}\right) & 0 & 1 & 0 & 0 & 0 & 0 \\
0 & -1 & 1 & 1 & 0 & 0 & 0 \\
\left(\sigma + \frac{\varphi+\alpha}{1-\alpha}\right) & 0 & 0 & 0 & 0 & 0 & 0 \\
0 & \frac{\varepsilon_p}{\lambda_p} & 0 & 0 & 1 & 0 & 1 \\
0 & 0 & \frac{\varepsilon_w(1-\alpha)}{\lambda_w} & 0 & 0 & 1 & -1 \\
0 & 0 & 0 & 0 & 0 & 0 & 1
\end{bmatrix}
$$

$$
\mathbf{A}_1^* \equiv
\begin{bmatrix}
0 & \beta & 0 & \lambda_p & 0 & 0 & 0 \\
0 & 0 & \beta & -\lambda_w & 0 & 0 & 0 \\
0 & 0 & 0 & 1 & 0 & 0 & 0 \\
0 & 0 & 0 & 0 & -\frac{\alpha \lambda_p}{1-\alpha} & -\lambda_w\left(\sigma + \frac{\varphi}{1-\alpha}\right) & 0 \\
0 & 0 & 0 & 0 & 1 & 0 & 0 \\
0 & 0 & 0 & 0 & 0 & 1 & 0 \\
0 & 0 & 0 & 0 & -\lambda_p & \lambda_w & \beta
\end{bmatrix}
$$

$$\mathbf{B}^* \equiv [0, 0, 1, 0, 0, 0, 0]'$$

References

Bénassy, Jean-Pascal (1995): "Money and Wage Contracts in an Optimizing Model of the Business Cycle," *Journal of Monetary Economics* 35, no. 2, 303–316.

Blanchard, Olivier J., and Lawrence W. Summers (1986): "Hysteresis and the European Unemployment Problem," in S. Fischer (ed.), *NBER Macroeconomics Annual 1986*, 15–78.

Christiano, Lawrence J., Martin Eichenbaum, and Charles L. Evans (2005): "Nominal Rigidities and the Dynamic Effects of a Shock to Monetary Policy," *Journal of Political Economy* 113, no. 1, 1–45.

Cooley, Thomas F., and Jang-Ok Cho (1995): "The Business Cycle with Nominal Contracts," *Economic Theory* 6, no. 1, 12–33.

Erceg, Christopher J., Dale W. Henderson, and Andrew T. Levin (2000): "Optimal Monetary Policy with Staggered Wage and Price Contracts," *Journal of Monetary Economics* 46, no. 2, 281–314.

Fischer, Stanley (1977): "Long-Term Contracts, Rational Expectations, and the Optimal Money Supply," *Journal of Political Economy* 85, no. 1, 191–206.

Giannoni, Marc P., and Michael Woodford (2003): "Optimal Inflation Targeting Rules," in B. Bernanke and M. Woodford (eds.), *The Inflation Targeting Debate*, Chicago University Press, Chicago, IL.

Huang, Kevin X. D., and Zheng Liu (2002): "Staggered Price-Setting, Staggered Wage-Setting, and Business Cycle Persistence," *Journal of Monetary Economics* 49, no. 2, 405–433.

Kim, Jinill (2000): "Constructing and Estimating a Realistic Optimizing Model of Monetary Policy," *Journal of Monetary Economics* 45, no. 2, 329–359.

Schmitt-Grohé, Stephanie, and Martin Uribe (2006): "Optimal Inflation Stabilization in a Medium Scale Macroeconomic Model," Duke University, Durham, NC, unpublished manuscript.

Smets, Frank, and Raf Wouters (2003): "An Estimated Dynamic Stochastic General Equilibrium Model of the Euro Area," *Journal of the European Economic Association* 1, no. 5, 1123–1175.

Taylor, John (1980): "Aggregate Dynamics and Staggered Contracts," *Journal of Political Economy*, 88, no. 1, 1–24.

Taylor, John B. (1999): "Staggered Price and Wage Setting in Macroeconomics," in J. B. Taylor and M. Woodford (eds.), *Handbook of Macroeconomics*, chap. 15, 1341–1397, Elsevier, New York.

Woodford, Michael (2003): *Interest and Prices: Foundations of a Theory of Monetary Policy*, Princeton University Press, Princeton, NJ.

Exercises

6.1 Optimal Monetary Policy in a Sticky Wage Economy

Assume a representative firm that is perfectly competitive and has access to a technology described by

$$y_t = a_t + n_t$$

where y_t, n_t, and a_t denote the logs of output, employment, and productivity, respectively. Prices are flexible. Assume

$$a_t = \rho\, a_{t-1} + \varepsilon_t.$$

The representative household's optimal labor supply is given by

$$w_t - p_t = \varphi\, n_t$$

where w_t and p_t denote the log of the wage and price levels, respectively.

a) Derive the equilibrium behavior of employment and output under the assumption of flexible wages and prices.

b) Next sticky wages are introduced. For each period, half the workers set the (log) nominal wage, which remains constant for two periods, according to

$$w_t^* = \frac{1}{2}\,(p_t + E_t\{p_{t+1}\}) + \frac{\varphi}{2}\,(n_t + E_t\{n_{t+1}\})$$

The average effective (log) wage paid by the firm in period t is thus

$$w_t = \frac{1}{2}\,(w_t^* + w_{t-1}^*).$$

Show that inflation evolves according to

$$\pi_t = E_t\{\pi_{t+1}\} + \varphi\,\tilde{n}_t + u_t$$

where $\tilde{n}_t \equiv n_{t-1} + E_{t-1}\{n_t\} + n_t + E_t\{n_{t+1}\}$ and $u_t \equiv -4a_t - (p_t - E_{t-1}\{p_t\})$.

c) Suppose that aggregate demand is given by the dynamic IS equation

$$y_t = -\frac{1}{\sigma}\,(i_t - E_t\{\pi_{t+1}\} - \rho) + E_t\{y_{t+1}\}$$

and assume that the optimal policy requires that the flexible wage allocation be replicated. Describe the equilibrium behavior of the interest rate, wage inflation, and price inflation under the optimal policy.

6.2   Optimal Monetary Policy with Wages Set in Advance

The representative firm is perfectly competitive and has access to a technology described by

$$y_t = a_t + n_t$$

where y, n, and a denote the logs of output, employment, and productivity, respectively. Prices are flexible. Assume

$$a_t = \rho_a\,a_{t-1} + \varepsilon_t^a.$$

The optimal labor supply satisfies

$$w_t - p_t = \varphi\,n_t$$

where w and p denote the log of the (nominal) wage and price levels, respectively. Aggregate demand is given by the dynamic IS equation

$$y_t = -\frac{1}{\sigma}\,(i_t - E_t\{\pi_{t+1}\} - \rho) + E_t\{y_{t+1}\}$$

where i_t denotes the nominal interest rate and $\pi_t \equiv p_t - p_{t-1}$ is the inflation rate.

a) Derive the equilibrium behavior of employment, output, and the real interest rate under the assumption of flexible wages and prices. Can one determine the corresponding equilibrium values for the nominal rate and inflation? Explain.

b) Next, wage stickiness is introduced by assuming that nominal wages are set in advance (i.e., at the end of the previous period), according to the rule

$$w_t = E_{t-1}\{p_t\} + \varphi\, E_{t-1}\{n_t\}.$$

c) Characterize the equilibrium behavior of output, employment, inflation, and the real wage under the assumption that the central bank follows the simple rule

$$i_t = \rho + \phi_\pi\, \pi_t.$$

d) Characterize the optimal policy and its associated equilibrium in the presence of sticky wages, and suggest an interest rate rule that would implement it. (Note: assume efficiency of the equilibrium allocation in the absence of sticky wages.)

6.3 Labor Market Institutions as a Source of Long Run Money Non-neutrality

As shown in Blanchard and Summers (1986), a perfectly competitive representative firm maximizes profits each period

$$P_t Y_t - W_t N_t$$

subject to a technology $Y_t = N_t^{1-\alpha}$. Assume that the desired labor supply is inelastic and equal to one. Equilibrium in the goods market is given by

$$Y_t = \frac{M_t}{P_t}$$

with the nominal money supply following an AR(1) process (in logs)

$$m_t = \rho_m\, m_{t-1} + \varepsilon_t$$

Derive the equilibrium process for (the log) of output y_t, employment n_t, prices p_t, and real wages $w_t - p_t$ under each of the alternative assumptions on the wage setting process:

a) Nominal wages are fully flexible and determined competitively

b) Nominal wages are set in advance, so that the labor market clears in expectation (i.e., $E_{t-1}\{n_t\} = 0$)

c) Nominal wages are set in advance by a union, so that in expectation only currently employed workers are employed (i.e., $E_{t-1}\{n_t\} = n_{t-1}$)

d) Discuss the empirical relevance of the three preceding scenarios in light of their implied properties (comovements, persistence) for real wages, employment, and output.

6.4   Monetary Policy and Real Wage Rigidities

Assume that the representative household's utility is given by $E_0 \sum_{t=0}^{\infty} \beta^t U(C_t, N_t)$ with $U(C_t, N_t) = C_t - \frac{1}{2} N_t^2$, where C_t denotes consumption and N_t denotes hours worked. Let firms' technology be given by the production function $Y_t = A_t N_t$, where Y_t denotes output and A_t is an exogenous technology parameter. All output is consumed.

Firms set prices in a staggered fashion à la Calvo, which results in the inflation dynamics equation

$$\pi_t = \beta \, E_t\{\pi_{t+1}\} + \lambda \, \widehat{mc}_t$$

where $\widehat{mc}_t \equiv mc_t - mc$ represents the log deviations of real marginal cost from its level in the zero inflation steady state.

a) Derive an expression for the (log) of the *efficient* level of output (which is denoted by y_t^*) as a function of (log) productivity a_t (i.e., the level of employment that a benevolent social planner would choose, given preferences and constraints).

b) Assume that the (log) nominal wage w_t is set each period according to the schedule $w_t = p_t + \frac{1}{1+\delta} n_t$, where $\delta > 0$ (the same assumption is maintained for parts (c), (d) and (e) below). Compare the behavior of the equilibrium real wage under that schedule with one that would be observed under competitive labor markets. In what sense can the condition $\delta > 0$ be interpreted as a "real rigidity"?

c) Derive the implied (log) *natural* level of output (denoted b y_t^n) defined as the equilibrium level of output under flexible prices (when all firms keep a constant (log) markup μ).

d) Derive an expression for the real marginal cost $\widehat{mc}_t$ as a function of the output gap $\tilde{y}_t \equiv y_t - y_t^n$.

e) Derive the inflation equation in terms of the welfare-relevant output gap $y_t - y_t^*$. Show how the presence of real wage rigidities ($\delta > 0$) generates a trade-off between stabilization of inflation and stabilization of the welfare-relevant employment gap.

f) Suppose that the monetary authority has a loss function given by $E_0 \sum_{t=0}^{\infty} \beta^t \, [\alpha(y_t - y_t^*)^2 + \pi_t^2]$. Solve for the equilibrium process for inflation and output under the optimal monetary policy under discretion (time-consistent solution), under the assumption of an i.i.d. technology process a_t. Explain the difference with the case of perfect competition in the labor market. (Note: for simplicity, assume that the frictionless markup μ is infinitesimally small when answering this question.)

7
Monetary Policy and the Open Economy

All the models analyzed in earlier chapters assumed a closed economy: households and firms were not able to trade in goods or financial assets with agents located in other economies. This chapter relaxes that assumption by developing an open economy extension of the basic New Keynesian model analyzed in chapter 3. The framework introduces explicitly the exchange rate, the terms of trade, exports, and imports, as well as international financial markets. It also implies a distinction between the consumer price index—that includes the price of imported goods—and the price index for domestically produced goods. Such a framework can in principle be used to assess the implications of alternative monetary policy rules for an open economy. Because the framework nests as a limiting case the closed economy model of chapter 3, it allows the exploration of the extent to which the opening of the economy affects some of the conclusions regarding monetary policy obtained for the closed economy model: in particular, the desirability of a policy that seeks to stabilize inflation (see chapter 4). It is also worth analyzing what role, if any, the exchange rate plays in the optimal design of monetary policy and/or what is the measure of inflation that the central bank should seek to stabilize. Finally, the framework can be used to determine the implications of alternative simple rules, as was done in chapter 4 for the closed economy.

The analysis of a monetary open economy raises a number of issues that a modeler needs to confront, and which are absent from its closed economy counterpart. First, a choice needs to be made between the modelling of a "large" or "small" economy, i.e., between allowing or not, respectively, for repercussions in the rest of the world of developments (including policy decisions) in the economy being modelled. Second, the existence of two or more economies subject to imperfectly correlated shocks generates an incentive to trade in assets between residents of different countries in order to smooth their consumption over time. Hence, a decision must be made regarding the nature of international asset markets and, more specifically, the set of securities that can be traded in those markets, with

---

This chapter is based on Galí and Monacelli (2005), with the notation modified for consistency with earlier chapters. Section 7.3 on the transmission of monetary policy shocks contains original material.

possible assumptions ranging from financial autarky to complete markets. Third, one needs to make some assumption about firms' abilities to discriminate across countries in the price they charge for the goods they produce ("pricing to market" versus "law of one price"). Furthermore, whenever discrimination is possible and prices are not readjusted continuously, an assumption must be made regarding the currency in which the prices of exported goods are set ("local currency pricing," i.e., prices are set in the currency of the importing economy versus "producer currency pricing," i.e., prices are set in the currency of the producer's country). Other dimensions of open economy modelling that require some choices include the allowance or not of nontradeable goods, the existence of trading costs, the possibility of international policy coordination, and so on.

A comprehensive analysis of those different modelling dimensions and how they may affect the design of monetary policy would require a book of its own, thus it is clearly beyond the scope of this chapter. The modest objective here is to present an example of a monetary open economy model to illustrate some of the issues that emerge in the analysis of such economies and which are absent from their closed economy counterparts. In particular, a small open economy model is developed, with complete international financial markets, where the law of one price holds. Then, in the discussion of the model's policy implications and in the notes on the literature in 7.6, a reference is made to a number of papers that adopt different assumptions, including a brief discussion of the extent to which this leads their findings to differ from those obtained here.

The framework below, originally developed in Galí and Monacelli (2005), models a small open economy as one among a continuum of (infinitesimally small) economies making up the world economy. For simplicity, and in order to focus on the issues brought about by the openness of the economy, the possible presence of either cost-push shocks or nominal wage rigidities is ignored. The assumptions on preferences and technology, combined with the Calvo price-setting structure and the assumption of complete financial markets, give rise to a highly tractable model and to simple and intuitive log-linearized equilibrium conditions. The latter can be reduced to a two-equation dynamical system consisting of a New Keynesian Phillips curve and a dynamic IS-type equation, whose structure is identical to the one derived in chapter 3 for the closed economy, though its coefficients depend on parameters that are specific to the open economy while the driving forces are a function of world variables (that are taken as exogenous to the small open economy). As in its closed economy counterpart, the two equations must be complemented with a description of how monetary policy is conducted.

After describing the model and deriving a simple representation of its equilibrium dynamics, section 7.3 analyzes the transmission of monetary policy shocks, emphasizing the role played by openness in that transmission. Section 7.4 turns to the issue of optimal monetary policy design, focusing on a particular case for which the flexible price allocation is efficient. Under the same assumptions it is straightforward to derive a second-order approximation to the consumer's utility, which can be used to evaluate alternative policy rules. Section 7.5 assesses the merits of two different Taylor-type rules, a policy that fully stabilizes the CPI, and an exchange rate peg. Section 7.6 concludes with a brief note on the related literature.

7.1 A Small Open Economy Model

The world economy is modelled as a continuum of small open economies represented by the unit interval. Since each economy is of measure zero, its performance does not have any impact on the rest of the world. Different economies are subject to imperfectly correlated productivity shocks, but it is assumed that they share identical preferences, technology, and market structure.

Next, the problem facing households and firms located in one such economy will be described in detail. Before doing so, a brief remark on notation is in order. Because the focus is on the behavior of a single economy and its interaction with the world economy, and in order to lighten the notation, variables *without* an i-index are used to refer to the small open economy being modelled. Variables with an $i \in [0, 1]$ subscript refer to economy i, one among the continuum of economies making up the world economy. Finally, variables with an *asterisk superscript* (*) correspond to the world economy as a whole.

7.1.1 Households

A typical small open economy is inhabited by a representative household who seeks to maximize

$$E_0 \sum_{t=0}^{\infty} \beta^t \, U(C_t, N_t) \tag{1}$$

where N_t denotes hours of labor, and C_t is a composite consumption index defined by

$$C_t \equiv \left[(1-\alpha)^{\frac{1}{\eta}} \, (C_{H,t})^{\frac{\eta-1}{\eta}} + \alpha^{\frac{1}{\eta}} \, (C_{F,t})^{\frac{\eta-1}{\eta}} \right]^{\frac{\eta}{\eta-1}} \tag{2}$$

where $C_{H,t}$ is an index of consumption of domestic goods given by the constant elasticity of substitution (CES) function

$$C_{H,t} \equiv \left(\int_0^1 C_{H,t}(j)^{\frac{\varepsilon-1}{\varepsilon}} \, dj \right)^{\frac{\varepsilon}{\varepsilon-1}}$$

where $j \in [0, 1]$ denotes the good variety.[1] $C_{F,t}$ is an index of imported goods given by

$$C_{F,t} \equiv \left(\int_0^1 (C_{i,t})^{\frac{\gamma-1}{\gamma}} \, di \right)^{\frac{\gamma}{\gamma-1}}$$

where $C_{i,t}$ is, in turn, an index of the quantity of goods imported from country i and consumed by domestic households. It is given by an analogous CES function

$$C_{i,t} \equiv \left(\int_0^1 C_{i,t}(j)^{\frac{\varepsilon-1}{\varepsilon}} \, dj \right)^{\frac{\varepsilon}{\varepsilon-1}}.$$

Note that parameter $\varepsilon > 1$ denotes the elasticity of substitution between varieties produced within any given country.[2] Parameter $\alpha \in [0, 1]$ can be interpreted as a measure of openness.[3] Parameter $\eta > 0$ measures the substitutability between domestic and foreign goods from the viewpoint of the domestic consumer, while γ measures the substitutability between goods produced in different foreign countries.

Maximization of (1) is subject to a sequence of budget constraints of the form

$$\int_0^1 P_{H,t}(j) \, C_{H,t}(j) \, dj$$

$$+ \int_0^1 \int_0^1 P_{i,t}(j) \, C_{i,t}(j) \, dj \, di + E_t\{Q_{t,t+1}D_{t+1}\} \le D_t + W_t N_t + T_t \quad (3)$$

for $t = 0, 1, 2, \ldots$ where $P_{H,t}(j)$ is the price of domestic variety j. $P_{i,t}(j)$ is the price of variety j imported from country i. D_{t+1} is the nominal payoff in period $t+1$ of the portfolio held at the end of period t (and which includes shares in firms), W_t is the nominal wage, and T_t denotes lump-sum transfers/taxes. The previous variables are all expressed in units of domestic currency. $Q_{t,t+1}$ is the stochastic discount factor for one-period-ahead nominal payoffs relevant to the domestic household. Assume that households have access to a complete set of contingent claims, traded internationally.

---

[1] As discussed below, each country produces a continuum of differentiated goods, represented by the unit interval.

[2] Notice that it is irrelevant to think of integrals like the one in (2) as including or not the corresponding variable for the small economy being modelled, because its presence would have a negligible influence on the integral itself (in fact, each individual economy has a zero measure). The previous remark also applies to many other expressions involving integrals over the continuum of economies (i.e., over i) that the reader will encounter below.

[3] Equivalently, $1 - \alpha$ is a measure of the degree of home bias. Note that in the absence of some home bias the households in the small open economy would attach an infinitesimally small weight to local goods, and consumption expenditures would be allocated to imported goods (except for an infinitesimally small share allocated to domestic goods).

The optimal allocation of any given expenditure within each category of goods yields the demand functions

$$C_{H,t}(j) = \left(\frac{P_{H,t}(j)}{P_{H,t}}\right)^{-\varepsilon} C_{H,t} \; ; \; C_{i,t}(j) = \left(\frac{P_{i,t}(j)}{P_{i,t}}\right)^{-\varepsilon} C_{i,t} \tag{4}$$

for all $i, j \in [0, 1]$, where $P_{H,t} \equiv \left(\int_0^1 P_{H,t}(j)^{1-\varepsilon} dj\right)^{\frac{1}{1-\varepsilon}}$ is the *domestic price index* (i.e., an index of prices of domestically produced goods) and $P_{i,t} \equiv \left(\int_0^1 P_{i,t}(j)^{1-\varepsilon} dj\right)^{\frac{1}{1-\varepsilon}}$ is a price index for goods imported from country i (expressed in domestic currency) for all $i \in [0, 1]$. Combining the optimality conditions in (4) with the definitions of price and quantity indexes $P_{H,t}$, $C_{H,t}$, $P_{i,t}$, and $C_{i,t}$ yields $\int_0^1 P_{H,t}(j) C_{H,t}(j) dj = P_{H,t} C_{H,t}$ and $\int_0^1 P_{i,t}(j) C_{i,t}(j) dj = P_{i,t} C_{i,t}$.

Furthermore, the optimal allocation of expenditures on imported goods by country of origin implies

$$C_{i,t} = \left(\frac{P_{i,t}}{P_{F,t}}\right)^{-\gamma} C_{F,t} \tag{5}$$

for all $i \in [0, 1]$ where $P_{F,t} \equiv \left(\int_0^1 P_{i,t}^{1-\gamma} di\right)^{\frac{1}{1-\gamma}}$ is the price index for *imported* goods, also expressed in domestic currency. Note that (5), together with the definitions of $P_{F,t}$ and $C_{F,t}$, implies that total expenditures on imported goods can be written as $\int_0^1 P_{i,t} C_{i,t} di = P_{F,t} C_{F,t}$.

Finally, the optimal allocation of expenditures between domestic and imported goods is given by

$$C_{H,t} = (1 - \alpha) \left(\frac{P_{H,t}}{P_t}\right)^{-\eta} C_t \; ; \; C_{F,t} = \alpha \left(\frac{P_{F,t}}{P_t}\right)^{-\eta} C_t \tag{6}$$

where $P_t \equiv [(1 - \alpha) (P_{H,t})^{1-\eta} + \alpha (P_{F,t})^{1-\eta}]^{\frac{1}{1-\eta}}$ is the CPI.[4] Note that under the assumption of $\eta = 1$ or, alternatively, when the price indexes for domestic and foreign goods are equal (as in the steady state described below), parameter α corresponds to the share of domestic consumption allocated to imported goods. It is also in this sense that α represents a natural index of openness.

Accordingly, total consumption expenditures by domestic households are given by $P_{H,t} C_{H,t} + P_{F,t} C_{F,t} = P_t C_t$. Thus, the period budget constraint can be rewritten as

$$P_t C_t + E_t\{Q_{t,t+1} D_{t+1}\} \leq D_t + W_t N_t + T_t. \tag{7}$$

---

[4] It is useful to notice, for future reference, that in the particular case of $\eta = 1$, the CPI takes the form $P_t = (P_{H,t})^{1-\alpha} (P_{F,t})^\alpha$, while the consumption index is given by $C_t = \frac{1}{(1-\alpha)^{(1-\alpha)}\alpha^\alpha} C_{H,t}^{1-\alpha} C_{F,t}^\alpha$.

As in previous chapters, the period utility function is specialized to be of the form $U(C, N) \equiv \frac{C^{1-\sigma}}{1-\sigma} - \frac{N^{1+\varphi}}{1+\varphi}$. Thus, the remaining optimality conditions for the household's problem can be rewritten as

$$C_t^\sigma \, N_t^\varphi = \frac{W_t}{P_t} \tag{8}$$

which is the standard intratemporal optimality condition. In order to derive the relevant intertemporal optimality condition note that the following relation must hold for the optimizing household in the small open economy

$$\frac{V_{t,t+1}}{P_t} \, C_t^{-\sigma} = \xi_{t,t+1} \, \beta \, C_{t+1}^{-\sigma} \, \frac{1}{P_{t+1}} \tag{9}$$

where $V_{t,t+1}$ is the period t price (in domestic currency) of an Arrow security, i.e., a one-period security that yields one unit of domestic currency if a specific state of nature is realized in period $t + 1$, and nothing otherwise, and where $\xi_{t,t+1}$ is the probability of that state of nature being realized in $t + 1$ (conditional on the state of nature at t). Variables C_{t+1} and P_{t+1} on the right side should be interpreted as representing the values taken by the consumption index and the CPI at $t + 1$ conditional on the state of nature to which the Arrow security refers to being realized. Thus, the left side captures the utility loss resulting from the purchase of the Arrow security considered (with the corresponding reduction in consumption), whereas the right side measures the expected one-period-ahead utility gain from the additional consumption made possible by the (eventual) security payoff. If the consumer is optimizing the expected utility gain, it must exactly offset the current utility loss.

Given that the price of Arrow securities and the one-period stochastic discount factor are related by the equation $Q_{t,t+1} \equiv \frac{V_{t,t+1}}{\xi_{t,t+1}}$, (9) can be rewritten as[5]

$$\beta \left(\frac{C_{t+1}}{C_t} \right)^{-\sigma} \left(\frac{P_t}{P_{t+1}} \right) = Q_{t,t+1} \tag{10}$$

which is assumed to be satisfied for all possible states of nature at t and $t + 1$.

Taking conditional expectations on both sides of (10) and rearranging terms, a conventional stochastic Euler equation can be derived

$$Q_t = \beta \, E_t \left\{ \left(\frac{C_{t+1}}{C_t} \right)^{-\sigma} \left(\frac{P_t}{P_{t+1}} \right) \right\} \tag{11}$$

where $Q_t \equiv E_t\{Q_{t,t+1}\}$ denotes the price of a one-period discount bond paying off one unit of domestic currency in $t + 1$.

---

[5] Note that under complete markets a simple no room for arbitrage argument implies that the price of a one-period asset (or portfolio) yielding a random payoff D_{t+1} must be given by $\sum V_{t,t+1} D_{t+1}$ where the sum is over all possible $t + 1$ states. Equivalently, that price can be written as $E_t\{\frac{V_{t,t+1}}{\xi_{t,t+1}} D_{t+1}\}$. Thus, the one-period stochastic discount factor can be defined as $Q_{t,t+1} \equiv \frac{V_{t,t+1}}{\xi_{t,t+1}}$.

For future reference, recall that (8) and (11) can be respectively written in log-linearized form as

$$w_t - p_t = \sigma\, c_t + \varphi\, n_t$$

$$c_t = E_t\{c_{t+1}\} - \frac{1}{\sigma}\, (i_t - E_t\{\pi_{t+1}\} - \rho) \tag{12}$$

where lowercase letters denote the logs of the respective variables, $i_t \equiv -\log Q_t$ is the short term nominal rate, $\rho \equiv -\log \beta$ is the time discount rate, and $\pi_t \equiv p_t - p_{t-1}$ is CPI inflation (with $p_t \equiv \log P_t$).

7.1.1.1 Domestic Inflation, CPI Inflation, the Real Exchange Rate, and the Terms of Trade: Some Identities

Next, several assumptions and definitions are introduced, and a number of identities are derived that are extensively used below. *Bilateral terms of trade* between the domestic economy and country i is defined as $S_{i,t} = \frac{P_{i,t}}{P_{H,t}}$, i.e., the price of country i's goods in terms of home goods. The *effective terms of trade* are thus given by

$$S_t \equiv \frac{P_{F,t}}{P_{H,t}}$$

$$= \left(\int_0^1 S_{i,t}^{1-\gamma}\, di \right)^{\frac{1}{1-\gamma}}$$

which can be approximated (up to first order) around a symmetric steady state satisfying $S_{i,t} = 1$ for all $i \in [0, 1]$ by

$$s_t = \int_0^1 s_{i,t}\, di \tag{13}$$

where $s_t \equiv \log S_t = p_{F,t} - p_{H,t}$.

Similarly, log-linearization of the CPI formula around the same symmetric steady state yields

$$p_t \equiv (1 - \alpha)\, p_{H,t} + \alpha\, p_{F,t}$$

$$= p_{H,t} + \alpha\, s_t. \tag{14}$$

It is useful to note, for future reference, that (13) and (14) hold *exactly* when $\gamma = 1$ and $\eta = 1$, respectively.

It follows that *domestic inflation*, defined as the rate of change in the index of domestic goods prices, i.e., $\pi_{H,t} \equiv p_{H,t+1} - p_{H,t}$, and *CPI inflation* are linked according to the relation

$$\pi_t = \pi_{H,t} + \alpha\, \Delta s_t \tag{15}$$

which makes the gap between the two measures of inflation proportional to the percent change in the terms of trade, with the coefficient of proportionality given by the openness index α.

Assume that the *law of one price* holds for individual goods at all times (both for import and export prices), implying that $P_{i,t}(j) = \mathcal{E}_{i,t}\, P_{i,t}^i(j)$ for all $i, j \in [0, 1]$, where $\mathcal{E}_{i,t}$ is the bilateral nominal exchange rate (the price of country i's currency in terms of the domestic currency), and $P_{i,t}^i(j)$ is the price of country i's good j expressed in terms of its own currency. Plugging the previous assumption into the definition of $P_{i,t}$ yields $P_{i,t} = \mathcal{E}_{i,t}\, P_{i,t}^i$, where $P_{i,t}^i \equiv \left(\int_0^1 P_{i,t}^i(j)^{1-\varepsilon} dj \right)^{\frac{1}{1-\varepsilon}}$ is country i's domestic price index. In turn, by substituting into the definition of $P_{F,t}$ and log-linearizing around the symmetric steady state,

$$p_{F,t} = \int_0^1 (e_{i,t} + p_{i,t}^i)\, di$$
$$= e_t + p_t^*$$

where $p_{i,t}^i \equiv \int_0^1 p_{i,t}^i(j)\, dj$ is the (log) domestic price index for country i (expressed in terms of its own currency), $e_t \equiv \int_0^1 e_{i,t}\, di$ is the (log) *effective nominal exchange rate*, and $p_t^* \equiv \int_0^1 p_{i,t}^i\, di$ is the (log) *world price index*. Notice that for the world as a whole, there is no distinction between CPI and domestic price level, nor between their corresponding inflation rates.

Combining the previous result with the definition of the terms of trade yields the expression

$$s_t = e_t + p_t^* - p_{H,t}. \tag{16}$$

Next, a relationship is derived between the terms of trade and the real exchange rate. First, the *bilateral real exchange rate* is defined with country i as $\mathcal{Q}_{i,t} \equiv \frac{\mathcal{E}_{i,t} P_t^i}{P_t}$, i.e., the ratio of the two countries' CPIs, both expressed in terms of domestic currency. Let $q_t \equiv \int_0^1 q_{i,t}\, di$ be the (log) *effective real exchange rate*, where $q_{i,t} \equiv \log \mathcal{Q}_{i,t}$. It follows that

$$q_t = \int_0^1 (e_{i,t} + p_t^i - p_t)\, di$$
$$= e_t + p_t^* - p_t$$
$$= s_t + p_{H,t} - p_t$$
$$= (1 - \alpha)\, s_t$$

where the last equality holds only up to a first-order approximation when $\eta \neq 1$.[6]

---

[6] The last equality can be derived by log-linearizing $\frac{P_t}{P_{H,t}} = [(1-\alpha) + \alpha\, \mathcal{S}_t^{1-\eta}]^{\frac{1}{1-\eta}}$ around a symmetric steady state, which yields $p_t - p_{H,t} = \alpha\, s_t$.

7.1.1.2 International Risk-Sharing

Under the assumption of complete markets for securities traded internationally, a condition analogous to (9) must also hold for the representative household in any other country, say country i

$$\frac{V_{t,t+1}}{\mathcal{E}_t^i P_t^i} (C_t^i)^{-\sigma} = \xi_{t,t+1} \beta (C_{t+1}^i)^{-\sigma} \frac{1}{\mathcal{E}_{t+1}^i P_{t+1}^i}$$

where the presence of the exchange rate terms reflects the fact that the security purchased by the country i's household has a price $V_{t,t+1}$ and a unit payoff expressed in the currency of the small open economy of reference, and hence, needs to be converted to country i's currency.

The previous relation can be written in terms of our small open economy's stochastic discount factor as

$$\beta \left(\frac{C_{t+1}^i}{C_t^i} \right)^{-\sigma} \left(\frac{P_t^i}{P_{t+1}^i} \right) \left(\frac{\mathcal{E}_t^i}{\mathcal{E}_{t+1}^i} \right) = Q_{t,t+1}. \tag{17}$$

Combining (10) and (17), together with the definition for the real exchange rate definition gives

$$C_t = \vartheta_i \, C_t^i \, Q_{i,t}^{\frac{1}{\sigma}} \tag{18}$$

for all t, and where ϑ_i is a constant that will generally depend on initial conditions regarding relative net asset positions. Henceforth, and without loss of generality, symmetric initial conditions are assumed (i.e., zero net foreign asset holdings and an ex-ante identical environment), in which case $\vartheta_i = \vartheta = 1$ for all i.

Taking logs on both sides of (18) and integrating over i yields

$$c_t = c_t^* + \frac{1}{\sigma} q_t \tag{19}$$

$$= c_t^* + \left(\frac{1-\alpha}{\sigma} \right) s_t$$

where $c_t^* \equiv \int_0^1 c_t^i \, di$ is the index for world consumption (in log terms), and where the second equality holds only up to a first-order approximation when $\eta \neq 1$. Thus, the assumption of complete markets at the international level leads to a simple relationship linking domestic consumption with world consumption and the terms of trade.

7.1.1.3 A Brief Detour: Uncovered Interest Parity and the Terms of Trade

Under the assumption of complete international financial markets, the equilibrium price (in terms of the small open economy's domestic currency) of a riskless bond denominated in country i's currency is given by $\mathcal{E}_{i,t} \, Q_t^i = E_t \{ Q_{t,t+1} \, \mathcal{E}_{i,t+1} \}$, where Q_t^i is the price of the bond in terms of country i's currency. The previous pricing equation can be combined with the domestic bond pricing equation $Q_t = E_t\{Q_{t,t+1}\}$ to obtain a version of the uncovered interest-parity condition

$$E_t\{Q_{t,t+1} \left[\exp\{i_t\} - \exp\{i_t^*\} \left(\mathcal{E}_{i,t+1}/\mathcal{E}_{i,t}\right)\right]\} = 0.$$

Log-linearizing around a perfect foresight steady state, and aggregating over i, yields the familiar expression

$$i_t = i_t^* + E_t\{\Delta e_{t+1}\}. \tag{20}$$

Combining the definition of the (log) terms of trade with (20) yields the stochastic difference equation

$$s_t = (i_t^* - E_t\{\pi_{t+1}^*\}) - (i_t - E_t\{\pi_{H,t+1}\}) + E_t\{s_{t+1}\}. \tag{21}$$

As shown in appendix 7.1, the terms of trade are pinned down uniquely in the perfect foresight steady state. That fact, combined with the assumption of stationarity in the model's driving forces and unit relative prices in the steady state, implies that $\lim_{T\to\infty} E_t\{s_T\} = 0$.[7] Hence, (21) can be solved forward to obtain

$$s_t = E_t \left\{ \sum_{k=0}^{\infty} \left[(i_{t+k}^* - \pi_{t+k+1}^*) - (i_{t+k} - \pi_{H,t+k+1}) \right] \right\} \tag{22}$$

i.e., the terms of trade are a function of current and anticipated real interest rate differentials.

It must be pointed out that while equations (21) and (22) provide a convenient (and intuitive) way of representing the connection between terms of trade and interest rate differentials, they do not constitute an additional independent equilibrium condition. In particular, it is easy to check that (21) can be derived by combining the consumption Euler equations for both the domestic and world economies with the risk sharing condition (19) and equation (15).

Next, attention is turned to the supply side of the economy.

---

[7] The assumption regarding the steady state implies that the real interest rate differential will revert to a zero mean. More generally, the real interest rate differential will revert to a constant mean, as long as the terms of trade are stationary in first differences. That would be the case if, say, the technology parameter had a unit root or a different average rate of growth relative to the rest of the world. Those cases would have persistent real interest rate differentials.

7.1.2 Firms

7.1.2.1 Technology

A typical firm in the home economy produces a differentiated good with a linear technology represented by the production function

$$Y_t(j) = A_t \, N_t(j)$$

where $a_t \equiv \log A_t$ follows the AR(1) process $a_t = \rho_a \, a_{t-1} + \varepsilon_t$, and where $j \in [0, 1]$ is a firm-specific index.[8]

Hence, the real marginal cost (expressed in terms of domestic prices) will be common across domestic firms and given by

$$mc_t = -v + w_t - p_{H,t} - a_t$$

where $v \equiv -\log(1 - \tau)$, with τ being an employment subsidy whose role is discussed later in more detail.

7.1.2.2 Price Setting

As in the basic model of chapter 3, it is assumed that firms set prices in a staggered fashion. In particular, a measure $1 - \theta$ of (randomly selected) firms sets new prices each period, with an individual firm's probability of reoptimizing in any given period being independent of the time elapsed since it last reset its price. As shown in chapter 3, the optimal price-setting strategy for the typical firm resetting its price in period t can be approximated by the (log-linear) rule

$$\overline{p}_{H,t} = \mu + (1 - \beta\theta) \sum_{k=0}^{\infty} (\beta\theta)^k \, E_t\{mc_{t+k} + p_{H,t+k}\} \qquad (23)$$

where $\overline{p}_{H,t}$ denotes the log of newly set domestic prices, and $\mu \equiv \log \frac{\varepsilon}{\varepsilon-1}$ is the log of the (gross) markup in the steady state (or, equivalently, the equilibrium markup in the flexible price economy).[9]

---

[8] An extension of the analysis to the case of decreasing returns considered in chapter 3 is straightforward. In order to keep the notation as simple as possible the analysis here is restricted to the case of constant returns.

[9] $\overline{p}_{H,t}$ is used to denote newly set prices instead of p_t^* (used in chapter 3), because in this chapter letters with an asterisk refer to world economy variables.

7.2 Equilibrium

7.2.1 Aggregate Demand and Output Determination

7.2.1.1 Consumption and Output in the Small Open Economy

Goods market clearing in the home economy requires

$$Y_t(j) = C_{H,t}(j) + \int_0^1 C^i_{H,t}(j) \, di = \left(\frac{P_{H,t}(j)}{P_{H,t}} \right)^{-\varepsilon} \tag{24}$$

$$\times \left[(1-\alpha) \left(\frac{P_{H,t}}{P_t} \right)^{-\eta} C_t + \alpha \int_0^1 \left(\frac{P_{H,t}}{\mathcal{E}_{i,t} P^i_{F,t}} \right)^{-\gamma} \left(\frac{P^i_{F,t}}{P^i_t} \right)^{-\eta} C^i_t \, di \right]$$

for all $j \in [0, 1]$ and all t, where $C^i_{H,t}(j)$ denotes country i's demand for good j produced in the home economy. Notice that the second equality has made use of (5) and (6) together with the assumption of symmetric preferences across countries, which implies $C^i_{H,t}(j) = \alpha \left(\frac{P_{H,t}(j)}{P_{H,t}} \right)^{-\varepsilon} \left(\frac{P_{H,t}}{\mathcal{E}_{i,t} P^i_{F,t}} \right)^{-\gamma} \left(\frac{P^i_{F,t}}{P^i_t} \right)^{-\eta} C^i_t$.

Plugging (24) into the definition of aggregate domestic output $Y_t \equiv \left[\int_0^1 Y_t(j)^{1-\frac{1}{\varepsilon}} \, dj \right]^{\frac{\varepsilon}{\varepsilon-1}}$ yields

$$Y_t = (1-\alpha) \left(\frac{P_{H,t}}{P_t} \right)^{-\eta} C_t + \alpha \int_0^1 \left(\frac{P_{H,t}}{\mathcal{E}_{i,t} P^i_{F,t}} \right)^{-\gamma} \left(\frac{P^i_{F,t}}{P^i_t} \right)^{-\eta} C^i_t \, di$$

$$= \left(\frac{P_{H,t}}{P_t} \right)^{-\eta} \left[(1-\alpha) C_t + \alpha \int_0^1 \left(\frac{\mathcal{E}_{i,t} P^i_{F,t}}{P_{H,t}} \right)^{\gamma-\eta} \mathcal{Q}^\eta_{i,t} C^i_t \, di \right]$$

$$= \left(\frac{P_{H,t}}{P_t} \right)^{-\eta} C_t \left[(1-\alpha) + \alpha \int_0^1 \left(\mathcal{S}^i_t \mathcal{S}_{i,t} \right)^{\gamma-\eta} \mathcal{Q}^{\eta-\frac{1}{\sigma}}_{i,t} \, di \right] \tag{25}$$

where the last equality follows from (18), and where $\mathcal{S}^i_t$ denotes the effective terms of trade for country i, while $\mathcal{S}_{i,t}$ denotes the bilateral terms of trade between the home economy and country i. Notice that in the particular case of $\sigma = \eta = \gamma = 1$ the previous condition can be written exactly as[10]

$$Y_t = C_t \, \mathcal{S}^\alpha_t. \tag{26}$$

---

[10] Here one must use the fact that under the assumption $\eta = 1$, the CPI takes the form $P_t = (P_{H,t})^{1-\alpha}(P_{F,t})^\alpha$, thus implying $\frac{P_t}{P_{H,t}} = \left(\frac{P_{F,t}}{P_{H,t}} \right)^\alpha = \mathcal{S}^\alpha_t$.

More generally, and recalling that $\int_0^1 s_t^i \, di = 0$, the following first-order log-linear approximation to (25) is derived around the symmetric steady state

$$y_t = c_t + \alpha\gamma \, s_t + \alpha\left(\eta - \frac{1}{\sigma}\right)q_t$$

$$= c_t + \frac{\alpha\omega}{\sigma}\, s_t \tag{27}$$

where $\omega \equiv \sigma\gamma + (1-\alpha)(\sigma\eta - 1)$. Notice that $\sigma = \eta = \gamma = 1$ implies $\omega = 1$.

A condition analogous to the one above will hold for all countries. Thus, for a *generic country i* it can be rewritten as $y_t^i = c_t^i + \frac{\alpha\omega}{\sigma}\, s_t^i$. By aggregating over all countries, a world market clearing condition can be derived as

$$y_t^* \equiv \int_0^1 y_t^i \, di$$

$$= \int_0^1 c_t^i \, di \equiv c_t^* \tag{28}$$

where y_t^* and c_t^* are indexes for world output and consumption (in log terms), and where the main equality follows, once again, from the fact that $\int_0^1 s_t^i \, di = 0$.

Combining (27) with (19) and (28) yields

$$y_t = y_t^* + \frac{1}{\sigma_\alpha}\, s_t \tag{29}$$

where $\sigma_\alpha \equiv \frac{\sigma}{1+\alpha(\omega-1)} > 0$.

Finally, combining (27) with Euler equation (12) gives

$$y_t = E_t\{y_{t+1}\} - \frac{1}{\sigma}(i_t - E_t\{\pi_{t+1}\} - \rho) - \frac{\alpha\omega}{\sigma} E_t\{\Delta s_{t+1}\}$$

$$= E_t\{y_{t+1}\} - \frac{1}{\sigma}(i_t - E_t\{\pi_{H,t+1}\} - \rho) - \frac{\alpha\Theta}{\sigma} E_t\{\Delta s_{t+1}\}$$

$$= E_t\{y_{t+1}\} - \frac{1}{\sigma_\alpha}(i_t - E_t\{\pi_{H,t+1}\} - \rho) + \alpha\Theta \, E_t\{\Delta y_{t+1}^*\} \tag{30}$$

where $\Theta \equiv (\sigma\gamma - 1) + (1-\alpha)(\sigma\eta - 1) = \omega - 1$. Note that, in general, the degree of openness influences the sensitivity of output to any given change in the domestic real rate $i_t - E_t\{\pi_{H,t+1}\}$, given world output. In particular, if $\Theta > 0$ (i.e., for relatively high values of η and γ), an increase in openness raises that sensitivity (i.e., σ_α is smaller). The reason is the direct negative effect of an increase in the real rate on aggregate demand and output is amplified by the induced real appreciation (and the consequent switch of expenditure toward foreign goods). This will be partly offset by any increase in CPI inflation relative to domestic inflation induced by the expected real depreciation, which would dampen the change in the consumption-based real rate $i_t - E_t\{\pi_{t+1}\}$—which is the one ultimately relevant for aggregate demand—relative to $i_t - E_t\{\pi_{H,t+1}\}$.

7.2.1.2 The Trade Balance

Let $nx_t \equiv \left(\frac{1}{Y}\right)\left(Y_t - \frac{P_t}{P_{H,t}} C_t\right)$ denote net exports in terms of domestic output, expressed as a fraction of steady state output Y. In the particular case of $\sigma = \eta = \gamma = 1$, it follows from (25) that $P_{H,t}Y_t = P_t C_t$ for all t, thus implying a balanced trade at all times. More generally, a first-order approximation yields $nx_t = y_t - c_t - \alpha s_t$, which combined with (27) implies a simple relation between net exports and the terms of trade

$$nx_t = \alpha \left(\frac{\omega}{\sigma} - 1\right) s_t. \tag{31}$$

Again, in the special case of $\sigma = \eta = \gamma = 1$, $nx_t = 0$ for all t, though the latter property will also hold for any configuration of those parameters satisfying $\sigma(\gamma - 1) + (1 - \alpha)(\sigma\eta - 1) = 0$. More generally, the sign of the relationship between the terms of trade and net exports is ambiguous, depending on the relative size of σ, γ, and η.

7.2.2 The Supply Side: Marginal Cost and Inflation Dynamics

7.2.2.1 Aggregate Output and Employment

Let $Y_t \equiv \left[\int_0^1 Y_t(j)^{1-\frac{1}{\varepsilon}} dj\right]^{\frac{\varepsilon}{\varepsilon-1}}$ represent an index for aggregate domestic output, analogous to the one introduced for consumption. As in chapter 3, one can derive an approximate aggregate production function relating the previous index to aggregate employment. Hence, notice that

$$N_t \equiv \int_0^1 N_t(j)\, dj = \frac{Y_t}{A_t} \int_0^1 \left(\frac{P_t(j)}{P_t}\right)^{-\varepsilon} dj.$$

As shown in chapter 3, however, variations in $d_t \equiv \int_0^1 \left(\frac{P_t(j)}{P_t}\right)^{-\varepsilon} dj$ around the perfect foresight steady state are of second order. Thus, and up to a first-order approximation, the following relationship between aggregate output and employment holds as

$$y_t = a_t + n_t. \tag{32}$$

7.2.2.2 Marginal Cost and Inflation Dynamics in the Small Open Economy

As was shown in chapter 3, the (log-linearized) optimal price-setting condition (23) can be combined with the (log linearized) difference equation describing the evolution of domestic prices (as a function of newly set prices) to yield an equation determining domestic inflation as a function of deviations of marginal cost from its steady state value

$$\pi_{H,t} = \beta \ E_t\{\pi_{H,t+1}\} + \lambda \ \widehat{mc}_t \tag{33}$$

where $\lambda \equiv \frac{(1-\beta\theta)(1-\theta)}{\theta}$. Thus, relationship (33) does not depend on any of the parameters that characterize the open economy. On the other hand, the determination of real marginal cost as a function of domestic output in the open economy differs somewhat from that in the closed economy, due to the existence of a wedge between output and consumption, and between domestic and consumer prices. Thus, in the present model,

$$
\begin{aligned}
mc_t &= -\nu + (w_t - p_{H,t}) - a_t \\
&= -\nu + (w_t - p_t) + (p_t - p_{H,t}) - a_t \\
&= -\nu + \sigma \ c_t + \varphi \ n_t + \alpha \ s_t - a_t \\
&= -\nu + \sigma \ y_t^* + \varphi \ y_t + s_t - (1 + \varphi) \ a_t
\end{aligned}
\tag{34}
$$

where the last equality makes use of (19) and (32). Thus, it can be seen that the marginal cost is increasing in the terms of trade and world output. Both variables end up influencing the real wage through the wealth effect on labor supply resulting from their impact on domestic consumption. In addition, changes in the terms of trade have a direct effect on the product wage for any given consumption wage. The influence of technology (through its direct effect on labor productivity) and of domestic output (through its effect on employment and, hence, the real wage for given output) is analogous to that observed in the closed economy.

Finally, using (29) to substitute for s_t, the previous expression for the real marginal cost in terms of domestic output and productivity, as well as world output, can be rewritten as

$$mc_t = -\nu + (\sigma_\alpha + \varphi) \ y_t + (\sigma - \sigma_\alpha) \ y_t^* - (1 + \varphi) \ a_t. \tag{35}$$

Generally, in the open economy, a change in domestic output has an effect on marginal cost through its impact on employment (captured by φ) and the terms of trade (captured by σ_α, which is a function of the degree of openness and the substitutability between domestic and foreign goods). World output, on the other hand, affects marginal cost through its effect on consumption (and, hence, the real wage as captured by σ) and the terms of trade (captured by σ_α). Note that the sign of its impact on marginal cost is ambiguous. Under the assumption of $\Theta > 0$ (i.e., high substitutability among goods produced in different countries), $\sigma > \sigma_\alpha$, implying that an increase in world output raises the marginal cost. This is so because in that case the size of the real appreciation needed to absorb the change in relative supplies is small with its negative effects on marginal cost more than offset by the positive effect from a higher real wage. Notice that in the special cases $\alpha = 0$ and/or $\sigma = \eta = \gamma = 1$, which imply $\sigma = \sigma_\alpha$, the domestic real marginal cost is completely insulated from movements in foreign output.

How does the degree of openness affect the sensitivity of marginal cost and inflation to changes in domestic and world output? Note also that, under the same assumption of high substitutability ($\Theta > 0$) considered above, an increase in openness reduces the impact of a change in domestic output on marginal cost (and, hence, on inflation), for it lowers the size of the required adjustment in the terms of trade. By the same token, it raises the positive impact of a change in world output on marginal cost by limiting the size of the associated variation in the terms of trade and, hence, its countervailing effect.

Finally, and for future reference, note that under flexible prices, $mc_t = -\mu$ for all t. Thus, the natural level of output in the open economy is given by

$$y_t^n = \Gamma_0 + \Gamma_a \, a_t + \Gamma_* \, y_t^* \tag{36}$$

where $\Gamma_0 \equiv \frac{v-\mu}{\sigma_\alpha+\varphi}$, $\Gamma_a \equiv \frac{1+\varphi}{\sigma_\alpha+\varphi} > 0$, and $\Gamma_* \equiv -\frac{\alpha\Theta\,\sigma_\alpha}{\sigma_\alpha+\varphi}$. Note that the sign of the effect of world output on the domestic natural output is ambiguous, depending on the sign of the effect of the former on domestic marginal cost, which in turn depends on the relative importance of the terms of trade effect discussed above.

7.2.3   Equilibrium Dynamics: A Canonical Representation

In this section the linearized equilibrium dynamics for the small open economy is shown to have a representation in terms of output gap and domestic inflation analogous to its closed economy counterpart.

Let $\tilde{y}_t \equiv y_t - y_t^n$ denote the domestic output gap. Given (35) and the fact that y_t^* is invariant to domestic developments, it follows that the domestic real marginal cost and the output gap are related according to

$$\widehat{mc}_t = (\sigma_\alpha + \varphi) \, \tilde{y}_t.$$

Combining the previous expression with (33) the following version of the New Keynesian Phillips curve for the open economy can be derived

$$\pi_{H,t} = \beta E_t\{\pi_{H,t+1}\} + \kappa_\alpha \, \tilde{y}_t \tag{37}$$

where $\kappa_\alpha \equiv \lambda \, (\sigma_\alpha + \varphi)$. Notice that for $\alpha = 0$ (or $\sigma = \eta = \gamma = 1$) the slope coefficient is given by $\lambda \, (\sigma + \varphi)$ as in the standard, closed economy New Keynesian Phillips curve. More generally, note that the form of the inflation equation for the open economy corresponds to that of the closed economy, at least as far as domestic inflation is concerned. The degree of openness α affects the dynamics of inflation only through its influence on the slope of the NKPC, i.e., the size of the inflation response to any given variation in the output gap. If $\Theta > 0$ (which obtains for "high" values of η and γ, i.e., under high substitutability of goods produced in different countries), an increase in openness lowers σ_α, dampening the real depreciation induced by an increase in domestic output and, as a result, the effect of the latter on marginal cost and inflation.

Using (30) it is straightforward to derive a version of the so-called dynamic IS equation for the open economy in terms of the output gap

$$\widetilde{y}_t = E_t\{\widetilde{y}_{t+1}\} - \frac{1}{\sigma_\alpha} (i_t - E_t\{\pi_{H,t+1}\} - r_t^n) \tag{38}$$

where

$$r_t^n \equiv \rho - \sigma_\alpha \Gamma_a (1 - \rho_a) a_t + \frac{\alpha \Theta \sigma_\alpha \varphi}{\sigma_\alpha + \varphi} E_t\{\Delta y_{t+1}^*\} \tag{39}$$

is the small open economy's natural rate of interest.

Thus, it is seen that the small open economy's equilibrium is characterized by a forward looking IS-type equation similar to that found in the closed economy. Two differences can be pointed out, however. First, as discussed above, the degree of openness influences the sensitivity of the output gap to interest rate changes. Second, openness generally makes the natural interest rate depend on expected world output growth, in addition to domestic productivity.

7.3 Equilibrium Dynamics under an Interest Rate Rule

Next, the equilibrium response of our small open economy to a variety of shocks is analyzed. In so doing, it is assumed that the monetary authority follows an interest rate rule of the form already assumed in chapter 3, namely

$$i_t = \rho + \phi_\pi \pi_{H,t} + \phi_y \widetilde{y}_t + v_t \tag{40}$$

where v_t is an exogenous component, and where ϕ_π and ϕ_y are non-negative coefficients chosen by the monetary authority.

Combining (37), (38), and (40), the equilibrium dynamics for the output gap and domestic inflation can be represented by means of the system of difference equations

$$\begin{bmatrix} \widetilde{y}_t \\ \pi_{H,t} \end{bmatrix} = \mathbf{A}_\alpha \begin{bmatrix} E_t\{\widetilde{y}_{t+1}\} \\ E_t\{\pi_{t+1}\} \end{bmatrix} + \mathbf{B}_\alpha (\widehat{r}_t^n - v_t) \tag{41}$$

where $\widehat{r}_t^n \equiv r_t^n - \rho$, and

$$\mathbf{A}_\alpha \equiv \Omega_\alpha \begin{bmatrix} \sigma_\alpha & 1 - \beta\phi_\pi \\ \sigma_\alpha \kappa_\alpha & \kappa_\alpha + \beta(\sigma_\alpha + \phi_y) \end{bmatrix}; \quad \mathbf{B}_T \equiv \Omega_\alpha \begin{bmatrix} 1 \\ \kappa_\alpha \end{bmatrix}$$

with $\Omega_\alpha \equiv \frac{1}{\sigma_\alpha + \phi_y + \kappa_\alpha \phi_\pi}$. Note that the previous system takes the same form as the one analyzed in chapter 3 for the closed economy, with the only difference lying in the fact that some of the coefficients are a function of the "open economy parameters" α, η, and γ, and that $\widehat{r}_t^n$ is now given by (39). In particular, the condition for a locally unique stationary equilibrium under rule (40) takes the same form as shown in chapter 3, namely

$$\kappa_\alpha \left(\phi_\pi - 1\right) + (1 - \beta)\, \phi_y > 0, \tag{42}$$

which is assumed to hold for the remainder of this section.

Section 7.3.1 uses the previous framework to examine the economy's response to an exogenous monetary policy shock, i.e., an exogenous change in v_t. Given the isomorphism with the closed economy model of chapter 4, many of the results derived there can be exploited.

The analysis of the effects of a technology shock (or a change in world output), which is not pursued below, goes along the same lines as in chapter 3. First, one should determine the implications of the shock considered for the natural interest rate $\widehat{r}_t^n$ and then proceed to solve for the equilibrium response of the output gap and domestic inflation exactly as done below for the case of a monetary policy shock, given the symmetry with which v_t and $\widehat{r}_t^n$ enter the equilibrium conditions.[11]

7.3.1   The Effects of a Monetary Policy Shock

Assume that the exogenous component of the interest rate v_t follows an AR(1) process

$$v_t = \rho_v\, v_{t-1} + \varepsilon_t^v$$

where $\rho_v \in [0, 1)$.

The natural rate of interest is not affected by a monetary policy shock so $\widehat{r}_t^n = 0$ for all t for the purposes of this exercise. As in chapter 3, let us guess that the solution takes the form $\widetilde{y}_t = \psi_{yv}\, v_t$ and $\pi_t = \psi_{\pi v}\, v_t$, where ψ_{yv} and $\psi_{\pi v}$ are coefficients to be determined. Imposing the guessed solution on (37) and (38) and using the method of undetermined coefficients,

$$y_t = \widetilde{y}_t$$
$$= -(1 - \beta\rho_v)\Lambda_v\, v_t$$

and

$$\pi_{H,t} = -\kappa_\alpha \Lambda_v\, v_t$$

where $\Lambda_v \equiv \frac{1}{(1-\beta\rho_v)[\sigma_\alpha(1-\rho_v)+\phi_y]+\kappa_\alpha(\phi_\pi-\rho_v)}$. It can be easily shown that as long as (42) is satisfied, $\Lambda_v > 0$. Hence, as in the closed economy, an exogenous increase in the interest rate leads to a persistent decline in output and inflation. The size

---

[11] Of course, as in chapter 3, it must be taken into account that a technology shock or a shock to world output also leads to a variation in the natural output level, thus breaking the identity between output and the output gap.

of the effect of the shock relative to the closed economy benchmark depends on the values taken by a number of parameters. More specifically, if the degree of substitutability among goods produced in different countries is high (i.e., if η and γ are high, then $\omega > 1$) then Λ_v can be shown to be increasing in the degree of openness, thus implying that a given monetary policy shock will have a larger impact in the small open economy than in its closed economy counterpart.

Using interest rate rule (40) can determine the response of the nominal rate, taking into account the central bank's endogenous reaction to changes in inflation and the output gap

$$i_t = \left[1 - \Lambda_v(\phi_\pi \kappa_\alpha + \phi_y(1 - \beta\rho_v))\right] v_t.$$

Note that as in the closed economy model, the full response of the nominal rate may be positive or negative, depending on parameter values. The response of the real interest rate (expressed in terms of domestic goods) is given by

$$r_t = i_t - E_t\{\pi_{H,t+1}\}$$
$$= \left[1 - \Lambda_v((\phi_\pi - \rho_v)\kappa_\alpha + \phi_y(1 - \beta\rho_v))\right] v_t$$

which can be shown to increase when v_t rises (because the term in square brackets is unambiguously positive).

Using (29) can uncover the response of the terms of trade to the monetary policy shock

$$s_t = \sigma_\alpha y_t$$
$$= -\sigma_\alpha(1 - \beta\rho_v)\Lambda_v \, v_t.$$

The change in the nominal exchange rate is given in turn by

$$\Delta e_t = \Delta s_t + \pi_{H,t}$$
$$= -\sigma_\alpha(1 - \beta\rho_v)\Lambda_v \, \Delta v_t - \kappa_\alpha \Lambda_v \, v_t.$$

Thus, a monetary policy contraction leads to an improvement in the terms of trade (i.e., a decrease in the relative price of foreign goods) and a nominal exchange rate appreciation.

Note that, in the long run, the terms of trade revert back to their original level in response to the monetary policy shock, while the (log) levels of both domestic prices and the nominal exchange rate experience a permanent change of size $-\frac{\kappa_\alpha \Lambda_v}{1-\rho_v}$ (given an initial shock of size normalized to unity).

Hence, the exchange rate will overshoot its long-run level in response to the monetary policy shock, if and only if,

$$\sigma_\alpha(1 - \beta\rho_v)(1 - \rho_v) > \kappa_\alpha \rho_v$$

which requires that the shock is not too persistent. It can be easily shown that the previous condition corresponds to that for an increase in the nominal interest rate in response to a positive v_t shock. Note that, in that case, the subsequent exchange rate depreciation required by the interest parity condition (20) leads to an initial overshooting.

7.4   Optimal Monetary Policy: A Special Case

This section derives and characterizes the optimal monetary policy for the small open economy described above, as well as the implications of that policy for a number of macroeconomic variables. The analysis, which follows closely that of Galí and Monacelli (2005), is restricted to a special case for which a second-order approximation to the welfare of the representative consumer can be easily derived analytically. Its conclusions should thus not be taken as applying to a more general environment. Instead, this exercise is presented as an illustration of the approach to optimal monetary design to an open economy.

Let us take as a benchmark the basic New Keynesian model developed in chapter 3. As discussed in that chapter, under the assumption of a constant employment subsidy τ that neutralizes the distortion associated with firms' market power, the optimal monetary policy is the one that replicates the flexible price equilibrium allocation. The intuition for that result is straightforward: With the subsidy in place, there is only one effective distortion left in the economy, namely, sticky prices. By stabilizing markups at their "frictionless" level, nominal rigidities cease to be binding, since firms do not feel any desire to adjust prices. By construction, the resulting equilibrium allocation is efficient, and the price level remains constant.

In an open economy—and as noted, among others, by Corsetti and Pesenti (2001)—there is an additional factor that distorts the incentives of the monetary authority beyond the presence of market power: the possibility of influencing the terms of trade in a way beneficial to domestic consumers. This possibility is a consequence of the imperfect substitutability between domestic and foreign goods, combined with sticky prices (that render monetary policy non-neutral). As shown below, and as discussed by Benigno and Benigno (2003) in the context of a two-country model, the introduction of an employment subsidy that exactly offsets the market power distortion is not sufficient to render the flexible price equilibrium allocation optimal, for, at the margin, the monetary authority would have an incentive to deviate from it to improve the terms of trade.

For the special parameter configuration $\sigma = \eta = \gamma = 1$ the employment subsidy that exactly offsets the combined effects of market power and the terms of trade distortions can be derived analytically, thus rendering the flexible price equilibrium allocation optimal. That result, in turn, rules out the existence of an average inflation (or deflation) bias and allows the focus on policies consistent with zero average inflation in a way analogous to the analysis for the closed economy found in chapter 4. Perhaps not surprisingly, and as shown below, the policy that maximizes welfare in that case requires that domestic inflation be fully stabilized, while allowing the nominal exchange rate (and, as a result, CPI inflation) to adjust as needed in order to replicate the response of the terms of trade that would be obtained under flexible prices.

One may wonder to what extent the optimality of strict domestic inflation targeting is specific to the special case considered here or whether it carries over to a more general case. The optimal policy analysis undertaken in Faia and Monacelli (2007), using a model nearly identical to the one considered here, suggests that while the optimal policy involves some variation in the domestic price level, the latter is almost negligible from a quantitative point of view, thus making strict domestic inflation targeting a good approximation to the optimal policy (or at least conditional on the productivity shocks considered here). Using a different approach, de Paoli (2006) reaches a similar conclusion, except when an (implausibly) high elasticity of substitution is assumed.[12] But even in the latter case, the losses that arise from following a domestic inflation targeting policy are negligible.[13] More generally, it is clear that there are several channels in the open economy that may potentially render a strict domestic inflation policy suboptimal, including a nonunitary elasticity of substitution, local currency pricing, incomplete financial markets, and so on, all of which are unrelated to the sources of policy tradeoffs that may potentially arise in the closed economy. The quantitative significance of the effects of those channels (individually or jointly) still needs to be explored in the literature, and its analysis is clearly beyond the scope of this chapter.

With that consideration in mind, let us next turn to the analysis of the optimal policy in the special case mentioned above.

7.4.1 The Efficient Allocation and Its Decentralization

Let us first characterize the optimal allocation from the viewpoint of a social planner facing the same resource constraints to which the small open economy is subject in equilibrium (in relation to the rest of the world), given the assumption of complete markets. In that case, the optimal allocation must maximize $U(C_t, N_t)$ subject to (i) the technological constraint $Y_t = A_t N_t$, (ii) a consumption/output possibilities set implicit in the international risk-sharing conditions (18), and (iii) the market clearing condition (25).

---

[12] Those results are conditional on productivity shocks being the driving force. Not surprisingly, in the presence of cost-push shocks of the kind considered in chapter 5, stabilizing domestic inflation is not optimal (as in the closed economy).

[13] In solving the optimal policy problem for the general case, de Paoli (2006) adopts the linear–quadratic approach originally developed in Benigno and Woodford (2005), which replaces the linear terms in the approximation to the households' welfare losses using a second-order approximation to the equilibrium conditions. Faia and Monacelli (2007) solve for the Ramsey policy using the original nonlinear equilibrium conditions as constraints of the policy problem.

Consider the special case of $\sigma = \eta = \gamma = 1$. In that case, (19) and (26) imply the exact expression $C_t = Y_t^{1-\alpha}(Y_t^*)^{\alpha}$. The optimal allocation (from the viewpoint of the small open economy, which takes world output as given) must satisfy

$$-\frac{U_n(C_t, N_t)}{U_c(C_t, N_t)} = (1-\alpha)\,\frac{C_t}{N_t}$$

which, under the assumed preferences and given $\sigma = 1$, can be written as

$$C_t\,N_t^{\varphi} = (1-\alpha)\,\frac{C_t}{N_t}$$

thus implying a constant employment $N = (1-\alpha)^{\frac{1}{1+\varphi}}$.

Notice, on the other hand, that the flexible price equilibrium in the small open economy (with corresponding variables denoted with an n superscript) satisfies

$$1 - \frac{1}{\varepsilon} = MC_t^n$$

$$= -\frac{(1-\tau)}{A_t}(S_t^n)^{\alpha}\,\frac{U_{n,t}^n}{U_{c,t}^n}$$

$$= \frac{(1-\tau)}{A_t}\,\frac{Y_t^n}{C_t^n}\,(N_t^n)^{\varphi}\,C_t^n$$

$$= (1-\tau)(N_t^n)^{1+\varphi}$$

where the term on the right side of the second equality corresponds to the real wage (net of the subsidy) normalized by productivity, and where the third equality follows from (26).

Hence, by setting τ such that $(1-\tau)(1-\alpha) = 1 - \frac{1}{\varepsilon}$ is satisfied or, equivalently, $v = \mu + \log(1-\alpha)$, the optimality of the flexible price equilibrium allocation is guaranteed. As in the closed economy case, the optimal monetary policy requires stabilizing the output gap (i.e., $\tilde{y}_t = 0$ for all t). Equation (37) then implies that domestic prices are also stabilized under that optimal policy (i.e., $\pi_{H,t} = 0$ for all t). Thus, in the special case under consideration, (strict) domestic inflation targeting (DIT) is indeed the optimal policy.

7.4.2 Implementation and Macroeconomic Implications

This section discusses the implementation of a domestic inflation targeting policy and characterizes some of its equilibrium implications. While that policy has been shown to be optimal only for the special case considered above, the implications of that policy for the general case will also be considered.

7.4.2.1 *Implementation*

As discussed above, full stabilization of domestic prices implies

$$\tilde{y}_t = \pi_{H,t} = 0$$

for all t. This in turn implies that $y_t = y_t^n$ and $i_t = r_t^n$ will hold in equilibrium for all t, with all the remaining variables matching their natural levels at all times.

For the reasons discussed in chapter 4, an interest rate rule of the form $i_t = r_t^n$ is associated with an indeterminate equilibrium, and hence, does not guarantee that the outcome of full price stability be attained. That result follows from the equivalence between the dynamical system describing the equilibrium of the small open economy and that of the closed economy of chapter 4. As shown there, the indeterminacy problem can be avoided, and the uniqueness of the price stability outcome restored by having the central bank follow a rule that makes the interest rate respond with sufficient strength to deviations of domestic inflation and/or the output gap from target. More precisely, the central bank can guarantee that the desired outcome is attained if it commits to a rule of the form

$$i_t = r_t^n + \phi_\pi \, \pi_{H,t} + \phi_y \, \tilde{y}_t \tag{43}$$

where $\kappa_\alpha \, (\phi_\pi - 1) + (1 - \beta) \, \phi_y > 0$. Note that, in equilibrium, the term $\phi_\pi \, \pi_{H,t} + \phi_y \, \tilde{y}_t$ will vanish (because $\tilde{y}_t = \pi_{H,t} = 0$), implying that $i_t = r_t^n$ for all t.

7.4.2.2 *Macroeconomic Implications*

Under strict domestic inflation targeting, the behavior of real variables in the small open economy corresponds to the one that would be observed in the absence of nominal rigidities. Hence, it is seen from the inspection of equation (36) that domestic output always increases in response to a positive technology shock at home. As discussed earlier, the sign of the response to a rise in world output is ambiguous, however, and it depends on the sign of Θ, which in turn depends on the size of the substitutability parameters γ and η and the risk aversion parameter σ.

The natural level of the terms of trade is given by

$$s_t^n = \sigma_\alpha \, (y_t^n - y_t^*)$$
$$= \sigma_\alpha \, (\Gamma_0 + \Gamma_a \, a_t - \Phi \, y_t^*)$$

where $\Phi \equiv \frac{\sigma + \varphi}{\sigma_\alpha + \varphi} > 0$. Thus, given world output, an improvement in domestic technology always leads to a real depreciation through its expansionary effect on domestic output. On the other hand, an increase in world output always generates an improvement in the domestic terms of trade (i.e., a real appreciation), given domestic technology.

Given that domestic prices are fully stabilized under DIT, it follows that $e_t^{DIT} = s_t^n - p_t^*$, i.e., the nominal exchange rate moves one for one with the (natural) terms of trade and (inversely) with the world price level. Assuming constant world prices, the nominal exchange rate will inherit all the statistical properties of the natural terms of trade. Accordingly, the volatility of the nominal exchange rate under DIT will be proportional to the volatility of the gap between the natural level of domestic output (in turn related to productivity) and world output. In particular, that volatility will tend to be low when domestic natural output displays a strong positive comovement with world output. When that comovement is low (or negative), possibly because of a large idiosyncratic component in domestic productivity, the volatility of the terms of trade and the nominal exchange rate under DIT will be enhanced.

The implied equilibrium process for the CPI can also be derived. Given the constancy of domestic prices it is given by

$$p_t^{DIT} = \alpha \ (e_t^{DIT} + p_t^*)$$
$$= \alpha \ s_t^n.$$

Thus, it is seen that under the DIT regime, the CPI level will also vary with the (natural) terms of trade and will inherit its statistical properties. If the economy is very open, and if domestic productivity (and hence, the natural level of domestic output) is not much synchronized with world output, CPI prices could potentially be highly volatile, even if the domestic price level is constant.

An important lesson emerges from the previous analysis: Potentially large and persistent fluctuations in the nominal exchange rate, as well as in some inflation measures (like the CPI), are not necessarily undesirable, nor do they require a policy response aimed at dampening such fluctuations. Instead, and especially for an economy that is very open and subject to large idiosyncratic shocks, those fluctuations may be an equilibrium consequence of the adoption of an optimal policy, as illustrated by the model above.

7.4.3 The Welfare Costs of Deviations from the Optimal Policy

Under the particular assumptions for which strict domestic inflation targeting has been shown to be optimal (i.e., log utility and unit elasticity of substitution between goods of different origin), it is relatively straightforward to derive a second-order approximation to the utility losses of the domestic representative consumer resulting from the optimal policy deviations. Those losses, expressed as a fraction of steady state consumption, can be written as

$$\mathbb{W} = - \frac{(1-\alpha)}{2} \sum_{t=0}^{\infty} \beta^t \left[\frac{\varepsilon}{\lambda} \ \pi_{H,t}^2 + (1+\varphi) \ \tilde{y}_t^2 \right]. \tag{44}$$

The derivation of (44) goes along the lines of that for the closed economy shown in appendix 4.1 of chapter 4. The reader is referred to Galí and Monacelli (2005) for the details specific to (44).

The expected period welfare losses of any policy that deviates from strict inflation targeting can be written in terms of the variances of inflation and the output gap

$$\mathbb{V} = -\frac{(1-\alpha)}{2}\left[\frac{\varepsilon}{\lambda}\, var(\pi_{H,t}) + (1+\varphi)\, var(\tilde{y}_t)\right]. \qquad (45)$$

Note that the previous expressions for the welfare losses are, up to the proportionality constant $(1-\alpha)$, identical to the ones derived for the closed economy in chapter 4, with domestic inflation (and not CPI inflation) being the relevant inflation variable. Below, (45) is used to assess the welfare implications of alternative monetary policy rules and to rank those rules on welfare grounds.

7.5 Simple Monetary Policy Rules for the Small Open Economy

This section analyzes the macroeconomic implications of three alternative monetary policy regimes for the small open economy. Two of the simple rules considered are stylized Taylor-type rules. The first has the domestic interest rate respond systematically to domestic inflation, whereas the second assumes that CPI inflation is the variable the domestic central bank reacts to. The third rule considered is one that pegs the effective nominal exchange rate. Formally, the domestic inflation-based Taylor rule (DITR, for short) is specified as

$$i_t = \rho + \phi_\pi\, \pi_{H,t}.$$

The CPI inflation-based Taylor rule (CITR, for short) is assumed to take the form

$$i_t = \rho + \phi_\pi\, \pi_t.$$

Finally, the exchange rate peg (PEG, for short) implies

$$e_t = 0$$

for all t.

Below, a comparison is provided of the equilibrium properties of several macroeconomic variables under the above simple rules for a calibrated version of the model economy. Such properties are compared to those associated with a strict DIT, the policy that is optimal under the conditions discussed above, and which is assumed to be satisfied in the baseline calibration. Much of this chapter's analysis draws directly from Galí and Monacelli (2005).

7.5.1   A Numerical Analysis of Alternative Rules

7.5.1.1   Calibration

This section presents some quantitative results based on a calibrated version of the small open economy. The baseline calibration set $\sigma = \eta = \gamma = 1$ in a way consistent with the special case considered above. It is assumed that $\varphi = 3$, which implies a labor supply elasticity of $\frac{1}{3}$. ε, the elasticity of substitution between differentiated goods (of the same origin) is set equal to 6, thus implying a steady state markup of 20 percent. Parameter θ is set equal to 0.75, a value consistent with an average period of one year between price adjustments. It is assumed that $\beta = 0.99$, which implies a riskless annual return of about 4 percent in the steady state. A baseline value for α (the degree of openness) is set at 0.4. The latter corresponds roughly to the import/GDP ratio in Canada, which is taken as a prototype small open economy. The calibration of the interest rate rules follows the original Taylor calibration and sets ϕ_π equal to 1.5.

In order to calibrate the stochastic properties of the exogenous driving forces, let us fit AR(1) processes to (log) labor productivity in Canada (the proxy for domestic productivity), and (log) U.S. GDP (taken as a proxy for world output), using quarterly, Hodrick-Prescott (HP) filtered data over the sample period 1963: 1–2002:4. The following estimates are obtained (with standard errors shown in parentheses)

$$a_t = \underset{(0.06)}{0.66}\, a_{t-1} + \varepsilon_t^a, \ \sigma_a = 0.0071$$
$$y_t^* = \underset{(0.04)}{0.86}\, y_{t-1}^* + \varepsilon_t^*, \ \sigma_{y^*} = 0.0078$$

with $corr(\varepsilon_t^a, \varepsilon_t^*) = 0.3$.

7.5.1.2   Impulse Responses

First described are the dynamic effects of a *domestic* productivity shock on a number of macroeconomic variables. Figure 7.1 displays the impulse responses to a unit innovation in a_t under the four regimes considered. By construction, domestic inflation and the output gap remain unchanged under the optimal policy (DIT). It is also seen that the shock leads to a persistent reduction in the domestic interest rate, as it is needed in order to support the transitory expansion in consumption and output consistent with the flexible price equilibrium allocation. Given the constancy of the world nominal interest rate, uncovered interest parity implies an initial nominal depreciation followed by expectations of a future appreciation, as reflected in the response of the nominal exchange rate. Given constant world prices and the stationarity of the terms of trade, the constancy of domestic prices implies a mean-reverting response of the nominal exchange rate.

It is interesting to contrast the implied dynamic behavior of the same variables under the optimal policy to the one under the two stylized Taylor rules (DITR

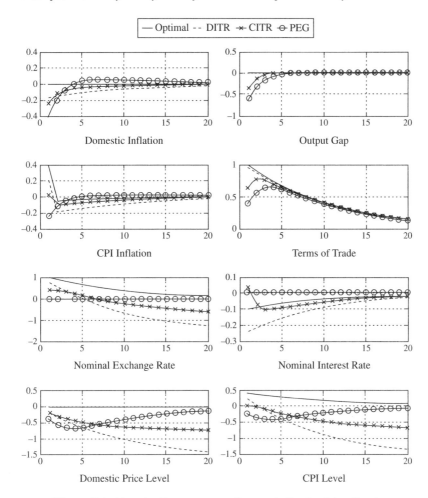

Figure 7.1   Impulse Responses to a Domestic Productivity Shock
under Alternative Policy Rules

and CITR). Notice, at first, that both rules generate, unlike the optimal policy, a permanent fall in both domestic and CPI prices. The unit root in domestic prices is then mirrored, under both rules, by the unit root in the nominal exchange rate.

A key difference between the two Taylor rules concerns the behavior of the terms of trade. Thus, under DITR there is a real depreciation on impact with the terms of trade reverting gradually to the steady state afterwards (mirroring closely the response under the optimal policy), while under CITR the initial response of the terms of trade is more muted and is followed by a hump-shaped pattern. The intuition is simple. Under both rules, the rise in domestic productivity and the required real depreciation lead, for *given domestic prices*, to an increase in CPI inflation. However, under CITR the desired stabilization of CPI inflation is partly achieved relative to DITR, by means of a more muted response of the terms of trade (since the latter affect the CPI), and a fall in domestic prices. The latter, in turn, requires a negative output gap and hence, a more contractionary monetary policy (i.e., a higher interest rate). Under the present calibration, that policy response takes the form of an initial rise in both the nominal and real interest rates, with the subsequent path of the real rate remaining systematically above that implied by the optimal policy or a DITR policy.

Finally, the same figure displays the corresponding impulse responses under the PEG policy. Notice that the responses of output gap and inflation are qualitatively similar to the CITR case. However, the impossibility of lowering the nominal rate and letting the currency depreciate, as would be needed in order to support the expansion in consumption and output required to replicate the flexible price allocation, leads to a very limited response in the terms of trade, and as a result, an amplification of the negative response of domestic inflation and the output gap. Interestingly, under a PEG, the complete stabilization of the nominal exchange rate generates stationarity of the domestic price level and, in turn, also of the CPI level (given the stationarity in the terms of trade). This is a property that the PEG regime shares with the optimal policy as specified above. The stationarity in the price level also explains why, in response to the shock, domestic inflation initially falls and then rises persistently above the steady state.

As discussed below, the different dynamics of the terms of trade are unambiguously associated with a welfare loss, relative to the optimal policy.

7.5.1.3   Second Moments and Welfare Losses

In order to complement the quantitative analysis, table 7.1 reports the standard deviations of several key variables under alternative monetary policy regimes. The numbers confirm some of the findings that were already evident from visual inspection of the impulse responses. Thus, it is seen that the critical element that distinguishes each simple rule relative to the optimal policy is the excess smoothness of both the terms of trade and the (first-differenced) nominal exchange

Table 7.1   Cyclical Properties of Alternative Policy Regimes

	Optimal	DI Taylor	CPI Taylor	PEG
Output	0.95	0.68	0.72	0.86
Domestic inflation	0.00	0.27	0.27	0.36
CPI inflation	0.38	0.41	0.27	0.21
Nominal interest rate	0.32	0.41	0.41	0.21
Terms of trade	1.60	1.53	1.43	1.17
Nominal depreciation rate	0.95	0.86	0.53	0.00

Note: Standard deviations expressed in percent.

Table 7.2 Contribution to Welfare Losses

	DI Taylor	CPI Taylor	PEG
Benchmark $\mu = 1.2, \varphi = 3$			
Var(Domestic inflation)	0.0157	0.0151	0.0268
Var(Output gap)	0.0009	0.0019	0.0053
Total	0.0166	0.0170	0.0321
Low steady state markup $\mu = 1.1, \varphi = 3$			
Var(Domestic inflation)	0.0287	0.0277	0.0491
Var(Output gap)	0.0009	0.0019	0.0053
Total	0.0297	0.0296	0.0544
Low elasticity of labor supply $\mu = 1.2, \varphi = 10$			
Var(Domestic inflation)	0.0235	0.0240	0.0565
Var(Output gap)	0.0005	0.0020	0.0064
Total	0.0240	0.0261	0.0630
Low markup and elasticity of labor supply $\mu = 1.1, \varphi = 10$			
Var(Domestic inflation)	0.0431	0.0441	0.1036
Var(Output gap)	0.0005	0.0020	0.0064
Total	0.0436	0.0461	0.1101

Note: Entries are percentage units of steady state consumption.

rate.[14] This in turn is reflected in too high a volatility of the output gap and domestic inflation under the simple rules. In particular, the PEG regime is the one that amplifies both output gap and inflation volatility to the largest extent, with the CITR regime lying somewhere in between. Furthermore, notice that the terms of trade are more stable under an exchange rate peg than under any other policy regime. That finding, which is consistent with the evidence of Mussa (1986), points to the existence of "excess smoothness" in real exchange rates under fixed exchange rates. That feature is a consequence of the inability of prices (which are sticky) to compensate for the constancy of the nominal exchange rate.[15]

Table 7.2 reports the welfare losses associated with the three simple rules analyzed in the previous section: DITR, CITR, and PEG. There are four panels in this table. The top panel reports welfare losses in the case of the benchmark parameterization, while the remaining three panels display the effects of lowering the steady state markup (as implied by an increase in ε), the elasticity of labor supply, and both of the aforementioned effects. All entries are to be read as percentage units of steady state consumption and in deviation from the first-best represented by DIT. Under the baseline calibration all rules are suboptimal because they involve

---

[14] Statistics are reported for the nominal *depreciation* rate, as opposed to the level, given that both DITR and CITR imply a unit root in the nominal exchange rate.

[15] See Monacelli (2004) for a detailed analysis of the implications of fixed exchange rates.

nontrivial deviations from full domestic price stability. Also, one result stands out clearly: Under all the calibrations considered, an exchange rate peg implies a substantially larger deviation from the first-best than DITR and CITR, as one may have anticipated from the quantitative evaluation of the second moments conducted above. However, and as is usually the case in welfare exercises of this sort found in the literature, the implied welfare losses are quantitatively small for all policy regimes.

Consider next the effect of lowering, respectively, the steady state markup to 1.1, by setting $\varepsilon = 11$ (which implies a larger penalization of inflation variability in the loss function), and the elasticity of labor supply to 0.1 (which implies a larger penalization of output gap variability). This has a general effect of generating a substantial magnification of the welfare losses relative to the benchmark case, especially in the third exercise where both parameters are lowered simultaneously. In the case of low markup and low elasticity of labor supply, the PEG regime leads to nontrivial welfare losses relative to the optimum. Notice also that under all scenarios considered here the two stylized Taylor rules, DITR and CITR, imply very similar welfare losses. While this points to a substantial irrelevance in the specification of the inflation index in the monetary authority's interest rate rule, the same result may once again be sensitive to the assumption of complete exchange rate pass-through.

7.6   Notes on the Literature

Earlier work on optimizing open economy models with nominal rigidities focused on the transmission of monetary policy shocks, typically represented as disturbances to an exogenous stochastic process for the money supply.[16] A key contribution in that area is Obstfeld and Rogoff (1995), who develop a two-country model where monopolistically competitive firms set prices before the realization of the shocks (i.e., one period in advance). The framework is used to analyze the dynamics of the exchange rate and other variables in response to a change in the money supply (and government spending) and the welfare effects resulting from that intervention. An earlier paper, by Svensson and van Wijnbergen (1989), contains a related analysis under the assumption of full risk-sharing among consumers from different countries.

Corsetti and Pesenti (2001) develop a version of the Obstfeld–Rogoff model that allows for home-bias in preferences, leading to terms of trade effects in response to shocks that are argued to have potentially important welfare effects. Betts and Devereux (2000) revisit the analysis in Obstfeld and Rogoff (1995) while departing from the assumption of the law of one price found in the latter paper. In particular, they allow firms to price discriminate across markets assuming they set prices (in advance) in terms of the currency of the importing country ("pricing to market").

---

[16] See Lane (1999) for an excellent survey of the early steps in that literature.

The effects of money supply shocks on the persistence and volatility of nominal and real exchange rates are analyzed under the assumption of staggered price setting in Kollmann (2001) and Chari, Kehoe, and McGrattan (2002).[17] The assumption of staggered price setting (and staggered wage setting in Kollmann's case) induces much richer and more realistic dynamics than that of price setting one period in advance.

A more recent strand of the literature has attempted to go beyond the analysis of the transmission of exogenous monetary policy shocks, and has focused instead on the implications of sticky price open economy models for the design of optimal monetary policy, using a welfare theoretic approach.[18] Early examples of papers analyzing the properties of alternative monetary policy arrangements in a two-country setting assumed that prices are set one period in advance. They include the work of Obstfeld and Rogoff (2002) and Benigno and Benigno (2003), both using the assumption of producer currency pricing. Bacchetta and van Wincoop (2000), Sutherland (2003), Devereux and Engel (2003), and Corsetti and Pesenti (2005) use the same assumption in the context of economies with local currency pricing.

More recent frameworks have instead adopted the staggered price-setting structure à la Calvo. Galí and Monacelli (2005), on which the analysis of this chapter is based, is an illustration of work along those lines for a small open economy. An extension of that framework, incorporating cost-push shocks, can be found in Clarida, Galí, and Gertler (2001). Kollmann (2002) considers a more general model of a small open economy with several sources of shocks, and carries out a numerical analysis of the welfare implications of alternative rules. Using a similar framework as a starting point, Monacelli (2005) shows that the introduction of imperfect pass-through generates a tradeoff between stabilization of domestic inflation and the output gap, leading to gains from commitment similar to those analyzed in chapter 5 for the closed economy.

Finally, the papers by Clarida, Galí, and Gertler (2002), Pappa (2004), and Benigno and Benigno (2006) depart from the assumption of a small open economy and analyze the consequences of alternative monetary policy arrangement in a two-country framework with staggered price setting à la Calvo, and with a special focus on the gains from cooperation.

Appendix

7.1 The Perfect Foresight Steady State

In order to show how the home economy's terms of trade are uniquely pinned down in the perfect foresight steady state, symmetry is invoked among all countries

---

[17] Kollmann (2001) assumes prices and wages are set à la Calvo—as in the model of this chapter—whereas Chari et al. (2002) assume price-setting à la Taylor, i.e. with deterministic price durations.

[18] Ball (1999) and Svensson (2000) carry out an analysis similar in spirit, but in the context of nonoptimizing models.

(other than the home country), and then the terms of trade and output in the home economy are determined. Without loss of generality, a unit value is assumed for productivity in all foreign countries with a productivity level A in the home economy. It is shown that in the symmetric case (when $A = 1$) the terms of trade for the home economy must necessarily be equal to unity in the steady state, whereas output in the home economy coincides with that in the rest of the world.

First, notice that the goods market clearing condition, when evaluated at the steady state, implies

$$Y = (1 - \alpha) \left(\frac{P_H}{P} \right)^{-\eta} C + \alpha \int_0^1 \left(\frac{P_H}{\mathcal{E}_i P_F^i} \right)^{-\gamma} \left(\frac{P_F^i}{P^i} \right)^{-\eta} C^i \, di$$

$$= \left(\frac{P_H}{P} \right)^{-\eta} \left[(1 - \alpha) C + \alpha \int_0^1 \left(\frac{\mathcal{E}_i P_F^i}{P_H} \right)^{\gamma - \eta} Q_i^\eta C^i \, di \right]$$

$$= h(S)^\eta C \left[(1 - \alpha) + \alpha \int_0^1 \left(S^i \, S_i \right)^{\gamma - \eta} Q_i^{\eta - \frac{1}{\sigma}} \, di \right]$$

$$= h(S)^\eta C \left[(1 - \alpha) + \alpha \, S^{\gamma - \eta} \, q(S)^{\eta - \frac{1}{\sigma}} \right]$$

where equation (18), as well as the relationship

$$\frac{P}{P_H} = \left[(1 - \alpha) + \alpha \int_0^1 (S_i)^{1 - \eta} \, di \right]^{\frac{1}{1 - \eta}}$$

$$= \left[(1 - \alpha) + \alpha \, (S)^{1 - \eta} \right]^{\frac{1}{1 - \eta}} \equiv h(S)$$

and where $Q = \frac{S}{h(S)} \equiv q(S)$. Notice that $q(S)$ is strictly increasing in S.

Under the assumptions above, the international risk sharing condition implies that the relationship

$$C = C^* \, Q^{\frac{1}{\sigma}}$$

$$= C^* \, q(S)^{\frac{1}{\sigma}}$$

must also hold in the steady state.

Hence, combining the two relations above and imposing the world market clearing condition $C^* = Y^*$ yields

$$Y = \left[(1 - \alpha) \, h(S)^\eta \, q(S)^{\frac{1}{\sigma}} + \alpha \, S^{\gamma - \eta} h(S)^\eta q(S)^\eta \right] Y^*$$

$$= \left[(1 - \alpha) \, h(S)^\eta \, q(S)^{\frac{1}{\sigma}} + \alpha \, h(S)^\gamma q(S)^\gamma \right] Y^*$$

$$\equiv v(S) \, Y^* \tag{46}$$

where $v(S) > 0$, $v'(S) > 0$, and $v(1) = 1$.

Furthermore, the clearing of the labor market in steady state implies

$$C^\sigma \left(\frac{Y}{A}\right)^\varphi = \frac{W}{P}$$

$$= A \frac{1 - \frac{1}{\varepsilon}}{(1 - \tau)} \frac{P_H}{P}$$

$$= A \frac{1 - \frac{1}{\varepsilon}}{(1 - \tau)} \frac{1}{h(\mathcal{S})}$$

which, when combined with the sharing condition above, yields

$$Y = A^{\frac{1+\varphi}{\varphi}} \left(\frac{1 - \frac{1}{\varepsilon}}{(1 - \tau)(Y^*)^\sigma \mathcal{S}}\right)^{\frac{1}{\varphi}}. \tag{47}$$

Notice that, conditional on A and Y^*, (46) and (47) constitute a system of two equations in Y and $\mathcal{S}$ with a unique solution given by

$$Y = Y^* = A^{\frac{1+\varphi}{\sigma+\varphi}} \left(\frac{1 - \frac{1}{\varepsilon}}{1 - \tau}\right)^{\frac{1}{\sigma+\varphi}}$$

and

$$\mathcal{S} = 1$$

which in turn must imply $S_i = 1$ for all i.

References

Bacchetta, Philippe, and Eric van Wincoop (2000): "Does Exchange Rate Stability Increase Trade and Welfare?" *American Economic Review* 90, no. 5, 1093–1109.

Ball, Laurence (1999): "Policy Rules for Open Economies," in J. B. Taylor (ed.), *Monetary Policy Rules*, University of Chicago Press, Chicago, IL.

Benigno, Gianluca, and Pierpaolo Benigno (2003): "Price Stability in Open Economies," *Review of Economic Studies* 70, no. 4, 743–764.

Benigno, Gianluca, and Pierpaolo Benigno (2006): "Designing Targeting Rules for International Monetary Policy Cooperation," *Journal of Monetary Economics* 53, no. 3, 473–506.

Benigno, Pierpaolo, and Michael Woodford (2005): "Inflation Stabilization and Welfare: The Case of a Distorted Steady State," *Journal of the European Economic Association* 3, no. 6, 1185–1236.

Betts, Caroline, and Michael B. Devereux (2000): "Exchange Rate Dynamics in a Model of Pricing-to-Market," *Journal of International Economics* 50, no. 1, 215–244.

Chari, V. V., Patrick Kehoe, and Ellen McGrattan (2002): "Monetary Shocks and Real Exchange Rates in Sticky Price Models of International Business Cycles," *Review of Economic Studies* 69, no. 3, 533–563.

Clarida, Richard, Jordi Galí, and Mark Gertler (2001): "Optimal Monetary Policy in Open vs. Closed Economies: An Integrated Approach," *American Economic Review* 91, no. 2, 248–252.

Clarida, Richard, Jordi Galí, and Mark Gertler (2002): "A Simple Framework for International Monetary Policy Analysis," *Journal of Monetary Economics* 49, no. 5, 879–904.

Corsetti, Giancarlo, and Paolo Pesenti (2001): "Welfare and Macroeconomic Interdependence," *Quarterly Journal of Economics* 116, no. 2, 421–446.

Corsetti, Giancarlo, and Paolo Pesenti (2005): "International Dimensions of Monetary Policy," *Journal of Monetary Economics* 52, no. 2, 281–305.

de Paoli, Bianca S. C. (2006): "Welfare and Macroeconomic Policy in Small Open Economies," Ph.D. Dissertation, London School of Economics, London, England.

Devereux, Michael B., and Charles Engel (2003): "Monetary Policy in the Open Economy Revisited: Exchange Rate Flexibility and Price Setting Behavior," *Review of Economic Studies* 70, no. 4, 765–783.

Faia, Ester, and Tommaso Monacelli (2007): "Optimal Monetary Policy in a Small Open Economy with Home Bias," mimeo.

Galí, Jordi, and Tommaso Monacelli (2005): "Monetary Policy and Exchange Rate Volatility in a Small Open Economy," *Review of Economic Studies* 72, no. 3, 707–734.

Kollmann, Robert (2001): "The Exchange Rate in a Dynamic Optimizing Current Account Model with Nominal Rigidities: A Quantitative Investigation," *Journal of International Economics* 55, no. 2, 243–262.

Kollmann, Robert (2002): "Monetary Policy Rules in the Open Economy: Effects on Welfare and Business Cycles," *Journal of Monetary Economics* 49, no. 5, 989–1015.

Lane, Philip R. (1999): "The New Open Economy Macroeconomics: A Survey," *Journal of International Economics* 54, 235–266.

Monacelli, Tommaso (2004): "Into the Mussa Puzzle: Monetary Policy Regimes and the Real Exchange Rate in a Small Open Economy," *Journal of International Economics* 62, no. 1, 191–217.

Monacelli, Tommaso (2005): "Monetary Policy in a Low Pass-Through Environment," *Journal of Money, Credit and Banking* 37, no. 6, 1048–1066.

Mussa, Michael (1986): "Nominal Exchange Rate Regimes and the Behavior of Real Exchange Rates," *Carnegie-Rochester Conference Series on Public Policy*, vol. 25, 117–213.

Obstfeld, Maurice, and Kenneth Rogoff (1995): "Exchange Rate Dynamics Redux," *Journal of Political Economy* 103, no. 3, 624–660.

Obstfeld, Maurice, and Kenneth Rogoff (2002): "Global Implications of Self-Oriented National Monetary Rules," *Quarterly Journal of Economics* 117, no. 2, 503–535.

Pappa, Evi (2004): "Should the Fed and the ECB Cooperate? Optimal Monetary Policy in a Two-Country World," *Journal of Monetary Economics* 51, no. 4, 753–780.

Sutherland, Alan (2003): "International Monetary Policy Coordination and Financial Market Integration," mimeo., University of St. Andrews.

Svensson, Lars E. O. (2000): "Open-Economy Inflation Targeting," *Journal of International Economics* 50, no. 1, 155–183.

Svensson, Lars E. O., and Sweder van Wijnbergen (1989): "Excess Capacity, Monopolistic Competition, and International Transmission of Monetary Disturbances," *The Economic Journal* 99, 785–805.

Exercises

7.1 A Small Open Economy Model

Consider a small open economy where no international trade in assets is allowed (implying that trade is always balanced). Hence,

$$p_t + c_t = p_{H,t} + y_t$$

where c_t denotes consumption, y_t is output, $p_{H,t}$ is the domestic price level, and p_t is the CPI (all in logs). Assuming a constant price level in the rest of the world ($p_t^* = 0$),

$$p_t = (1 - \alpha)\, p_{H,t} + \alpha\, e_t$$

where e_t is the nominal exchange rate.

Let $s_t \equiv e_t - p_{H,t}$ denote the terms of trade. Under the assumption of a unit elasticity of substitution between foreign and domestic goods,

$$s_t = y_t - y_t^*$$

where y_t^* is (log) output in the rest of the world (assumed to evolve exogenously). The domestic aggregate technology can be written as

$$y_t = a_t + n_t$$

where a_t is an exogenous technology process. Assume perfect competition in both goods and labor markets with flexible prices and wages. The labor supply takes the form

$$w_t - p_t = \sigma\, c_t + \varphi\, n_t.$$

Finally, assume a money demand function $m_t - p_t = c_t$.

a) Determine the equilibrium processes for output, consumption, the terms of trade, and the nominal exchange rate in the small open economy as a function of productivity a_t, foreign output y_t^*, and the money supply under the assumption that the latter evolves exogenously. Discuss the implications of assuming $\sigma = 1$.

b) How would your answer have to be modified if a fixed, nominal exchange rate regime were in place?

c) Discuss, in words, how some of the results in (a) and (b) would change qualitatively in the presence of imperfect competition and sticky prices.

7.2 The Effects of Technology Shocks in the Open Economy

Consider the small open economy model described in this chapter. The equilibrium dynamics for domestic inflation $\pi_{H,t}$ and the output gap $\tilde{y}_t$ are described by the equations

$$\pi_{H,t} = \beta E_t\{\pi_{H,t+1}\} + \kappa_\alpha \, \tilde{y}_t$$

$$\tilde{y}_t = E_t\{\tilde{y}_{t+1}\} - \frac{1}{\sigma_\alpha}\,(i_t - E_t\{\pi_{H,t+1}\} - r_t^n)$$

and where r_t^n is given by

$$r_t^n = \rho - b\,a_t.$$

Natural output is in turn given by

$$y_t^n = d\,a_t.$$

The technology parameter follows a stationary AR(1) process

$$a_t = \rho_a\,a_{t-1} + \varepsilon_t^a$$

where $\rho_a \in [0, 1)$.

Assume that the monetary authority follows the simple interest rate rule

$$i_t = \rho + \phi_\pi\,\pi_{H,t}$$

where $\phi_\pi > 1$.

a) Determine the response of output, domestic inflation, the terms of trade, and the nominal exchange rate to a positive domestic technology shock (Note: for the purposes of this exercise assume $y_t^* = p_t^* = 0$ for all t).

b) Suppose that the central bank pegs the nominal exchange rate so that $e_t = 0$ for all t. Characterize the economy's response to a technology shock in that case.

8

Main Lessons and Some Extensions

The previous chapters have provided an introduction to the New Keynesian model and its use for monetary policy evaluation. Throughout this book examples have been restricted to relatively simple versions of that framework in order to keep the analysis tractable. In recent years, however, larger versions of the model have been developed incorporating many features so as to provide a better fit of the data.[1] Thus, and in addition to the staggered price and wage setting analyzed in chapter 6, the resulting frameworks allow for habit formation, capital accumulation with investment adjustment costs, backward-looking indexation of wages and prices, and a variety of structural shocks, including markup shocks, neutral and investment specific technology shocks, preference shocks, and so on. Many central banks have already started using versions of those models in simulation and forecasting exercises, a development that can only add further discipline to their decision-making and communication processes.

Their simplicity notwithstanding, the models discussed in this book suffice to convey the main policy insights generated by the new vintage of monetary models. Some of those insights represent important differences with the traditional macroeconometric models that preceded the new vintage. In that respect, the New Keynesian research program has gone beyond the mere provision of microfoundations to the traditional macro models.[2]

In particular, there are two key implications of the new framework that are worth emphasizing in this concluding chapter:

1. *The importance of expectations.* The transmission of monetary policy depends critically on private sector expectations on the future path of the central bank's policy instrument, i.e., the short term interest rate. This dependence is central to the New Keynesian model. Thus, as was seen in chapter 3 and subsequent chapters, aggregate demand and output depend at any point

---

Many of the ideas contained in this chapter are based on my paper "Macroeconomic Modeling for Monetary Policy Evaluation," coauthored with Mark Gertler and forthcoming in the *Journal of Economic Perspectives*.

[1] See, e.g., Christiano, Eichenbaum, and Evans (2005) and Smets and Wouters (2003, 2007).

[2] See Galí and Gertler (2007) for an extensive discussion of the differences between the two vintages of models. The following discussion draws heavily on that paper.

in time on expectations about future short term interest rates and inflation. Current inflation, in turn, is a function of current and expected levels of economic activity. As a consequence, the current values of aggregate output and inflation depend not only on the central bank's current choice of the short term interest rate, but also on the anticipated future path of this instrument. Thus, the central bank's management of private sector expectations about its future policy settings is an important factor in determining the overall effectiveness of monetary policy. In other words, the policy process is as much, if not more, about communicating the future intentions of policy, as it is about choosing the current policy instrument. In this respect, the new framework provides a clear rationale for the trend toward greater transparency pursued by central banks around the globe. In particular, the inflation targeting framework adopted by a large number of central banks places a large weight on the publication of a quantitative objective for inflation, supplemented with an active communications policy (press conferences, inflation reports, speeches, and so on) aimed at explaining how the central bank intends to attain the inflation target. The regular publication by some central banks of their own projections regarding the future path of the policy rate provides the clearest example of the importance attached by policymakers to the correct public understanding of their intended policy actions.

2. *The importance of the natural levels of output and the interest rate*, i.e., the values for those variables that would arise in the equilibrium without nominal rigidities. As argued in earlier chapters, those variables are important reference points for monetary policy, in part because they reflect the constrained efficient level of economic activity, but also because monetary policy cannot create persistent departures from those natural values without inducing either inflationary or deflationary pressures. Within traditional frameworks, the natural levels of output and the real interest rate were typically modelled by means of smooth trends. Within the new framework they are instead determined by economic factors, and correspond, roughly speaking, to the values of output and the real interest rate that a frictionless real business cycle model would generate, given the assumed preferences and technology. As RBC theory suggests, further, those assumptions can vary considerably, given that the economy is continually buffeted by "real" shocks including oil price shocks, shifts in the pace of technological change, tax changes, and so on. Thus, these new models identify tracking the natural equilibrium of the economy, which is not directly observable, as an important challenge for central banks. The development and use of estimated DSGE models may play a key role in meeting that challenge.

8.1 Extensions

In the remainder of this concluding chapter a number of extensions of the basic New Keynesian model are mentioned that have been the focus of much research over the past few years, but which were ignored in the previous chapters. Each extension includes a list of readings, with no attempt to be exhaustive.

- **State-dependent pricing.** In the models analyzed in the previous chapters, the timing of price readjustments for any given firm is exogenous and, hence, independent of the gap between its current and desired prices. In such models, which are known as *time-dependent models*, the fraction of firms adjusting prices in any given period is independent of the state of the economy (e.g., the rate of inflation). In a seminal paper, Caplin and Spulber (1987) alerted to the potentially misleading implications of time-dependent models by developing an example of an economy in which each firm chooses optimally the timing of each adjustment, incurring a menu cost whenever it changes its price. Despite that stickiness at the micro level in the Caplin–Spulber model, the aggregate price level varies in proportion to the money supply, rendering changes in the latter fully neutral. Its simplicity and strong assumptions notwithstanding, the Caplin–Spulber model yields an important insight: When firms choose optimally the timing of their price adjustments, a selection effect emerges; firms whose prices are more out of line with their target prices are more likely to adjust their price, and do so by a larger amount. As a result, the response of the aggregate price level to shocks is likely to be larger than under the assumption that the adjusting firms are chosen randomly.

  Recently, there has been a renewed effort to develop models with state-dependent pricing, in which the latter is fully integrated into a general equilibrium framework. In contrast with the earlier literature, the new vintage of state dependent models are more amenable to a quantitative analysis, i.e., to a calibration and evaluation of their quantitative predictions in light of the existing evidence, both micro and macro. Influential examples of this recent literature are Danziger (1999), Dotsey, King, and Wolman (1999), Dotsey and King (2005), Golosov and Lucas (2007), Midrigan (2006), Gertler and Leahy (2006), and Nakamura and Steinsson (2006) who have all developed tractable quantitative models and assessed their ability to match different dimensions of the data. Gertler and Leahy (2006), in particular, show how it is possible to derive an inflation equation in a model with state-dependent pricing and infrequent firm-specific productivity shocks that is very similar in form to the New Keynesian Phillips curve derived in chapter 3 in the context of a model with time-dependent pricing.

- **Labor Market Frictions and Unemployment.** The framework analyzed in this book does not incorporate unemployment explictly, and, hence, it is silent about the determinants of its level and fluctuations, or its potential role in the design of monetary policy. On the other hand, a long-standing and highly influential literature has sought to understand unemployment and labor flows in the context of models with search frictions (see, e.g., Pissarides (2000) for an overview of that literature). Given the real nature of those models, that literature had nothing to say about monetary policy and its interaction with unemployment. More recently, however, a number of authors have tried to bridge the gap between the two literatures and have developed extensions of the New Keynesian model that combine nominal rigidities with labor market frictions giving rise to involuntary unemployment. Early papers along these lines focused on the ability of the augmented models to account for the persistent effects of monetary policy shocks (see, e.g., Walsh 2005 and Trigari 2006). Recent work has been motivated by the justification for wage rigidities provided by the presence of labor market frictions in search models of unemployment.[3] Thus, while the combination of labor market frictions and wage rigidities generally leads to inefficient unemployment fluctuations, the introduction of those features in a model with nominal rigidities makes room for the central bank policies to reduce those inefficiencies, though the latter motive has to be traded off with the desire to stabilize inflation, for the reasons discussed in chapter 4. That tradeoff gives rise to a meaningful monetary policy problem that can be tackled with some of the tools developed here (see, e.g., Blanchard and Galí 2006, Faia 2006, and Thomas 2007). The analysis of alternative specifications of wage rigidities and labor market frictions in the context of New Keynesian models and an assessment of their empirical relevance is likely to be an active research area in the coming years.[4]

- **Imperfect Information and Learning.** Underlying the monetary policy analysis contained in the previous chapters are the assumptions of perfect information and rational expectations, i.e., that both private agents and the central bank know the structure of the economy (specification and parameter values), are able to observe the shocks impinging on the latter, and form expectations in a way consistent with that (correct) model. A great deal of research in macroeconomics over the past decade has sought to relax some of those assumptions, which are widely regarded as unrealistically

---

[3] See, e.g., Hall (2005) for a discussion of the range of wage paths consistent with equilibrium in the context of a real model with search and matching frictions. Shimer (2005) and Gertler and Trigari (2005) explore the ability of search models with real wage rigidities to account for the volatility of unemployment and labor flows.

[4] See Gertler, Sala, and Trigari (2007) for an early example of work in that direction.

strong. Much of that work has focused on monetary applications and has adopted a normative perspective, exploring the implications of imperfect information and learning for the optimal design of monetary policy. Many of those applications are being cast in the context of the New Keynesian model developed in previous chapters.[5]

Some papers in this literature have focused on imperfect information and learning by private agents, studying the implications for monetary policy design of having private sector expectations being formed with some adaptive learning algorithm (e.g., recursive least squares). In particular, some authors have studied the conditions that an interest rate rule has to satisfy in that case for the economy to converge to the rational expectations equilibrium (see, e.g., Bullard and Mitra 2002 and Evans and Honkapohja 2003). Other authors have characterized the optimal monetary policy in such an environment and shown how that policy tries to "influence" the learning process in order to improve the tradeoff facing the central bank, typically by anchoring inflation expectations through an aggressive response to any surge in inflation (e.g., Gaspar, Smets, and Vestin 2006).[6] Within the same class of models, Woodford (2005b) investigates the nature of the optimal robust monetary policy when the central bank does not know with certainty the mechanism used by the private sector to form expectations. It is known that the latter does not differ "too much" from their rational counterpart (an assumption that Woodford terms *near-rational expectations*), and finds that many of the qualitative features of the optimal policy under rational expectations carry over to this environment (including the importance of commitment and history dependence).

Other authors have focused instead on the implications of the central bank's imperfect knowledge of the structure of the economy or limited observability of shocks or endogenous variables (e.g., Aoki 2003 and Svensson and Woodford 2003, 2004). Other work has sought to characterize the optimal policy rules when the policymaker faces uncertainty regarding the model's parameters, and seeks to minimize its expected losses given a prior on the parameters' distribution or, alternatively, under a worst-case parameter configuration (e.g., Giannoni 2006).

- **Endogenous Capital Accumulation.** For the sake of simplicity, all the models analyzed in the previous chapters have abstracted from capital and

---

[5] A smaller but highly influential literature has adopted instead a positive perspective, seeking to interpret some features of the data (e.g., the rise and fall of inflation in the postwar period) as a consequence of a policymaker's learning about the structure of the economy. See Sargent (1999) for a prominent example in that tradition.

[6] See Orphanides and Williams (2005) for another key reference in that literature, though in a framework with a supply side specification that differs from the one associated with the standard New Keynesian model emphasized here.

its accumulation. The introduction of endogenous capital accumulation in New Keynesian models poses no major difficulty if one is willing to assume the existence of a competitive rental market where capital services can be purchased by firms, as found in many versions of the New Keynesian model (e.g., Yun 1996 and Christiano, Eichenbaum, and Evans 2005). Further complications arise if capital is assumed to be firm-specific, with investment decisions being made by the same firms that adjust prices infrequently, for in that case the price set by any firm depends on its own current and expected capital stock, which will generally differ across firms, given differences in price-setting history (e.g., Sveen and Weinke 2004 and Woodford 2005a). In that case, the conditions that a Taylor-type interest rate rule needs to satisfy in order to guarantee a unique equilibrium must be modified, with the Taylor principle no longer offering a reliable criterion (e.g., Sveen and Weinke 2005).

- **Financial Market Imperfections.** The baseline New Keynesian model developed in the previous chapters assumes that capital markets are perfect. In many instances, this approximation may be reasonable. However, there are many situations where financial market frictions may be relevant. In this regard, there is an ongoing effort to incorporate financial factors within the New Keynesian framework, with the aim of better understanding the appropriate role of monetary policy in mitigating the effects of financial crises. A reference model combining nominal rigidities and credit frictions has been developed in Bernanke, Gertler, and Gilchrist (1999). That model features a "financial accelerator" property, whereby any shocks affecting the net worth of borrowers see their effects on aggregate demand and output amplified through their impact on the "external finance premium" paid by borrowing firms, which is inversely related to their net worth. Other recent papers have explored the policy implications of the coexistence of nominal rigidities with different types of credit frictions, including collateral-based borrowing constraints (e.g., Iacoviello 2005 and Monacelli 2006) or the presence of a fraction of households with no access to financial markets (e.g., Galí, López-Salido, and Vallés 2004, 2007).

- **Zero Lower Bound on Nominal Interest Rates.** The analysis of monetary policy throughout this book has ignored the fact that in actual economies nominal interest rates on a riskless asset cannot be negative, for otherwise the corresponding assets would be dominated by currency, whose interest rate is zero and has the same risk properties. In periods of low or even negative inflation, that zero lower bound constraint may become binding, in which case the central bank may not be able to stimulate the economy as much as it would wish to, as the experience of Japan between 1999 and 2006 has shown. A number of recent papers have studied how the problem of optimal monetary policy design is affected by the presence of that constraint, using a New Keynesian model as a framework of reference (see, e.g., Eggertson and Woodford 2003, Jung, Teranishi, and Watanabe 2005, Adam and Billi 2006, 2007, and Nakov 2006). Furthermore, whenever the central bank follows an interest rate rule that makes the nominal rate a continuous, increasing function of inflation, the zero lower bound constraint implies the existence of two steady states, one of which is characterized by a failure of the Taylor principle to hold, with the resulting indeterminate equilibrium dynamics emerging in its neighborhood (Benhabib, Schmitt-Grohé, and Uribe 2001).

It is still too early to tell which, if any, of the previous features will be permanently incorporated in empirical, larger-scale versions of the New Keynesian model. Most likely, those models will continue to evolve as more data is accumulated and more economic shocks are experienced. It may be very well the case that important new features are introduced and that ones that are central for performance today are less so in the future. At the same time, while the models are expected to change, the general approach will not: Quantitative macroeconomic modelling, along with its role in the policy-making process, is here to stay.

References

Adam, Klaus, and Roberto Billi (2006): "Optimal Monetary Policy under Commitment with a Zero Bound on Nominal Interest Rates," *Journal of Money, Credit and Banking* 38, no. 7, 1877–1905.

Adam, Klaus, and Roberto Billi (2007): "Discretionary Monetary Policy and the Zero Bound on Nominal Interest Rates," *Journal of Monetary Economics* 54, no. 3, 728–752.

Aoki, Kosuke (2003): "On the Optimal Monetary Policy Response to Noisy Indicators," *Journal of Monetary Economics* 50, no. 3, 501–523.

Benhabib, Jess, Stephanie Schmitt-Grohé, and Martin Uribe (2001): "The Perils of Taylor Rules," *Journal of Economic Theory* 96, no. 1–2, 40–69.

Bernanke, Ben, Mark Gertler, and Simon Gilchrist (1999): "The Financial Accelerator in a Quantitative Business Cycle Framework," in J. B. Taylor and M. Woodford (eds.), *Handbook of Macroeconomics* 1C, 1341–1397, Elsevier, New York.

Blanchard, Olivier J., and Jordi Galí (2006): "A New Keynesian Model with Unemployment," MIT, mimeo.

Bullard, James, and Kaushik Mitra (2002): "Learning About Monetary Policy Rules," *Journal of Monetary Economics* 49, no. 6, 1105–1130.

Caplin, Andrew, and Daniel Spulber (1987): "Menu Costs and the Neutrality of Money," *Quarterly Journal of Economics* 102, no. 4, 703–725.

Christiano, Lawrence J., Martin Eichenbaum, and Charles L. Evans (2005): "Nominal Rigidities and the Dynamic Effects of a Shock to Monetary Policy," *Journal of Political Economy* 113, no. 1, 1–45.

Danziger, Lief (1999): "A Dynamic Economy with Costly Price Adjustments," *American Economic Review* 89, no. 4, 878–901.

Dotsey, Michael, and Robert G. King (2005): "Implications of State Dependent Pricing for Dynamic Macroeconomic Models," *Journal of Monetary Economics* 52, no. 1, 213–242.

Dotsey, Michael, Robert G. King, and Alexander L. Wolman (1999): "State Dependent Pricing and the General Equilibrium Dynamics of Money and Output," *Quarterly Journal of Economics* 114, no. 2, 655–690.

Eggertson, Gauti, and Michael Woodford (2003): "The Zero Bound on Interest Rates and Optimal Monetary Policy," *Brookings Papers on Economic Activity* 1, no. 1, 139–211.

Evans, George W., and Seppo Honkapohja (2003): "Adaptive Learning and Monetary Policy Design," *Journal of Money, Credit and Banking* 35, no. 6, 1045–1072.

Faia, Ester (2006): "Optimal Monetary Policy Rules in a Model with Labor Market Frictions," ECB WP#698.

Galí, Jordi, and Mark Gertler (2007): "Macroeconomic Modeling for Monetary Policy Evaluation," *Journal of Economic Perspectives*, forthcoming.

Galí, Jordi, David López-Salido, and Javier Vallés (2004): "Rule of Thumb Consumers and the Design of Interest Rate Rules," *Journal of Money, Credit, and Banking* 36, no. 4, 739–764.

Galí, Jordi, David López-Salido, and Javier Vallés (2007): "Understanding the Effects of Government Spending on Consumption," *Journal of the European Economics Association* 5, no. 1, 227–270.

Gaspar, Vitor, Frank Smets, and David Vestin (2006): "Adaptive Learning, Persistence and Optimal Monetary Policy," *Journal of the European Economic Association* 4, no. 2–3, 376–385.

Gertler, Mark, and John Leahy (2006): "A Phillips Curve with an S-s Foundation," NBER Working Paper No. 11971.

Gertler, Mark, and Antonella Trigari (2005): "Unemployment Fluctuations with Staggered Nash Wage Bargaining," mimeo.

Gertler, Mark, Luca Sala, and Antonella Trigari (2007): "An Estimated Monetary DSGE Model with Labor Market Frictions," IGIER, mimeo.

Gianonni, Marc P. (2006): "Robust Optimal Policy in a Forward-Looking Model with Parameter and Shocks Uncertainty," *Journal of Applied Econometrics* 22, no. 1, 179–213.

Golosov, Mikhail, and Robert E. Lucas (2007): "Menu Costs and Phillips Curves," *Journal of Political Economy* 115, no. 2, 171–199.

Hall, Robert E. (2005): "Employment Fluctuations with Equilibrium Wage Stickiness," *American Economic Review* 95, no. 1, 50–65.

Iacoviello, Matteo (2005): "House Prices, Borrowing Constraints and Monetary Policy in the Business Cycle," *American Economic Review* 95, no. 3, 739–764.

Jung, Taehun, Yuki Teranishi, and Tsutomo Watanabe (2005): "Optimal Monetary Policy at the Zero Interest Rate Bound," *Journal of Money, Credit and Banking* 37, no. 5, 813–835.

Midrigan, Virgiliu (2006): "Menu Costs, Multi-Product Firms, and Aggregate Fluctuations," Ohio State University, unpublished manuscript.

Monacelli, Tommaso (2006): "Optimal Monetary Policy with Collateralized Household Debt and Borrowing Constraints," in J. Campbell (ed.), *Asset Prices and Monetary Policy*, University of Chicago Press, Chicago, IL.

Nakamura, Emi, and Jón Steinsson (2006): "Monetary Non-Neutrality in a Multi-Sector Menus Cost Model," Harvard University, unpublished manuscript.

Nakov, Anton (2006): "Optimal and Simple Monetary Policy Rules with a Zero Floor on the Nominal Interest Rate," Banco de España, Working Paper No. 637.

Orphanides, Athanasios, and John Williams (2005): "Imperfect Knowledge, Inflation Expectations and Monetary Policy," in B. Bernanke and M. Woodford (eds.), *The Inflation Targeting Debate*, University of Chicago Press, Chicago, IL.

Pissarides, Christopher (2000): *Equilibrium Unemployment Theory*, second edition, MIT Press, Cambridge, MA.

Sargent, Thomas (1999): *The Conquest of American Inflation*, Princeton University Press, Princeton, NJ.

Shimer, Robert (2005): "The Cyclical Behavior of Equilibrium Unemployment and Vacancies," *American Economic Review* 95, no. 1, 25–49.

Smets, Frank, and Raf Wouters (2003): "An Estimated Dynamic Stochastic General Equilibrium Model of the Euro Area," *Journal of the European Economic Association* 1, no. 5, 1123–1175.

Smets, Frank, and Raf Wouters (2007): "Shocks and Frictions in U.S. Business Cycles: A Bayesian DSGE Approach," *American Economic Review* 97, no. 3, 586–606.

Sveen, Tommy, and Lutz Weinke (2004): "Pitfalls in the Modelling of Forward-Looking Price Setting and Investment Decisions," Norges Bank Working Paper 2004/1.

Sveen, Tommy, and Lutz Weinke (2005): "New Perspectives on Capital, Sticky Prices and the Taylor Principle," *Journal of Economic Theory* 123, no. 1, 21–39.

Svensson, Lars E. O., and Michael Woodford (2003): "Indicator Variables for Optimal Policy," *Journal of Monetary Economics* 50, no. 3, 691–720.

Svensson, Lars E. O., and Michael Woodford (2004): "Indicator Variables for Optimal Policy under Asymmetric Information," *Journal of Economic Dynamics and Control* 28, no. 4, 661–690.

Thomas, Carlos (2007): "Search and Matching Frictions and Optimal Monetary Policy," London School of Economics, mimeo.

Trigari, Antonella (2006): "The Role of Search Frictions and Bargaining of Inflation Dynamics," IGIER Working Paper No. 304.

Walsh, Carl (2005): "Labor Market Search, Sticky Prices, and Interest Rate Rules," *Review of Economic Dynamics* 8, no. 4, 829–849.

Woodford, Michael (2005a): "Firm-Specific Capital and the New Keynesian Phillips Curve," *International Journal of Central Banking* 1, no. 2, 1–46.

Woodford, Michael (2005b): "Robustly Optimal Monetary Policy with Near-Rational Expectations," NBER Working Paper No. 11896.

Woodford, Michael (2007): "Inflation-Forecast Targeting: A Monetary Standard for the Twenty First Century?" *Journal of Economic Perspectives*, forthcoming.

Yun, Tack (1996): "Nominal Price Rigidity, Money Supply Endogeneity, and Business Cycles," *Journal of Monetary Economics* 37, no. 2, 345–370.

Index